ILLINOIS AND ST. LOUIS BRIDGE COMPANY.

REPORT

OF THE

CHIEF ENGINEER.

OCTOBER, 1870.

ST. LOUIS:
GEORGE KNAPP & CO., PRINTERS AND BINDERS.
1870.

CHIEF ENGINEER'S REPORT.

ST. LOUIS, October 1st, 1870.

To the President and Directors of the St. Louis and Illinois Bridge Company:

GENTLEMEN: I have the honor to submit the following report:

THE WEST ABUTMENT.

The masonry of the west abutment has been completed from the bed-rock of the river to a point thirty-one feet above low-water mark. From the bed-rock to the top of the masonry, the height is now forty-four feet. Eight courses of granite are laid on it and two courses, or five feet, are required to complete it to the skewbacks against which the steel ribs of the western span will rest. This mass of solid masonry stands upon the lower edge of the wharf in St. Louis, and measures at its base, in the direction of the river current, ninety-four feet, and transversely sixty-two feet nine inches, and contains at this time six thousand three hundred and eighty cubic yards of masonry. When completed to the carriage-way, it will be one hundred and fifteen feet high, above the bed-rock of the river, and will then contain eleven thousand eight hundred and sixty cubic yards of masonry.

The work on it is going steadily forward in a satisfactory manner.

Although the bed-rock at the site of this abutment is seventy-three and a half feet higher than at the east pier, the difficulties encountered in building its foundation were of a much more perplexing and tedious character than those encountered at either of the others. Its site had been for over sixty years a part of the steamboat wharf of the city, and as such had received every kind of useless material thrown overboard from the various steamers lying over it during that time. The old sheet-iron enveloping their furnaces, worn-out grate-bars, old fire-bricks, parts of smoke-stacks, stone-coal cinders and clinker, and every manner of things entering into the construction of a Mississippi steamer seemed to have found a resting place at this spot, and constituted a deposit averaging twelve feet in depth over the rock. During the memorable fire of 1849, when twenty-nine steamers were destroyed at the levee, the wrecks of two of them sunk upon the site of this abutment. One of these was partly covered by the hull of the other, which probably sunk immediately afterwards. The lower one was but two or three feet above the bed-rock. After this terrible conflagration, the city authorities determined to widen the wharf. Its front was extended to a line inclosing about one-half of these two wrecks, by filling in with stone and rubbish from the city. During this extension, several other vessels were burnt at the wharf, and the wreck of one of these also sunk upon the site of the abutment. The coffer-dam, constructed to enclose the site, had to be put down through these three wrecks, the hulk of either of which was not probably less than four hundred tons measurement. Their bottom planking was all of oak, three or four inches in thickness. To drive the sheet piling down through these hulks, an oak beam six by ten inches square, armed with a huge steel chisel, was first driven down as far as a steam pile-driver could force it. It was then withdrawn and a sheet-pile, five by ten inches square, was driven down in its place. The coffer-dam was formed of two courses of sheet-piling, six feet apart, which were filled in between with clay. When this was completed, the water pumped out and the excavation prosecuted within it, the discovery was made that from one-third to one-half of the length of each of these three steamboat hulks was enclosed within the dam, and that some of the sheet-piling had not been driven through the lower one, owing to the great resistance of the hulk and the mass above it. Before the space between the lower wreck and the bed-rock could be made secure on the inner side of the dam, the water came through and flooded the inclosure. A stream from a powerful Gwynne pump, having an eight-inch diameter of jet, was then directed against the material deposited over these wrecks on the outer side of the dam, where the water was fifteen feet deep, and enough of the deposit was washed away to enable another course of sheet-piling to be driven down six feet beyond the dam, through all of the wrecks to the rock. After this, that part of the wrecks enclosed between this last course of piling and the dam, was removed by a diver and the space filled in with clay, and the inclosure again pumped out. This portion of the dam, about fifty feet in length, was by this construction, made double. As the excavation within progressed, it revealed the fact that another portion of the dam had been built and made water-tight through and over a water wheel of one of the wrecks. The crank of an engine of seven feet stroke attached to the head of the shaft of the wheel, was just within the inclosure, while the flanges, arms and braces of the wheel were within the walls formed by the sheet-piling. From the inclosure within the dam were taken parts of several old and burnt steamboat engines, the iron parts of some of which had to be cut off at the dam. Four wrecks of barges, some of them in use doubtless before the era of steam, were also found within it; likewise several oak sawlogs, some anchors, chains and a great variety of smaller articles lost or thrown overboard from the river craft, or dumped in from the city.

This incongruous deposit made it exceedingly difficult to maintain the integrity of the dam, which at times had to resist a pressure of thirty feet of water. Frequent floodings consequently occurred, which delayed and increased the cost of the work. These difficulties were however, finally overcome, and the bed-rock within was at last exposed to view.

On the 25th day of February, 1868, after thoroughly testing the solidity of the rock by drilling, the first stone of your Bridge was laid in this abutment fifty-five feet below high water mark, about four months after commencing the construction of the dam.

THE EAST PIER.

The caisson for sinking the east pier described in my published report, September 1st, 1869, having been completed, and the requisite guide piles, air and sand pumps, hoisting machinery, etc., being made ready, it was launched from the ways at Carondelet, on the 18th of October, 1869, and was towed up to its position in the river and duly secured within the guide piles on the same day. Some days more were occupied in securing the caisson to the suspension screws that were to steady it until it reached the sandy bed of the river, and in connecting the various air and water-pipes with it. On the 25th day of October, the first stone was laid upon it, from which moment until it reached the bed-rock of the river, on the 28th of February last, (one hundred and twenty-eight feet below high water mark, or one hundred and twenty feet below the city directrix,) the progress of its descent and the working of the machinery connected with it, were marked by an almost total freedom from accident.*

During low water the normal depth of sand over the bed-rock at this pier is about eighty feet. A rise in the river causes it to scour down, whilst a subsidence of the flood permits the moving sands from above to deposit rapidly and again raise the sand bed. At the time of placing the caisson in position the water in the river was thirty-five feet deep, and sixty-eight feet of sand were then overlying the rock. As the caisson descended, the current sweeping under its bottom at the rate of about three and a half miles per hour, caused a further scour of five feet, leaving an irregular surface of sand, averaging about sixty-three feet deep above the rock. When the caisson had fairly entered the sand a deposit was made rapidly around it, especially in the eddy created below the caisson. The sides of the caisson were swept to some extent by the current, otherwise the derrick boats on each side of it would have grounded on the deposit. This deposit was increased by the discharge from the sand pumps, and by the completion of the ice-breaker above the pier, so that for twenty or thirty days before it reached the rock, the sand was visible above the water, both above and below the caisson. The iron walls of the caisson had consequently a severe external pressure upon them from this mass of sand, and as the sides of the pier were inclined whilst the walls of the caisson were vertical, a space was left between the two. This space was at first occupied with bracings against the masonry to sustain the walls. As the pier descended and the pressure increased, sand from the pumps was discharged into it and in this way the walls were relieved; the height of sand inside, between the caisson walls and the pier, being maintained at the level of the sand on the outside. The design was to keep the masonry constantly built up above water, as the pier descended. The failure of the granite company to deliver in time the granite which was intended to form the exterior of the pier above low water mark, prevented me from following out this design. At the time the

* An inspection of the lithographic plates in the Appendix will give the reader a clearer idea of the method and appliances used in sinking the east and west piers.

granite was wanted, the river was from ten to twelve feet above low water mark, and there was left only the alternative of stopping the descent of the caisson that much above the bed-rock and awaiting the receipt of the granite, or else allowing the pier to descend and trust to the walls of the caisson to exclude the water above the top of the pier. Three courses of granite, each two feet thick, were received in time, but when the pier reached the bed-rock the top of the masonry was about six feet below the surface of the water.

To prevent danger to the workmen in the air-chamber, in the event of the walls of the caisson giving way under a pressure of water and condition of things deemed possible, but not expected, the shafts or wells through the masonry, by which access was obtained to the air-locks which were at the bottom of the pier, were kept securely built up above the level of the water. On one or two occasions leaks occurred in the caisson walls, causing the top of the masonry to be flooded. But this precaution prevented a suspension of the work of filling the air-chamber under the pier with concrete, in consequence of such accidents, as the shafts remained free of water. During the month of April however, the river rose to within nine feet six inches of the City Directrix, and was nineteen feet six inches above the top of the masonry. From the moment the caisson touched the rock up to this time, the filling of the air-chamber with concrete had been progressing almost without interruption. When the water reached this point, the walls of the caisson suddenly sprung a leak, and the pier was again flooded in a few moments. As the flooding of the pier usually increased the leakage in the shafts very much, it was not found practicable to continue work in the air-chamber when it happened, if the depth over the pier exceeded a few feet. When this accident occurred, the men were immediately signalled to come up from the air chamber, then one hundred and ten and a half feet below the surface of the river. This they did with entire safety. A suspension of work on the pier was then ordered until the water should subside.

Examinations of the caisson walls were made by our diver, Capt. Quigley, and careful soundings were made to ascertain the depth of the sand on the inside and outside of the caisson. It was then discovered that fifty-five feet in depth of the sand on the east side of the caisson (on the outer side) had been scoured away by the action of the current, the soundings showing but thirty-five feet of sand remaining above the bed-rock. This had reversed the strains on the caisson walls; the corresponding fifty-five feet of sand on the inside between the pier and the caisson, had by its gravity burst out the eastern wall of the caisson, now no longer supported by the sand on the outside. This wall was of plate iron ⅜ of an inch in thickness. This rupture rendered the further use of the caisson as a coffer-dam, forever after totally impracticable. The upper portion of it was consequently removed, and in its stead there was secured around the pier a wooden dam, joined together in sections corresponding to the sides and ends of the pier, and having a large cushion near its lower edge, on the inner side, to fit against the fourth joint of the masonry below the top course of the pier. This work was admirably executed under the direction of the Superintendent of Construction, Mr. W. K. McComas; the submarine work being very skillfully performed by Capt. Quigley. On the 13th of August the water was again pumped off from the top of the masonry. Since this time the pier has been carried up to the height of one hundred and seventeen feet above the bed-rock on which it rests, and is now (October 1st) nineteen feet nine inches above the present level of the river surface. The coffer-dam has been removed from around it, and no apprehension of further trouble from water during its completion need be entertained. It measures at its base, in the direction of the current, eighty-two feet in length, and transversely sixty feet, and on the top at its present height, seventy-five feet seven inches by thirty-five feet one inch. It now contains thirteen thousand two hundred and forty cubic yards of masonry, concrete and brick work. The vertical wells or shafts through it, were lined with brick work from thirteen to twenty-two inches in thickness. These openings were carefully filled up with concrete and the entire pier is now one solid mass of masonry.

In addition to the almost constant presence of the Superintendent of Construction, in charge of all the works, it was made the duty of three civil engineers, familiar with the plans, machinery, etc., to give their personal superintendence to the sinking of the pier; one being constantly on duty, watching the progress of the work, and keeping a record of everything of interest occurring. The necessary number of steam engineers, machinists and firemen, were employed for keeping the engines at work night and day, and the machinery in perfect order, so that the work could go on without any interruption whatever. To accomplish this desirable object, sufficient duplicate pumps, engines, boilers etc., were provided, so that the failure of any one piece of the machinery would cause no stoppage in the progress of the work. The pier was placed on the rock in one hundred and twenty-six days after the laying of the first stone, which period included the most inhospitable season of the year. The mason work was suspended during twenty days of this time on account of bad weather. During fifteen days it was impossible to tow a barge of stone to the pier on account of the running ice.

TELEGRAPH.

When this pier had reached the depth of sixty-six feet, a telegraphic instrument was placed in the air-chamber, and a wire was led to the office of the Superintendent of Construction on one of the derrick boats at the pier, and also to the office of the Chief Engineer in the city. By this means messages were transmitted to and from the air-chamber, and between the offices of the Superintendent of Construction and that of the Chief Engineer, by which I was, when not present, regularly advised of the progress and condition of the work during the sinking of the pier. The knowledge that a means of communication with the upper world was constantly at hand in the air-chamber, and one which was not likely to be interrupted by any accident endangering the lives of the workmen in it, was productive of a very salutary moral effect upon them.

These telegraphic arrangements were courteously put up complete under the gratuitous superintendence of Col. Chas. H. Haskins, General Superintendent of the Pacific and Atlantic Telegraph Company. The instruments were of the kind known as "alphabetical," and were easily understood and operated by those placed in charge of them in the service of the Bridge Company.

FILLING THE AIR-CHAMBER.

The filling of the air-chamber was executed in the most careful and substantial manner under the immediate direction of the Superintendent of Construction. The preparation and disposition of the concrete were made in the air-chamber, (from one hundred and three to one hundred and ten and a half feet beneath the surface of the river,) under the immediate supervision of Mr. Rud. Wieser, C. E., Chief Inspector of Masonry, and his assistants, Mr. Rich. Richardson and Mr. Fritz Eberley, master masons, one or the other being constantly on duty. From frequent personal inspection, I am warranted in saying that this part of the work is unsurpassed in excellence by that of any part of the masonry above water.

The filling of the air-chamber with concrete commenced on the second day of last March, and was finished on the 27th of last May. The working time being fifty-three days. The space filled may be fairly stated at nearly thirty-six thousand cubic feet. The area of the base of the pier is four thousand and twenty square feet and the height of the chamber nine feet. The caisson was stopped as soon as it touched the bed-rock. This was at its southwest corner. At the northwest corner its edge was eight inches from the rock. The northeast corner was sixteen inches and the southeast corner eight inches. It will be seen from this that the rock was fortunately, very nearly level. The sand beneath the edge of the caisson was removed, the rock laid bare and the space filled carefully with concrete, the air pressure being sufficient to prevent a more rapid infiltration of the water under the edge of the caisson than could be managed by the pumping arrangements within it. The sand seemed packed so firmly that no trouble was taken to barricade it out of this space between the rock and the edge of the caisson. When the entire edge of the caisson and the space under its two great girders were thus concreted, the rock in its interior was gradually cleared of sand and the concrete placed directly upon it in layers of nine or ten inches in thickness, the closing courses under the roof of the chamber being stoutly rammed in place. The air-locks were then filled with the same material, and finally the shafts. The concrete was made of broken limestone thoroughly washed, the interstices being filled with mortar made of equal parts of Akron cement and pure sand.

During the sinking of the pier the sand pumps designed by me for this special purpose, gave great satisfaction and proved entirely successful. One pump of three and one-half inches bore was found quite capable of raising twenty cubic yards of sand one hundred and twenty feet high per hour; the water pressure required to supply the jet being about one hundred and fifty pounds per square inch.

PRESSURE IN THE AIR-CHAMBER.

The pressure of air in the air-chamber was very accurately determined by the depth of the caisson below the surface. Any greater pressure than that due to the depth, caused the air to escape beneath it, but when the caisson had penetrated into the sand to a considerable distance, it was discovered that the water level formed by the air under or across the bottom of the chamber was nearly a foot lower than the bottom edge of the caisson. When the caisson was but a few feet in the sand, the air forced its way up by its sides in one or two currents of large volume, but as it penetrated more deeply, the passage of the air through the sand evidently became more difficult, and it appeared in small bubbles sixty or seventy feet distant from the caisson. This retardation of the escapement of the air from beneath the caisson, caused an increase of air pressure by which the water was held at a greater or lesser depth below the line of the bottom of the air-chamber. The sand inclosed in the air-chamber and forming its floor was usually one or two feet more elevated than the lower edge of the chamber, and was entirely devoid of water, the air pressure expelling the water from it down below the edge of the caisson as just stated. The distance to which it was thus expelled and maintained, was at no time discovered to exceed ten inches, and generally it was not over eight inches. This would give an air pressure equal to nearly one foot more than the depth of the caisson, or about one-third of a pound per square inch more. This difficulty of escapement of the air through the sand was increased somewhat by concreting under the edge of the caisson on the rock, and the actual air pressure could then be no longer accurately determined by the height of the water above. The pressure gauges usually indicated a pressure of one or two pounds more than the depth of water would give by calculation. This was caused in a great measure however, by the friction of the air in the pipes, the gauges being at the pumps and not in the air-chamber. A column of water one hundred and ten feet six inches in height would be equal to a pressure of 47.96 pounds per square inch, assuming the weight of the water to be 62.5 pounds per cubic foot. The greatest pressure marked by the gauges was fifty-two pounds, and it is not probable that the pressure in the air-chamber ever exceeded fifty or fifty-one pounds.

EFFECTS OF COMPRESSED AIR ON THE MEN.

The first symptom manifesting itself, caused by the pressure of the air, is painfulness in one or both ears. The Eustachian tubes extending from the back of the mouth to the bony cavities over which the drums of the ears are distended, are so minute as not to allow the compressed air to pass rapidly through them to these cavities, and when the pressure is increased rapidly, the external pressure on the drums causes pain. These tubes constitute a provision of nature to relieve the ears of such barometric changes as occur in the atmosphere in which we live. The act of swallowing facilitates the passage of the air through them and thus equalizes the pressure on both sides of the drums, and prevents the pain. The pressure may be admitted into the air-lock so rapidly that this natural remedy will not in all cases relieve it. By closing the nostrils between the thumb and fingers, shutting the lips tightly and inflating the cheeks, the Eustachian tubes are opened and the pressure on the inner and outer surfaces of the tympanum is equalized, and the pain prevented. This method must be used and repeated from time to time as the pressure is let on, if it be increased rapidly. No inconvenience is felt by the reaction when the pressure is let off, as the compressed air within the drums has a tendency to open the tubes, and thus facilitates its escape through them; whereas increasing the pressure has the effect of collapsing them and therefore makes it more difficult to admit the compressed air within the cavities of the ears. It frequently occurs however, from some abnormal condition of these tubes, as when inflamed by a cold in the head, that neither of these remedies will relieve the pain. To continue the admission of compressed air into the lock, under such circumstances, would intensify the suffering, and possibly rupture the tympanum, therefore the lock tenders were particularly instructed to shut off the compressed air at the moment any one in the lock experienced pain about the ears; and then, if it could not be relieved by the above means, the lock was opened and the person was not permitted to go through into the air-chamber. Sometimes fifteen minutes were occupied in passing persons through the first time, after which they usually had no further trouble from this cause.

The fact that the depth penetrated by the air-chamber was considerably greater than that hitherto reached in any similar work, left me without any benefit from the experience of others, in either guarding against any injurious effects of this great pressure upon the workmen and engineers subjected to it, or of availing myself of any known specific for relieving those affected by it. When the depth of sixty feet had been attained, some few of the workmen were affected by a muscular paralysis of the lower limbs. This was rarely accompanied with pain, and usually passed off in the course of a day or two. As the penetration of the pier progressed, the paralysis became more difficult to subdue. In some cases the arms were involved, and in a few cases the sphyncter muscles and bowels. The patients also suffered much pain in the joints when the symptoms were severe. An average of at least nine out of ten of those affected, suffered no pain whatever, but soon recovered, and generally returned to the work.

The duration of the watches in the air-chamber was gradually shortened from four hours to three, and then to two, and finally to one hour.

The use of galvanic bands or armor seemed, in the opinion of the Superintendent of Construction, the foremen of the chamber, and the men, to give remarkable immunity from these attacks. They were all ultimately provided with them. These bands were made of alternate scales of zinc and silver, and were worn around the wrists, arms, ankles and waist, and also under the soles of the feet. Sufficient moisture and acidity were supplied by the perspiration to establish galvanic action in the armor, and as the opinion among those most accustomed to the chamber was almost unanimous in favor of this remedy, I am very much inclined to believe it valuable.

Immediately on the manifestation of greater severity in the symptoms, a hospital boat was fitted up at the pier, and one of the ablest physicians in the city (Dr. A. Jaminet) was engaged to attend those affected, and also to institute such sanitary measures as his judgment should dictate. A careful examination of the health and bodily condition of every workman was daily made, and none were permitted to engage in the work without the approval of Dr. Jaminet. Those most severely affected were sent to the City Hospital and had the benefit of the advice and treatment of its resident physician, Prof. E. A. Clark. The total number of men employed in the air-chamber of this pier was three hundred and fifty-two. Of this number about thirty were seriously affected. Notwithstanding the care and skill with which those most severely attacked were treated, twelve of the cases proved fatal. Each one of these, without exception I believe, was made the subject of careful inquest by the coroner, aided by an autopsy conducted usually by some of our most skillful surgeons and physicians. Whilst the exciting cause in all of these cases was doubtless the exposure of the system to the pressure of the condensed air of the chamber, the habits and condition of several of those who died were at the time they went to work, such as would have excluded them from it if subjected to the examination of Dr. Jaminet, and the verdict in about one-half of the cases gave a totally different cause for the death of the patient. Nearly or quite all of these deaths happened to men unaccustomed to the work; several of them to men who had worked but one watch of two hours. In contrast to this, is the fact that quite a large number of the men (certainly one-half of those constantly employed,) commenced with the work at its inception and remained throughout its continuance entirely without injury or inconvenience.

The gentlemen composing the engineer corps of the bridge all visited the air chamber, some of them quite often, either in the discharge of their professional duties, or from motives of curiosity, and none of them suffered any injury whatever.

Much diversity of opinion was expressed by the medical gentlemen who investigated the symptoms and held autopsies of the deceased. Some of these gentlemen maintained that a slower transition from the abnormal to the natural pressure would have been less injurious; others claimed on the contrary, that it was from the too rapid application of pressure in passing from the natural into the compressed air. The fact that the air-lock tenders were in no case affected, although subjected many times during a watch of two hours in the air-lock to rapidly alternating conditions of the atmosphere, at one moment in its normal state in the lock, and five minutes later exerting a pressure of fifty pounds per square inch upon every part of the body, would seem to prove both of these theories unsound, and lead us to believe that in the length of time to which the human system is subjected to this extraordinary pressure, exists the real source of danger, and not from any rapid alternations of pressure to which it is exposed. After the caisson reached the rock, I have frequently, when passing through the air-lock, admitted the compressed air into it so quickly that none but those well accustomed to it could relieve the pressure upon their ears, and yet I felt no ill effects whatever from this rapidly increased pressure ; and in going out I have let the pressure off so fast that the temperature in the lock has fallen thirty-two degrees (Fahrenheit) in consequence. These transitions occupied but three or four minutes.

The fact that the air-chamber was briefly visited by thousands of persons, including many delicate ladies,even after it had reached the bed-rock, some remaining as long as an hour in it without any of them experiencing the slightest ill effects from the pressure, and the fact that no cases of any importance whatever occurred among the workmen after the watches were reduced to one hour, satisfies me that this is the true cause of the paralysis, and that by lessening still more the duration of the watches, a depth considerably greater can be reached without injury to the workmen. Too long a continuance in the air-chamber was almost invariably followed by symptoms of exhaustion and paralysis. Dr. Jaminet, on one occasion, remained in two and three quarter hours when the depth was over ninety feet, and was dangerously attacked soon after reaching home.

Symptoms of paralysis rarely occurred in the shaft, but generally after the stairs were ascended, and never in the air-lock or air-chamber.

A large amount of money has been gratuitously expended by the company in assisting and providing for those who were seriously affected, and in relieving the wants of their families during their illness.

As a merited recognition of the courage, fidelity and services of the men employed in the air-chamber of the east pier ; and as an evidence of my personal appreciation of their faithfulness and good conduct, I have placed in the appendix to this report, the names of those engaged in the work when the pier reached the rock.

THE WEST PIER.

The sinking of the west pier began on the fifteenth day of January of last year, that being the day on which the first stone was laid on the caisson. As it was commenced twelve weeks later than the east pier, advantage could be taken of the experience gained in sinking the latter. On the east pier the interruption and annoyance caused by the necessity of riveting on the iron plates outside of the masonry to exclude the water, as the pier descended, led me to devise some means whereby this inconvenience might be prevented and the cost of the iron saved. The design of the west caisson was so modified that the use of these plates could be abandoned after the first twenty-nine feet; nine feet of this height being the air-chamber, and the remaining twenty feet enveloping the masonry above the chamber. This height of plate iron was deemed requisite to give such rigidity to the caisson as would insure it against any twisting or straining that would endanger the bond of the masonry. After a depth of forty or fifty feet was reached by the east pier, it was found evident that brick linings in the shafts, although surrounded by many feet of masonry carefully laid in hydraulic cement, were not sufficient to exclude the water, which at this depth filtered through quite rapidly. To prevent this and enable the iron around the outside of the pier to be dispensed with on the west pier, its shafts were lined with white pine staves, three inches thick in the centre shaft, which was ten feet in diameter, and two and a half inches thick in the smaller wells, which were four feet nine inches in diameter. This device answered admirably, and the estimated saving in plate iron over the original design was about $10,000. The lower staves were however, found to be too weak to sustain the high water of the Spring freshet without expansion bands of 1x3 inch bar iron, which were placed against them in the shafts in time to avoid any disaster. This novel feature of wooden linings and no exterior envelope for the masonry, will be introduced in the east abutment. The caisson for it is however, made so strongly, that the iron will only be brought up to a height of twelve feet around the base of the masonry. The lining staves in its wells will be so much stronger that they will require no internal supporting rings of iron.

Nothing could have exceeded the perfect working of these economic improvements in sinking the west pier, had not the contractors failed to deliver the granite for it in time. When the point was reached at which the granite became necessary, the surface of the masonry was six or eight feet above water and the base of the pier eighteen or twenty feet from the rock. A judicious view of the case, having reference solely to the cost of constructing this pier, would have dictated a suspension of the work until the stone should have arrived, rather than continue the sinking of the pier and suffer the top of the masonry to descend below the surface of the water. Other questions however, were involved of a more serious nature. It was universally conceded that any effort to negotiate the securities of the company would be fruitless unless preceded by an absolute demonstration of the practicability of putting down the channel piers of your Bridge upon the bed rock of the Mississippi, through the unusual depths of water and sand that were to be encountered. The east pier was in a similar condition at this time, and there remained no alternative but to continue sinking both, to do which, it was necessary to build up and brace out the iron plates which had been carried up from the air-chamber around the masonry of the last pier, and thus dam out the water from covering the top of the masonry as it descended below the surface of the Mississippi, so as to be able to resume the laying of stone when the granite should arrive; and as the west pier was without any such iron envelope, it became necessary to attach the wooden walls of a coffer-dam to its sides in such a manner as to exclude the water from the top of the pier. This was done by padding the lower edge of the dam and attaching its sides securely to the masonry, several courses below the top. This answered very well until the last nine inches of this pier was sunk to the rock. Some of the bolts holding down the dam at the south end of the pier gave way, and the friction of the sand, then fourteen feet high on the outside of the dam and nearly to the surface of the water, prevented the settlement of the dam with the pier at this particular point. Two outside courses of the limestone to which it was attached was held up by the dam nearly across the entire end of the pier. This mishap made it necessary to pump away the sand outside this end of the dam, and put down a large pad or wooden covering reaching below the two disturbed courses, then pump out the dam and relay them. This was done at a depth of about seventeen feet below the surface. The dam was not pumped out till the granite arrived, as the water over the pier did not prevent the work in the chamber, access to it being obtained through the wooden shafts or wells which passed down through the water that was over the masonry. This unexpected trouble, and that at the east pier, were caused solely by the failure of the Richmond Granite Co. to deliver the granite in time. Its delivery was due several months before it was needed, and yet it was not delivered until several months after it was wanted. The loss to your company, resulting from this failure, I estimate to amount to at least $50,000.

THE EAST ABUTMENT PIER.

The complete success which attended the sinking of the east pier convinced me of the practicability of sinking the east abutment pier to the rock in the same manner. The original plans of the bridge did not contemplate resting this abutment on the rock. It was believed quite practicable to protect its foundation with rip-rap stone, and to secure stability and safety by resting it on piles, which were to have been driven to a distance of fifty feet below low water mark. When the Directory of the company were assured of the practicability of resting this abutment upon the bed-rock itself, and of thus terminating forever all doubts as to the absolute stability of each one of the four great piers of your Bridge, the desire that this, the largest of them all, should be placed on the rock also, was unanimous; although the excess in cost involved over that of the original design was understood to be about $175,000. No less than ten thousand additional cubic yards of masonry *below* the line of the tops of the piling on which it was originally intended to start the masonry, are required to sink the pier to the rock. Consequently below this line, it will require nearly as much masonry as will be contained in the west abutment when the latter is completed.

This abutment, when completed, will contain twenty-two thousand four hundred and fifty-three cubic yards of masonry, including concrete and brick work, and will measure in height, from the rock to the top of its cornice, one hundred and ninety six feet nine inches.

The depth of the rock at the site of the abutment was ascertained by careful borings to be eight feet lower than that at the east pier, or one hundred and thirty-six feet below high water mark.

It is not probable that we shall have to contend with much deeper water or much greater air pressure than that encountered in sinking the east pier. The bed-rock at this abutment is ninety-four feet below extreme low water mark, and the river is not likely to be more than eighteen feet above that during the seasons occupied in sinking the pier. Extreme low water mark is only reached when the river is gorged with ice above the city, and the volume of water below the gorge becomes in consequence greatly lessened. The ordinary low water rarely reaches a point within five feet of low water mark.

In accordance with the wish of the Directory, preparations for sinking this abutment to the rock were commenced, and are now nearly completed. The caisson is nearly ready for launching, after which it will be immediately towed into position, and be made ready for sinking. It will cover when on the rock, five thousand square feet of surface, and is therefore about one quarter larger than the base of the east pier. A large trestlework has been erected immediately east of the site of this abutment extending a few feet above high water mark, on which is being placed a portion of the necessary machinery for sinking the caisson. This trestle-work was rendered necessary because of the shallowness of the water on that side of the abutment. On the west side of the caisson one of the derrick boats used at the east pier will be located, and on the trestle work will be placed much of the machinery of the other derrick boat, which was used on the other side of the east pier.

THE EAST ABUTMENT CAISSON.

This caisson will have several novel features in its construction, which I think will make it superior to those used for the east and west piers. The main shaft will have at the bottom two air-locks, each eight feet in diameter, instead of one of but six feet. The main shaft will be carried down into the air chamber ten feet in diameter, instead of but five feet.

The east pier caisson had six other shafts of four feet nine inches in diameter, with air-locks of the same diameter at the bottom of each. This caisson will have but two other shafts of four feet in diameter, with an air-lock at the bottom of each, eight feet in diameter. These last two shafts are enlarged below the roof of the air-chamber to eight feet in diameter each. The increased diameter of the locks will contribute to the health of the men, as it is sometimes necessary for twelve or fourteen of them to be in one of them at the same time, for several minutes, until the pressures are equalized. As all four of these locks are within the air chamber, and also the lower ends of the three shafts, and as about one thousand eight hundred cubic feet of space is occupied by them, there will be that much less space to fill in the compressed air when the pier is down.

The centre shaft alone will be used for the workmen, unless some unforeseen accident should render it necessary for them to use one or the other of the side shafts, which are provided almost solely for safety. The extra size of the locks makes either one of them capable of holding in an emergency all the men that will be in the air chamber at one time, and hence their security will be increased.

To avoid the labor of walking up a circular stairway about one hundred and twenty feet high after leaving the air chamber, the main shaft, in addition to the stairway, will have an elevator or lift to bring the men up. This, it is believed, will contribute greatly to their health. When they are at work in a pressure of forty-five or fifty pounds above that of the natural atmosphere, there ensues a rapid exhaustion of the physical energies. When relieved from duty, a considerable degree of prostration is frequently manifested, and the foremen of the different gangs were in consequence instructed by the physician to cause the men to ascend the stairs leisurely, to avoid increasing it. I confidently believe therefore, that by bringing the men to the surface in the elevator, there will be much less danger of injury occurring from their employment in the air-chamber.

LIGHTING THE CAISSON.

A different method of lighting the air chamber will likewise be adopted. In the other caissons much inconvenience was experienced on account of the particles of unburned carbon thrown off from the flames of the candles used. The consumption of the candles under the action of the compressed air was much more rapid than in the normal atmosphere. At the depth of one hundred feet, they were found to be consumed in about three-fifths of the time required in the open air. Large quantities of smoke were emitted from the flames, and the air was filled with particles of floating carbon which could only be removed thoroughly, by placing a rose jet on the nozzle of a water hose in the chamber, and discharging the spray in every direction. Some amelioration of the evil was obtained by burning the candles under an inverted funnel or chimney, communicating with one of the shafts by a small outlet pipe, through which the escape of the compressed air was regulated by a cock, thus creating a draft above the flame by which the smoke was carried off.

The calcium light would probably prove the most satisfactory one which could be employed in the chamber, were it not for the excessive cost of it in this city. For the one hundred and fifty days which will be required in sinking this pier and completing its foundation on the rock, the cost of lighting the three compartments of the chamber with calcium lights would be at least $5,000. By the means devised for the purpose the cost cannot exceed one-fifth of that sum.

The difficulty of extinguishing a flame in an atmosphere of such density, caused me to forbid the use of oil lamps in the chamber before a depth of eighty feet had been reached. The clothing of two of the men having taken fire from contact with some of the hand lamps or candles used in the caisson, it was found exceedingly difficult to extinguish the flames. One of them was severely burned, although his garments were almost entirely woolen. It was deemed unsafe to risk the danger of having the clothing of the men saturated with oil from the accidental breaking of a lamp which might, by the same casualty, ignite their garments and thus endanger their lives. The use of oil was therefore forbidden.

At the depth of eighty feet it was found that the flame of a candle would immediately return to the wick after being blown out with the breath. At the depth of one hundred and eight and one-half feet below the surface of the river, I blew out the flame of one of them thirteen consecutive times in the course of half a minute, and each time excepting the last, it returned to its wick. Almost as long as a small portion of the wick remained incandescent, the flame would return, and when the glowing particle of two separate candles failed to possess sufficient heat to restore the flame to either, it would reappear at once by placing the luminous portions of the two wicks in contact.

The chamber of this caisson will be lighted by candles contained within glass globes of similar construction to those used in lighting railway carriages. The glass will be of strength sufficient to sustain the external pressure of the condensed air. The chimney will consist of an outlet pipe of one inch diameter, communicating with one of the shafts, and the compressed air will only be admitted within the globe in which the candle is placed, through a small regulating valve. The candle will therefore be burning under the normal pressure of air. A stop-cock in the chimney will prevent the escape of air from the chamber through the globe, when it is desirable to put in another candle, or to clean the glass.

TIMBER WORK.

Beneath the masonry piers of suspension and truss bridges, it is quite common to employ a considerable amount of timber. Where the pressure upon the pier is a vertical one, this economical substitute for stone is admissable, but in the piers of an arched bridge, where some one span is at times loaded while the others are unloaded, the thrust of the loaded arch has a tendency to oscillate the piers, and with a few feet in thickness of a material so elastic as wood under their bases, this oscillation would prove a dangerous feature. In the abutment piers where the thrust is only from one side, and oscillation is prevented by the works on shore, timber may be safely used to a considerable extent. To give the desired stiffness to the caisson for this abutment and avoid the more costly use of iron, the roof of the air chamber is made of timber four feet and ten inches in thickness. A large amount of timber is also used in constructing and stiffening the sides of the air chamber, which are ten feet high, and in forming two horizontal trusses or girders through the air chamber. These two girders are each ten feet thick at the top, three and one-half feet at the base and nine feet in height. They are about seventy-three feet long, and are interlocked at each end with the sides of the air-chamber. They divide this chamber into three nearly equal compartments in the direction of the length of the Bridge. Communication is made between these compartments by means of two openings through each girder.

The sides of the chamber are eight and one-half feet thick at the top and eighteen inches at the bottom, and are composed of timbers, some placed vertically, others horizontally, and some inclined at an angle of about forty-five degrees, and the whole, including roof and girders, thoroughly interlocked together, and bolted with large iron bolts. All of the timber is of the very best white oak, and was squared up with two steam planers belonging to the company. In addition to the iron bolting used, these timbers are thoroughly secured together with large white oak tree-nails.

The wood work of the caisson has been most admirably executed under the superintendence of Mr. John Dunlap, master of ship-carpenters.

PLATE IRON WORK.

Enveloping this entire wooden structure is an iron covering riveted together to prevent the escape of the air which is to supply the workmen. This is of three-eighth inch plate iron, and its sides are increased in thickness at the bottom edge to three inches, by riveting four three-quarter inch plates together. These extend several feet up the sides. This iron edge extends ten inches down below the wooden sides and forms the cutting edge of the caisson. Every two feet the iron sides are strengthened by vertical angle irons three by seven inches in size, riveted on flat wise on the outside of the caisson. Through these angle bars, bolts one and a half inches in diameter are inserted, and by them the iron and wooden sides are strongly held together. This iron covering extends over the wooden top of the air chamber and forms a floor on which the masonry will be laid. The three shafts passing through this floor, by which access to the chamber is obtained, are tightly riveted to it.

The iron sides are carried up twelve feet above this floor, where they will terminate. The masonry above this point will therefore have no exterior envelope such as the east pier had.

Nearly all of the iron used in this envelope was obtained from the hull of the iron gun-boat Milwaukie, the wreck of which was purchased about eighteen months ago. This iron work has been executed by Capt. Wm. S. Nelson, the skillful and energetic contractor who built the caissons of the two channel piers.

WATER TIGHT LININGS.

The water penetrating the masonry will be excluded from the three shafts by white pine linings, arranged like the staves of a cask. The staves composing this lining in the main well or shaft, which is ten feet in diameter, will be ten inches thick in the lower part, and will be gradually diminished to three inches at the top. In sinking the pier, the top of the masonry and shafts, will be kept constantly built up above the surface of the river.

FILLING THE AIR CHAMBER.

The most valuable improvement in the design of the caisson will I think, be found in the method devised for filling the chamber when it has reached the rock. It is a well established fact that sand constitutes one of the most reliable and durable materials for foundations known, if availed of in positions where it can be securely retained under the structure erected upon it. It is an equally well established fact that timber, when entirely submerged in fresh water foundations, is indestructible. These two facts will be relied upon in filling the air-chamber and fixing the foundation of this pier upon the rock. Instead of concrete, sand will be chiefly used for filling the chamber. The sides of the caisson are of great thickness, and are thoroughly interlocked at the corners of the air-chamber, and at the ends of the girders. The possibility of the sand surrounding the pier ever being scoured out to the rock, at the site of this abutment, is a very remote one. It is certainly much more improbable than that it may be scoured thus deeply at the sites of the two channel piers. To avoid all danger from this very remote possibility throughout all time, whatever space there may be existing between the timber walls of the caisson and the bed-rock, after the caisson shall have reached it, will be thoroughly concreted, so that these walls will have a substantial bearing upon a solid material which cannot be affected by any current that may possibly wash the base of the pier. The walls of the air-chamber are so framed as to be sufficiently strong to resist the bursting pressure of the sand within the chamber, caused by the weight of the masonry of the pier and half the side span upon it, even after all the iron used in it shall have been corroded away. The base of the pier is 5,000 square feet in area, and the weight of the entire pier including one-half of the span, will be about 46,500 tons. The pressure per square foot on the rock would, therefore, be 18,600 pounds. The area of the wooden edge of the caisson, including that of the bottom of the girders, air-locks and shafts, is about 1,250 square feet. This area alone would be capable of sustaining the pier, without any additional support from the sand contained within the air-chamber. Without this sand filling, the pressure upon the wooden base of the caisson (including the locks and shafts) would be about 74,000 pounds per square foot, or 514 pounds per square inch. This pressure is not beyond the power of good white oak to resist, nor would it be sufficient to crush the concrete that will be used in filling the small space between the oak and the rock.

Tests made with our testing machine upon a number of blocks of concrete only six weeks old, gave an average resistance to crushing, equal to one thousand two hundred pounds per square inch. Of course, with the integrity of the exterior of the caisson unimpaired, the escape of sand from the interior would be impossible. With the interior compactly filled, the pressure of the superincumbent mass must necessarily be very nearly equally distributed over every part of the caisson, and hence it cannot exceed about 16,000 pounds per square foot.

The tedious process used in concreting the air-chamber of the channel piers, together with the objections to working men at such great depths, induced me to devise some method by which a smaller amount of manual labor could be made to accomplish equally good results. By the plan determined on in this case, I confidently hope to accomplish the necessary work in the air-chamber with a fifth or sixth of the manual labor which was required under the east pier.

This method is so simple as to be readily explained. So soon as the rock shall have been struck by the iron edge of the caisson the space then remaining between the wooden walls of the caisson and the rock, will be thoroughly concreted. The sand under the two girders will be left intact. The borings indicate that the rock is quite level, and it is not probable that inequalities of more than eighteen inches will be found in it. It is estimated that one hundred cubic yards of concrete will be sufficient to support these walls, forming a bed of an average width of three feet six inches, by two feet six inches in height. This concreting being done, all of the pipes passing vertically through various parts of the pier, and used for air, water and sand-pumps, will be closed at the top, and the pumps valves and pipes connected with them in the air-chamber will then be taken off. There will be nineteen of these vertical pipes, each either four or six inches in diameter, the lower ends of which will be enlarged conically through five feet of their lengths. These pipes being opened at their lower extremities, and one of the inner doors of an air-lock being secured from being clogged by sand, the air from the chamber will be permitted to escape, and the chamber will be filled with water. This being done, sand will be introduced through the various vertical pipes mentioned. By means of plummets in these pipes, we shall be able to determine the height of the sand discharged in them, and when it is near the roof of the chamber the air will be again pumped in, and workmen will be sent in to level it off. By repeating this process two or three times, the chamber can be filled nearly to the roof with sand compacted in the water, which will insure its solidity. The remaining space can then be filled with concrete rammed in under the roof of the chamber. The great thickness of the walls and of the girders where they join the roof reduces the area of the upper part of the chamber very greatly. The upper three feet of it measures only two thousand and twenty-five cubic feet in area exclusive of the air-locks and shafts.

To fill the air-chamber of the east pier required one thousand three hundred and forty cubic yards of concrete which was placed in position by manual labor, under an air pressure of nearly fifty pounds per square inch. This pier is twenty-five per cent. larger, and will require only about two hundred cubic yards of concrete to be placed in it under similar conditions; hence the work required to be done in this chamber will be greatly less than in that of the east pier.

WEST APPROACH.

In this approach, which will be entirely of stone, there will be five arches of twenty-six feet eleven inches span, and forty-two feet ten inches in height above the level of the street. The foundations for the piers to support these arches, all rest upon the rock underlying the wharf. These foundations are nine feet by forty-six feet six inches. The one next to the west abutment is the deepest of the five, the rock being forty-one feet eight inches below the City Directrix. This foundation is already completed and will soon receive the Missouri rock-faced red granite, which will form the base for the fine cut sand stone, of which the approaches, on each side of the river, will be built. The foundation for the second pier of this approach has just been commenced. The foundation for the third and fourth piers are completed and are ready for the sand stone. The masonry already laid in these three approach piers measures nine hundred cubic yards.

The foundation for the fifth pier, will be in the line of the houses fronting the wharf, and has not yet been commenced. The cellars of the houses, where it is to stand, have been blasted out of the solid rock, and this pier will be rapidly and easily constructed when commenced.

THE EAST APPROACH.

The piers for this approach will be built upon pile foundations none of which have yet been commenced.

There will be no difficulty in completing this approach within the desired time, and it will be more convenient and economical to begin it after the work on the west approach is more advanced. In design it is almost exactly like the west one.

SAND STONE.

In the selection of sand stone, the greatest possible care has been exercised. This selection was more especially supervised by Col. W. Milnor Roberts, Associate Chief Engineer, who, personally visited and carefully inspected every sand stone quarry of any note, within available distance of the work. The one selected lies close to the Mississippi river, near St. Genevieve, and is distant about sixty-five miles from St. Louis. The stone is a pure sand stone, of a warm yellowish tint. It is of uniform color, free from blemishes, and from the tests made of it promises great durability.

A force has been at work for some time getting out and cutting the stone, and no fear of delay is entertained on account of non-delivery of it in time.

GRANITE.

Col. Roberts has also devoted much of his time to the selection of the granite used, and to be used, in the construction of your Bridge. Several examinations were made by him of the Eastern granites, and almost every quarry from Richmond to Buck's Harbor in Maine was visited by him, with a view to obtaining the best and cheapest that could be had. A contract for the first seven hundred cubic yards was made by him with the Richmond Granite Company, for gray granite. Subsequently, another was made with Messrs. Thomas Westcot & Son, of Maine, for all the gray granite that will be required for the two abutments and the two channel piers. All four of these piers will be faced with granite ashlar above extreme low water mark, except those parts of their sides which are above the springing of the arches and beneath the roadway, and inclosed between the spandrels of the arches. This portion, which is much less exposed to the weather and to view, will be of cut sand stone.

Missouri red granite will also be used as ashlar, but only in the bases of the approaches, and on the T walls of the abutments, and will appear only to the height of the curb stone on the St. Louis wharf, which is nearly the level of the City Directrix. For this purpose about fourteen hundred cubic yards will be required. This granite promises to be equally as durable as the gray, and that which is already laid up in the work is greatly admired, on account of the richness and beauty of its color.

It is to be regretted that proof could not have been given, at an earlier date, of the capacity of a Missouri quarry to supply a material so excellent and desirable. One of the good results of your enterprise, is the discovery and developement of this extensive quarry, owned by Hon. B. Gratz Brown, with whom a contract was made last April for 1,400 cubic yards of the stone, a great part of which has been already delivered. This quarry is distant ninety miles from St. Louis and three miles from the Iron Mountain Railroad.

Several hundred dollars were expended by the Bridge Co., in fruitless endeavors to obtain the proper quality of gray granite from a quarry in this state, prior to this contract and this discouragement, together with the unfavorable results of examinations made of other unproved quarries in this state, created a reasonable assurance that no suitable granite would be discovered in Missouri, in time for our wants. Hence, no alternative remained, but to seek for it elsewhere.

TESTS OF GRANITE.

In the Appendix will be found two interesting reports, one from Prof. Felix McArdle and the other from Dr. Eno Sander, chemists of high standing in St. Louis, giving the chemical tests applied by them, and the results produced by these tests upon the samples of red granite now being used in the construction of your Bridge.

The very careful experiments and report of Prof. McArdle were made gratuitously.

A resolution thanking him for this generous manifestation of his interest in your enterprise was passed by the Board of Directors of ~~your~~ Bridge Company.

MAGNESIAN LIMESTONE.

The interior of all the masonry will be of magnesian limestone from the Grafton quarries. None of this stone will be exposed to the weather. It is remarkably strong. Many tests of its compressive strength have been made in the company's testing machine, where its resistance has, in several instances, exceeded 17,000 pounds per square inch, which is equal to that of granite.

A curious fact has been developed by these tests, which is that, the modulus of elasticity of this stone is about the same as that of wrought iron. That is, a given weight placed upon a wrought iron column and on a column of the Grafton stone of the same size, will produce an equal shortening in both; while the elastic limit (or breaking point) of the stone is not far below the limit at which the wrought iron would be permanently shortened. A column of the stone two inches in diameter and eight inches long, was shortened under compression in the testing machine nearly one quarter of an inch without fracturing it. When the strain was removed the piece recovered its original length.

TESTING MACHINE.

The testing machine, the design of which was made by Col. Henry Flad, Chief Assistant Engineer, has been in operation for several months, and has given the greatest satisfaction. By means of a very simple little instrument, suggested by Chancellor Chauvenet, and matured by Col. Flad, the most delicate changes in the length of the specimen can be accurately recorded, with a degree of minuteness never before obtained or even approximated, in any testing machine, so far as my information extends. By this instrument it is perfectly easy to detect a change in the length of the piece equal to the two hundred thousandth part of an inch.

A brass collar is slipped over each end of the specimen, and these are secured by three pointed set screws in each collar. Any shortening or lengthening of the piece, will of course, alter the distance between the two collars. One collar has on the side of it a small flat surface or vertical table. Against this table is placed a little vertical steel cylinder, which is held against the table by the end of a little flat horizontal bar that is secured at its other end to the other collar. This bar is held against the steel cylinder by a spring, having sufficient strength to keep the cylinder from falling. It is evident now that if one collar be brought nearer, or is moved farther away from the other, the steel cylinder will be rotated, as one side of the cylinder is pressed against the table, which is attached to one collar, while the other side is pressed by the little bar that is fastened to the other collar. If the specimen be subjected to pressure it will be shortened and the collars will approach each other. If tension be applied to the specimen, the piece will be stretched according to its intensity, and in either case, the rotation of the little steel cylinder will indicate the measure of the disturbance that has occurred between the two collars, and it will give it absolutely without any element of error entering into it from any change of the dimensions of parts of the machine under strain. By placing on the top of this little cylinder a small vertical mirror, the extent to which the cylinder has been rotated may be determined in the following manner: Twenty-five feet from the mirror, an arc of a circle is struck, the little steel cylinder being the centre of the arc. On this arc is erected a scale of inches with decimal subdivisions. This scale being illuminated by gas-light can be easily read in the mirror by means of a small telescope placed immediately above the scale. The angles of incidence and reflection at the surface of the mirror being equal, it follows, that one-fourth of a complete rotation of the mirror, would be equal to a half circuit of the circle of which the arc is a part; or, in other words, a movement of the mirror of but one degree would be shown on the scale, by the reading of a space equal to two degrees, or the one hundredth part of an inch on the scale, would really be only half so much, or the two hundredth part of an inch, when seen in the mirror. The diameter of the little cylinder is so proportioned to the radius of the arc as to make the smallest subdivision of the scale equal to the twenty thousandth part of an inch, but the observer, after a little practice, can subdivide these divisions, which are magnified by the telescope, so as to observe the two hundred thousandth part of an inch.

The power is applied to the specimen under trial by means of a hydraulic press, the ram of which moves horizontally. The ram has a steel rod extension passing through the rear end of the cylinder. Specimens for testing by tension have one of their ends secured to this steel rod, and the other to the end of a scale beam. Specimens for crushing are placed at the other end of the cylinder and are compressed between the end of the ram and a crosshead. This crosshead is attached to the end of the scale beam before mentioned, by four powerful rods of steel surrounding the cylinder and leading back to a crosshead attached to the beam. This latter crosshead is detached from the beam when tensile experiments are being made.

It will be obvious, on reflection, that when a piece is being crushed by the thrust of the ram, the four bolts sustaining the crosshead against this thrust must stretch in proportion to the power applied, and hence the specimen will be moved bodily in the same direction, and that this will affect the accuracy of the readings of the mirror, as it too will be moved horizontally with the specimen to which it is attached. To correct this minute error in the readings, a second mirror and scale are used to ascertain the extent of this horizontal movement. The table holding this second mirror, against which the little cylinder rotates, is secured to the frame of the testing machine, which has no strain on it, and the little bar for rotating the cylinder is attached to the crosshead; of course, any movement of this head causes a rotation of this second mirror by which the extent of the movement can be at once ascertained.

It is equally important to know the exact weight applied to the specimen as well as the change of form assumed by it when subjected to the weight. Having no faith in the accuracy and durability of the ordinary mercury and spring gauges for such high pressures as are required in a hydrostatic testing machine, I determined that the absolute strain on the piece must be weighed on the balance. This, Col. Flad has very ingeniously accomplished by a system of levers, balanced on hardened chrome steel knife edges and boxings, sufficiently powerful to stand a strain of one hundred tons, and yet so delicate as to be turned by the weight of one-half of an ordinary cedar covered drawing-pencil when placed in the balance. One pound weight placed in the balance, equals a ton of two thousand pounds weight on the specimen.

I feel safe in asserting that the company have a testing machine which can scarcely be excelled in the accuracy, delicacy and minuteness of its results.

It has been placed in charge of Mr. Paul Dalhgren, C. E., by whom a carefully tabulated record is kept of all tests made with it. A great variety of these have already been made upon specimens of steel, iron, woods of various kinds, granite, brick, limestone, concrete, cement, models of tubes, trusses, &c., &c. Much valuable information having direct reference to the work in hand, has been already obtained by these experiments.

SUPERSTRUCTURE.

On twenty-sixth day of February last, a contract was made with the Keystone Bridge Company of Pittsburg, for the construction and erection of the superstructure of your Bridge, including that of the approaches. By this contract the Keystone Bridge Company undertakes to furnish all materials at the same prices per pound and per foot, at which they were estimated in my published report of May, 1868, excepting cast steel work, which is to be furnished at $20.00 per ton less than the cost set forth in that report. There will be about two thousand five hundred tons of steel used, therefore the saving on this item will amount to about $50,000. The contracting party will, however, receive $40,000 more for erecting the three spans than the estimate in the report. Every other item of cost as set forth in the report referred to, is the price per pound or foot to be paid the Keystone Bridge Company. The amounts set forth under the head of engineering and contingencies, in that report, and aggregating $149,512 14, for superstructure of Bridge and approaches, are reserved by your company, and will be ample to cover any excess of materials required over the amounts estimated, and for engineering expenses, &c.

By the terms of the contract with the Keystone Bridge Co., it agrees under a severe forfeiture in case of failure, to complete the structure ready for use in all its parts in seventeen months from the time working drawings, were furnished to it: provided it is not delayed by masonry work after the first of March next. In case of such delay, the time of completion is to be extended no longer than the time it is so delayed. Completed working drawings were not furnished until the first of July as the completion of certain parts of them was dependent upon data that were obtained from the testing machine, and which could not be ascertained at an earlier period. This delivery of drawings fixes the time for completion of the Bridge on the first of December of next year. I have no apprehensions that the masonry will not be completed in season to prevent any claim for an extension of time on the part of the Keystone Bridge Company.

I have been informed that the Keystone Bridge Company has contracted with the Wm. Butcher Steel Works Company, of Philadelphia, to furnish the cast steel that will be required in the work.

Specifications for the cast-steel work will be found in the Appendix to this report.

I have tested so many samples of steel made by this company which surpassed in strength the requirements set forth in these specifications, that I have no fear of its not being able to supply the quality required. Several pieces of this steel have shown limits of elastic reaction ranging from seventy thousand to ninety-three thousand pounds per square inch.

Since my report, 1st May, 1868, in which the plan of superstructure was described, I have made several modifications in the general arrangement of the arches and in the details of their construction, which will considerably improve the architectural appearance of the Bridge and simplify its fabrication.

These changes consist mainly in using but one cast-steel tube of eighteen inches diameter, instead of two of nine inches, in forming the upper and lower members of each one of the four ribbed arches composing each span ; and in increasing the depth of each one of the arches from eight feet to twelve feet from centre to centre of these tubes.

The railways (which are below the roadway) are raised four feet so that in no place will they appear below the arches, as they did in the original design. In that design the railways were eight feet lower than the centre of the middle span. By deepening the arch four feet and raising the tracks four feet, they are brought level with the centre of this span, or above the soffit of the arch. The lower ribs or tubes of the arches spring from the piers at their original level, consequently the arch has four feet less versed sine or rise than before. To lessen the grade of the railways it was necessary that the tracks should descend each way from the centre of the middle span. This would cause them to fall below the centres of the side spans, to avoid which the level of the springing of these two spans has been lowered eighteen inches at each abutment. That is the ends of the arches of the side spans resting against the abutment piers, will be eighteen inches lower than the other ends which rest against the channel piers. These arches, like the central ones, have four feet less rise than as originally designed, and by lowering their shore ends as stated an additional gain of nine inches depression is obtained at their centres, by which the gradients of the tracks are proportionately lessened towards the ends of the Bridge.

Raising the tracks to the height of the centres of the arches will unquestionably improve the appearance of the structure, and it is generally conceded that the alteration in the level of the springing of the shore ends of the side spans is likewise an architectural improvement. The effect upon the eye caused by it, will be somewhat similar to that produced by the camber of the Bridge.

Of course these changes involved the necessity of revising the former investigations and results, so as to ascertain the difference in the strains, and to determine the alterations required in the sectional areas of the various members of the structure, when thus modified. An entirely new set of detail and general drawings were likewise required in consequence of these changes.

The lithographic view of the Bridge in the appendix is a very correct representation of the structure as it has been definitely determined upon, and is now being constructed. This view also shows the depth of the bed rock at the site of the different piers, and the depth of sand overlying it during ordinary stages of water.

CONDEMNATION OF LAND FOR APPROACHES.

Since my last printed report, the land required in Illinois for the eastern approach to the Bridge has been obtained by condemnation, and paid for by the company.

Judicial proceedings have been commenced in this State for the condemnation of the requisite ground for the approach on this side of the river. About one-fifth part of that which will be required has already been obtained by purchase. A commission has been appointed by the Court to fix the values upon the remaining pieces wanted. No delay in obtaining possession of all the land required is anticipated. These matters are entirely under the control and in the charge of the Executive Committee.

WIDENING THE AVENUES TO THE BRIDGE.

During the last session of the General Assembly of the State of Missouri, a law was passed requiring an election to be held by the citizens of St. Louis to decide upon the question of taxing the city with a sum not exceeding $500,000.00, to defray the cost of widening the streets leading directly to the Bridge. This election was decided affirmatively by a very handsome majority. Steps have already been taken by the Mayor of St. Louis, Hon. Nathan Cole, to carry the will of the people, thus expressed, into effect.

Washington avenue is the most centrally located avenue in St. Louis, and is also one of the most beautiful. It runs nearly in the direction of the Bridge, which is located at its eastern terminus. By the Bridge this avenue is virtually extended across the Mississippi river into the State of Illinois. The law referred to requires this avenue, which is eighty feet wide, to be widened at Third street, where the roadway of the Bridge begins, to 140 feet, and at Fourth street to 117 feet.

Third street which is intersected by the roadway of the Bridge is at this point only sixty feet wide, and immediately south of the

Bridge it is only thirty-eight feet wide. The law contemplates the condemnation of the fronts of seven blocks on this street, three on one side and four on the other side, so that it will be 116 feet wide at the Bridge. This width will be maintained throughout two blocks north, and one block south of the Bridge. From this latter point it will be gradually narrowed from one hundred and sixteen feet to seventy-six feet, in the length of the second block south. Thence south, Third street is but forty or fifty feet wide. The widening of Washington avenue will however, afford easy access to Fourth street, which extends southwardly from the Bridge a mile or more in one uninterrupted width of eighty feet, by which the southern travel will be conveniently accommodated. North of the Bridge, Third street, or Broadway, as it is called, will afford one grand highway, one hundred feet wide, to the northern limits of the city.

These improvements will no doubt be completed by the city authorities as soon as the Bridge is finished. They will contribute greatly to the appearance and beauty of it, and will vastly promote the convenience of the public. The wisdom and liberality of those who voted in favor of providing these magnificent highways to accommodate the vast tides of travel that will hereafter flow to and from the Bridge, will be more fully appreciated when the structure is completed.

CHANGES IN THE BED OF THE RIVER.

I think the propriety of placing the channel piers of the Bridge upon the bed-rock can be no longer questioned, if we consider the facts developed in sinking them. The remarkable scour of fifty-one feet below low water line made in the bed of the stream at the east pier, by the freshet of last April, is sufficient to prove that the scour extends much deeper than was supposed to be possible by many distinguished engineers. The depth of scour was assumed by them as never exceeding thirty feet below low water mark. At more than twice this distance below low water mark, (sixty-six feet,) pieces of bituminous coal, as large as a cocoanut were found imbedded in the sand at the site of the east pier. This coal had evidently been mined by man and had not been carried any great distance by the current, as its surfaces were brilliant and the angles which had been formed by fracture were sharp and perfect. From these facts it would seem evident that the coal must have been carried by the current to where it was found, after the era of steam navigation, as we have no knowledge of stone coal having been used on the Mississippi before that period. These pieces of coal had doubtless been lost from some steamer navigating the river above the city and lodged where they were found during a deep scour, resulting from some unusual under current acting upon the bed of the stream. These currents, I am convinced, extend to a greater depth in the winter season, than in time of floods, which occur in the spring and early in the summer.

The channel opposite this city is very narrow and during severe winters it usually freezes over very firmly before many wider places above are closed. From these open parts floes and fields of ice float down and are driven under the fixed and frozen crust at this point. The floating ice, being lighter than the water, occupies the part of the channel immediately beneath the frozen crust and there stops, and as this engorgement in the narrow channel is increased by constant accessions from above, the current must be gradually forced deeper and deeper. In this way it is not at all improbable that where these gorges occur in the river, its sand deposit may be totally removed in mid-channel, and the bed-rock exposed to the action of the current. When this occurs a continuance of the supply of floating ice soon chokes the passage of the water between the rock and the gorged ice, and thus a natural dam is created across the stream. Sudden rises of the river above these gorges, attaining in a few hours several feet in height, are not at all unusual on the Missouri and Mississippi during severe winters. When they occur, the immense pressure of the water finally sweeps away the obstruction, and fills the open spaces in the river below, for miles distant, with ice so discolored with river sediment as to be scarcely capable of flotation, and giving ample evidence of its imprisonment beneath the surface.

Col. Roberts found a bone in the sand within a foot or two of the bed-rock, under the east pier. It is a part of the femur or thigh-bone of an animal larger than man, and is not petrified; from which fact I assume that it could not, probably, have been in the place where it was found during any long period of time.

While on this subject I will state, as an interesting geological fact that a piece of the bed-rock was broken off in which is found a considerable amount of white coral. It appears on the surface of the piece, which is about three inches thick, and extends through it, appearing on the lower or fractured side. The walls of the cells are incrusted with quartz, the crystals of which are so minute that they can only be seen through a lens.

Beneath the west pier logs partly charred were met with at the depth of fifty feet below low water mark. During the last pumping of sand from the east air-chamber, eighty-four feet below low water mark, particles of charcoal were constantly discharged from the pumps with the sand.

The bed-rock was found to be of dark colored limestone or marble of such close texture as to admit of a moderate degree of polish. Its surface was worn smooth and covered with corrugations of from three to six inches in size, evidently proving that it had been exposed to the direct and constant action of the current, probably at some very remote period.

THE ICE-BREAKERS.

The lateness of the season when the sinking of the east pier commenced, made it absolutely necessary to provide some adequate protection for the requisite boats, machinery, &c., at the site of the pier, against the heavy floating ice which invariably makes its appearance here during the winter. This floating ice frequently attains a thickness of ten or twelve inches, and often covers the entire surface of the river, moving along at the rate of about three or three and a half miles per hour. In proportion as the weather becomes more intensely cold, the volume of the ice increases, and the rate of its movement decreases, until it finally comes to a full stop and then quickly freezes over, affording, even within a few hours afterwards, a safe highway across for pedestrians. In a day or two later the frozen mass becomes so strong as to support the largest and most heavily loaded wagons.

The freezing over of the river at St. Louis is not however an invariable rule, as it does not occur, perhaps, oftener than three in every four years on an average. Last winter was fortunately an exception to the rule. For several days however the floating ice was so heavy and compact that it was with the utmost difficulty that the most powerful steam ferry boats, built expressly to meet such contingencies, could force a passage through it. One or two trips across during an entire day, being all that they could accomplish, frequent attempts in the meantime proving abortive.

To establish in mid-channel any temporary works to withstand an element so apparently resistless, and of such exhaustless volume, was an untried experiment on the Mississippi that presented several very discouraging features. The two chief difficulties were first, to place any construction above the pier that would not be quickly scoured out by the current, and second, to make such construction so strong as to resist the power of the ice to sweep it away. The method devised by me to accomplish the desired result will be fully understood by the following description.

About two hundred feet above the pier at a point from whence the current would flow to the centre of the pier, a pile was driven which formed the apex of a triangular system of piles shaped like the letter A. From this pile two lines of other piles were driven at distances of eight feet. These two lines extended down stream to the distance of two hundred feet and represented the two sides of the letter A. At their lower extremities these two sides were about one hundred and eighty feet distant from each other. The triangle thus formed was filled in with other piles driven in transverse lines from side to side at distances of about fourteen feet, and the tops of the entire system were then thoroughly braced together with hewn oak timbers ten by ten inches square, well bolted to the piles, which were of cypress.

The water was from forty to forty-seven feet deep, when this part of the work was executed, and many of the piles were washed up as the work progressed. It was difficult to drive them into the sand more than twenty feet deep, even with a steam pile driver of 3,500 pounds weight.

About fifty feet above this triangle was placed a clump of nine piles driven close together, and this was encased in sheet iron throughout about twelve feet of its length to prevent the ice cutting the piles, About one hundred and fifty feet above this clump of piles, a large iron pile made of the shell of an old cylindrical steam boiler five-sixteenths of an inch thick, twenty-eight feet long, and forty-two inches in diameter, was sunk nearly to its full length into the sand vertically. From the middle of this iron pile twelve feet below the river bed, was attached before sinking, a wire cable of one and seven-eighths inches in diameter. This cable was led over the clump of piles and firmly secured to it, and from thence it was carried down to the apex of the triangular system below, where it was hauled taught and securely fastened. The object of the rope was to aid in holding the piles steady until the entire protective system was completed; and also to form a cutting edge on which the large floes of ice could be raised and broken asunder before striking the works below. To the triangular system of piles the caisson was secured, and was held by it against the current until it entered the sand.

The iron pile was open through six feet of its lower part to form a sand chamber into which one of the sand pumps was introduced to withdraw the sand and permit it to sink. Above this chamber, the pile was filled with ore from the Iron Mountain of Missouri to insure its sinking in the sand. A central tube fourteen inches in diameter, made of an old boiler flue, enabled the sand pump to be passed through the pile to the sand chamber at the bottom; the ore being contained in the annular space surrounding this tube. The water was about thirty-five feet deep at the site of this pile when it was sunk. After its lower end had penetrated to a point about sixty-two feet below the surface of the water, and the cable had been tightly stretched, fifty or sixty cubic yards of large rubble stone were thrown in around the pile to protect it from scour.

After this work had progressed thus far, a subsidence of about ten feet in the river, enabled us to bolt on to each side of the triangle of piles, about ten feet below their tops, a longitudinal timber about ten inches square, running the entire length of the system. These two longitudinal timbers placed near the surface of the water, and well secured to the sides of the triangle, constituted hinges by which two enormous ice aprons were attached, one on each side, to the triangle.

The object of these aprons, which will be presently described, was to present an inclined surface on each side of the triangle of piles on which the impact of the ice should be received. Any obstruction opposing a vertical surface to the action of the ice would be soon crushed to pieces or ground away, whereas by presenting an inclined one, the ice would slide up on it and be broken to pieces, and be thus made to pass off harmless from it just as the soil does from the plowshare and mould board.

To protect the piles from the scouring action of the current it was necessary to provide some means of keeping the current from them. To do this with broken stone would be very expensive as well as unreliable, and would besides create an obstruction much larger than the pier, which would be difficult and costly to remove after the masonry was completed. By planking the ice-aprons down their inclined sides to the very bottom of the river, the current could be deflected by them from the piles below, and the ice from them above, and thus both objects be attained. This was done.

The ice-aprons were two hundred feet long and sixty feet wide. It was necessary to place them beneath the water at an angle of forty-five degrees, and with the lower edge or side of each resting on the sand, and to make them of such strength as not only to resist a powerful current, but also to withstand the great pressure of the ice which might by the fluctuations of the stream be made to impinge as low down on their sides as to the middle of their surfaces, as well as at twelve or fifteen feet above that point.

The frames of the aprons were made of strong squared oak timber placed transversely at intervals of eight feet, so that the upper end of each one of them would rest by the side of a pile, and on the longitudinal timbers before mentioned. The transverse timbers were each sixty feet long, and were held in place by three equidistant string pieces, each two hundred feet long, bolted beneath them. Two of these skeleton frames were thus constructed on shore, above the works, and were launched with sufficient pine timber beneath to float them. They were then towed, one to each side of the pile structure, and the end of each transverse timber on the side next the piles was placed on the longitudinal timber or hinge before named and secured temporarily to them by chains. The outer edges of these frames were then secured to barges placed alongside of them, and the pine floats under the frames were then taken out. In this position as the two frames lay on the water, they were planked with three inch oak plank. On that part where the ice was expected to impinge, No. 16 sheet iron was placed over the planking. A space on each apron about twelve feet wide and extending their entire length was thus covered with iron. Below this iron covering some openings were left through the aprons for the current to pass, to prevent the formation of a bar of sand below the structure in the eddy that would be created by the ice aprons, after they should be in place.

When the aprons were both completed the lines holding up their outside edges at the barges, were simultaneously cut away; these edges then quickly disappeared beneath the current and were swept by it to the bottom. Both aprons assumed the desired angle. The upper extremities of the transverse timbers forming them, then rested upon the longitudinal timbers forming the hinge by which their lower ends were rotated down to the bed of the stream. The upper ends of these transverse timbers were then each bolted to its respective pile, and that portion of the sides of the pile system extending vertically above the aprons, was planked with two or three strakes of ten by ten oak timber, at the part nearest the aprons, and above that point with lighter oak plank. At the apex of the breakwater thus formed, about one hundred and fifty cubic yards of rubble stone were thrown in, to thoroughly close any space left between the upper ends of the two aprons.

This structure sufficed to completely turn the ice during the winter and made a thorough protection to the works and barges about the pier. A deposit of sand rapidly formed behind the ice aprons which gave great support to them, whilst they in turn, protected this deposit once formed, from the action of the current.

Before our magnetic telegraph was erected, the ice was so heavy for several days as to completely suspend intercourse between the workmen at the pier and the shore. This contingency had been provided for by provisioning the men with two weeks' rations and providing them with bedding.

During the greatest severity of the ice, Mr. McComas, who remained at the pier, continued to operate the sand pumps, and every morning and evening reported the progress of the work in a conspicuous place and in characters so large as to be read by telescope from the shore. The closing sentence of the report was constantly "Ice-breaker all right."

This structure was duplicated at the west pier with equally successful results. Both ice-breakers are still standing having successfully withstood the April flood which attained a height of twenty-six and a half feet above low water mark, and although the current is much increased by them and the river scoured out in proportion, the original angles assumed by the aprons seems to be almost entirely unaltered.

CONCLUSION.

I avail myself of this opportunity to express my thanks to the several gentlemen assisting me in the various departments of the Engineer and Construction Corps of the Bridge, and to commend them to the kind consideration of the Company, for the faithful and efficient discharge of the important duties assigned them.

Respectfully submitted,

JAMES B. EADS,

Chief Engineer.

APPENDIX.

SPECIFICATIONS FOR CAST-STEEL WORK.

The steel shall be of the kind known in commerce as Crucible Cast Steel. It will be required to stand the following tests; and failure to stand any one of such tests will be sufficient cause for the rejection of the piece.

The staves composing the tubes will be required to stand a compressive strain of sixty thousand (60,000) pounds and a tensile strain of forty thousand (40,000) pounds per square inch of section, without permanent set.

They must stand a tensile strain of one hundred thousand (100,000) pounds per square inch without fracture.

The modulus of Elasticity shall not be less than twenty-six million(26,000,000) nor more than thirty million (30,000,000) pounds. This variation should be avoided if possible; in which case the lower amount will be preferable. If a variation occurs in the modulus, bars having the same modulus must be selected in making up the tubes, so that one side of a tube shall not have a greater power of resistance than the opposite one. Those having the same modulus shall be placed in the same tube. Each bar will be tested by the contractor, and the modulus stamped on it by the Illinois and St. Louis Bridge Company's Inspector.

The steel pins will be required to stand without permanent set, a tensile strain of forty thousand (40,000) pounds per square inch and an ultimate tensile strain, without fracture, of one hundred thousand (100,000) pounds. As it will be inconvenient to test these pieces, the Engineer will require to have two or more of them made in one piece, and of sufficient length to cut from the middle or ends of the piece a sample for testing. In such case, failure of the sample will cause the rejection of the entire piece.

Rods, bolts, eye washers, rivets, &c., will be required to bear an ultimate tensile strain of one hundred thousand (100,000) pounds per square inch without fracture, and forty thousand (40,000) pounds per square inch without permanent set; such parts of the work will not be tested in tension beyond forty thousand (40,000) pounds, sample pieces only being subjected to ultimate tests. Such tests as in the judgment of the Engineer or Inspector may be necessary to detect flaws or other imperfections, when the pieces cannot be conveniently subjected to trial in the testing machine, may be used, and any flaw or other imperfection existing in any piece, will be sufficient cause for its rejection, if in the opinion of the Engineer or Inspector it is injured thereby.

The one-quarter (1-4) inch plate steel for enveloping the staves will be required to have a resistance to compression and tension, without set, equal to forty thousand (40,000) pounds per square inch, and an ultimate tensile strength of one hundred thousand (100,000) pounds.

The staves must be so accurately formed that when six short sections of the same bar two (2) inches in length are bound together by an elastic hoop, they will fit accurately at the joints, and form a true circle seventeen and half (17 1-2) inches outside diameter. They must be as straight as it is possible to make them, without planing them.

Steel templates will be provided by the contractor, under the direction of the Engineer, and will be verified and stamped by the Engineer before being used. The various parts of the work must be made to fit these templates with the greatest attainable accuracy, and it will be the duty of the Inspector to reject any piece which in size and direction of its parts, shows the least imperfection.

All holes through the steel work must be drilled, and all bolts turned, unless otherwise directed by the Inspector, in writing. Wrought-iron bands on tubes must be turned on the inside, and faced on each edge, as shown in drawings, and must be heated and shrunk on.

The steel pins will be accurately finished according to the drawings. The central part, where it is reduced in size, will not require turning off. The conical portions must be large enough to fill tightly the holes in the tube couplings. The couplings for tubes may be of rolled steel. The portions next to the main braces of the arch, must be true and parallel, to insure accurate contact and adjustment of the braces to them; but these surfaces and the outside of the couplings need not be finished work.

The surfaces of these pieces coming in contact with each other, or in contact with all other parts of the work, except the main braces, must be accurately finished.

Pieces of the material of these couplings will be subjected to the same test as the pins.

Only the six (6) bolts nearest the centre of tubes, extending through and through, are to be put into them before erection. The caulking of the iron bands on the tubes and the remainder of the through bolts, must be put in after the superstructure is erected. Four (4) one and three-eighths (1 3-8) inch steel bolts will pass through the ends of each set of main braces, and will be tapped into the tube couplings. This work must also be done after erection of superstructure; the object of these bolts being to prevent any movement of the braces around the pins and of the braces on each other.

The tube envelopes must have their edges planed and brought closely together to insure accuracy of diameter of the tubes before riveting on the butt straps. These latter will be caulked.

Each piece, after being examined and accepted by the Inspector is to be covered with a coating of paint or other material, as may be directed by the Inspector, to prevent rusting.

CHEMICAL TESTS OF GRANITE.

Capt. J. B. Eads, *Chief Engineer, Illinois and St. Louis Bridge Company:*

Sir:—I have submitted the samples of granite to a series of experiments, with a view of determining their capacity for the absorption of moisture; the effects of the action of alternate freezing and thawing; and their resistance to decomposing influences, with the following results.

The absorptive per cent., or the amount of water taken up by one hundred parts by weight, was determined in each instance by immersing the sample in boiling water for fifteen minutes, and removing the superficial moisture before weighing.

No. of Expe'mt	RED GRANITE. Per cent. of absorption in 100 parts by weight.	GRAY GRANITE. Per cent. of absorption in 100 parts by weight.
1	.194700	.341673
2	.189670	.341942
3	.233641	.345082
4	.253420	.351791
5	.275892	.364073
6	.233641	.351912
7	.195640	.342510
8	.194520	.342089
9	.194591	.341783
10	.194702	.341599
11	.194711	.341690
12	.194794	.341687

After the twelfth trial the absorptive percentage was found to be constant and therefore the absorptive power of the red granite is determined to be .1947 of one per cent. in every one hundred parts by weight, and the absorptive power of the gray granite is .3416 of one per cent. in every one hundred parts by weight; a difference of .1469 of one per cent. in favor of the red.

The per cent. of loss was calculated from the effect produced by the disintegrating power of the sulphate of soda whilst crystallizing. A boiling saturated solution of the salt being used in which each sample was immersed for fifteen minutes, and when taken out the sulphate of soda was allowed to crystallize thoroughly, then the salt was washed out with boiling water and the loss in weight noted.

No. of Expe'mt	RED GRANITE. Per cent. of loss in 100 parts by weight.	GRAY GRANITE Per cent. of loss in 100 parts by weight.
1	.566511	.335821
2	.456282	.343314
3	.524111	.369341
4	.614235	.341107
5	.767891*	.380140
6	.513218	.344316
7	.524106	.339149
8	.531620	.338555
9	.541510	.336032
10	.559102	.335619
11	.565901	.335739
12	.566010	.335793

After the twelfth trial the percentage of loss appeared constant being for the red granite .566 of one per cent. and for the gray .3357 of one per cent. or in the proportion of 88 (gray) to 147 (red) as calculated from the specific gravities. The specific gravity of the red granite being 2.62038 and the specific gravity of the gray granite 2.64224.

The disintegrating effect of nitre was tried in the same manner; the average loss of the red granite in five experiments was .5597 of one per cent. and the average loss of the gray granite was .38994 of one per cent.

The great disparity between the absorptive and loss percentages of the red granite is explained when the large size of the crystals of quartz and feldspar composing it is taken into consideration; the loss being due to the bodily separation of the crystals from the surface of the specimen. In a specimen, the surface of which was ground, the loss by the disintegrating force of the above solutions amounted to .3089 of one per cent.; and a hammered specimen treated in like manner lost .384702 of one per cent.

*Loss partly mechanical, by handling.

The gray granite further suffers a loss from the solvent action of water alone; a sample of it immersed in distilled water for a number of days at the ordinary temperature was found to give to the distilled water traces of lime and the alkalies, and the bottom of the vessel containing the water was covered with a delicate layer of silica. This was not the case with the red.

The disintegration of granitic material may be produced by the agency of chemical change, which change is undergone by some foreign substance accidentally present, such as iron pyrites, garnet, etc., or the disintegration by chemical agency may proceed through the decomposition of the normal constituents, mica and feldspar. The disintegration of a granite may be safely assumed to commence always in the chemical decomposition of the feldspar when foreign substances are absent. The decomposition of the feldspar may be effected in different ways; first, by water containing free carbonic acid; second, by the action of sulphurous acid; and third, by water holding traces of alkaline or other substances in solution.

The red varieties of fieldspar are less affected by these agencies than the white varieties, since the red varieties contain a large quantity of sesquioxide of iron, and in some cases the alumina is altogether replaced by sesquioxide of iron; whenever this occurs the feldspar obstinately resists the decomposing agencies above recited.

The superior durability and resistance to chemical change of granitic material containing the red varieties of feldspar over that composed of the white varieties of feldspar is clearly shown in the case of these two granites.

The red granite lost after three days immersion in water containing free carbonic acid frequently renewed, .0913 of one per cent. in one hundred parts by weight; the gray granite treated in the same manner lost .64087 of one per cent. in one hundred parts by weight.

Treated with a weak solution of sulphurous acid for three days, the red granite lost .1456 of one per cent. of its weight; and the gray granite .4253 of one per cent. by weight. Exposed to an alkaline solution for four days the red granite lost .2287 of one per cent. of its weight, and the gray granite lost .7349 of one per cent.

of its weight. An atmosphere of carbonic acid or sulphurous acid gas causes an appreciable change in the gray granite, whilst it has apparently no influence on the red. In recording the results of the examination the term "granite" has been retained on account of its familiarity and common application.

With a view of determining the joint effect of the mechanical and chemical disintegrating agencies, the samples, after treatment with carbonic and sulphurous acids and with alkaline solutions, were again severally subjected to the action of boiling water, (to determine the increase or decrease of the absorptive per cent.,) and to the action of the sulphate of soda solution (to determine the loss percentage).

After treatment with solution of carbonic acid the absorptive per cent. was found to average in the red granite .2037 of one per cent. and in the gray granite .6601 of one per cent. in one hundred parts by weight; the loss percentage averaging in the red .53041 of one per cent. and in the gray .9764 of one per cent. After treatment with solution of sulphurous acid, the absorptive per cent. averaged in the red .2399 of one per cent. and in the gray .7731 of one per cent; the loss per cent. in the red was .63021 of one per cent. and in the grey .8999 of one per cent.

After treatment with alkaline solutions the absorptive per cent. of the red granite averaged .21227 of one per cent. and of the gray .38419 of one per cent; the loss percentage being respectively .70121 and .97929 of one per cent.

The destructive forces, therefore, most to be feared are not those of the rain and the frost, but the acid-laden air of the great city and the alkaline waters of the great river. These are constant, those only periodical.

I am, very respectfully, your obedient servant,

FELIX McARDLE, M. D.

St. Louis, March 30, 1870.

AUGUST 4th, 1870.

CAPT. JAMES B. EADS, *Chief Engineer, of Illinois and St. Louis Bridge Company:*

DEAR SIR:—It was a peculiar task with which you have honored me by asking a chemical examination of several specimens of granite with a view to determine as far as it could be done, not only their comparative value as a building material for the piers of the bridge under your supervision, but especially whether or not they might equally and successfully resist the decomposing influence of an atmosphere, impregnated, like ours, with the smoke and gases produced by the combustion of the vast amount of fuel consumed in a city of such dimensions as St. Louis has already acquired, and which will continue to increase with her manufacturing interests.

Would it be possible to arrive by experiments of but a few weeks' duration in the laboratory, and by the aid of chemical reagents, at a result in any degree similar to the slow but steady and continuous action of the combined influences of moisture, change of temperature, the mechanical force of wind and rain, and the obnoxious and deleterious gases, which are engaged incessantly in the immense laboratory of nature in producing the final decomposition of all matter? It was obvious, that if chemical researches would yield any results at all, they could be only approximate, and would have to be produced by substituting for the slow action of time, the strong and immediate influence of the same, or similar forces as act in the atmosphere but in a more concentrated form, which, although they could not insure precisely the same condition of things, would at least test the resisting power of the materials to which they were applied. With such reflections I commenced my investigations.

There was a considerable difference in the external appearance of the three specimens; while the Richmond Granite, with its fine grain and smooth appearance, seemed to be suitable, almost, for fine works of architecture, it shared with the granite from Maine, only the similarity of its gray color; for the structure of the latter was much coarser, resembling in this respect, more the sample from the Iron Mountain, which again differed from it widely in regard to its pinkish color. The firmness and compactness of the rock seemed to be the same in the three samples, which were broken up into small pieces of about two square inches each, and thus exposed to the action of the reagents, the result of which is hereby submitted to your consideration.

Although the rock of the piers will never be exposed to the action of acids, I thought it would manifest at least its quality, if their influence upon it should be ascertained, and consequently immersed a piece of each separately in diluted muriatic, nitric, and sulphuric acids. After ten days' immersion, they were examined and found uneffected; then they were boiled in the same solutions for about an hour, replenishing the evaporated water. After cooling, no visible change could be discovered on either piece, nor did its strength seem to be the least impaired; the remaining liquor however, from the Iron Mountain granite contained iron, which must have been uniformly dissolved from its surface, for the rock was apparently as firm as ever, and even stood well the following accident. While one of its specimens was being boiled with diluted nitric acid, it became accidentally neglected, the liquid evaporated entirely and left the granite dry and hot; but nevertheless, its surface remained intact, and even its sharp corners had retained their firmness.

I had received but a small quantity of Maine granite, barely sufficient for the foregoing experiments; it could not, therefore, be included in the other series of tests.

In order to determine the probable action of the gases produced by the combustion of fuel, which are mostly sulphurous and carbonic compounds, several pieces of each specimen of granite were treated with a slow current of a mixture of street gas, sulphurous acid, carbonic oxide and carbonic acid, and as it is recognized in nature, that moisture increases the force of the most powerful agencies for decomposition, it was believed that the destroying efficacy of these gases would also be increased by keeping the rock moist during the whole process. This experiment was continued for nearly two weeks, and when the specimens were taken from the apparatus, their surfaces were closely examined, but no sign of decay was visible, nothing could be discovered to indicate that the adhesion of the component parts had been loosened and the validity of the rock destroyed; its edges even remained firm and sharp.

In the foregoing experiments, the gases referred to were administered pure and without any admixture of air, smoke, etc., but as it might be inferred that their action would be modified when applied in the same state as they are discharged from the furnaces into the atmosphere, I considered it my duty also to determine the concentrated action of such mixture. The best place for such a test seemed to me the front of the flues of a boiler, through which the gases pass directly from the fire, with all the smoke and undecomposed air, and where the temperature rises and falls from sixty to two hundred degrees, and more according to the amount of fuel and the rapidity with which it is consumed. The specimens intended for this test were put into a dish with water, and then placed into the front of a boiler-flue, so that all the smoke and the gases had to pass over and touch and envelope them. The water was allowed to evaporate and dry up occasionally before being replenished, and the rock was thus exposed to all the imaginable changes attendant on such a situation. On the expiration of twelve days, the dish was removed from its position. The rocks showed no signs of decomposition and were hard and firm yet. It must be mentioned however, that I succeeded in loosening a few fragments from the edges of both samples, which from all appearances seemed to have been disintegrated by the sledge when the samples were broken up into smaller pieces.

It remained yet to test the influence, upon the samples, of frost and mild temperature. One piece of each granite was soaked in water and then repeatedly exposed, alternately to the low temperature of a freezing mixture, and the atmosphere of 55 deg. F., before they were placed into the dish in the flue where they remained several days. The treatment had made no apparent influence upon the rock.

If you will now recapitulate and compare the results of the experiments fully and minutely described in the foregoing paragraphs, you will find that there was no test made which has not terminated in the favor of the resistive power of either specimen of granite, against the decomposing influences of the reagents, and if any such experiments and tests are of any value whatever, or give permission to draw conclusions in regard to the technical value of the material experimented upon, it is manfested beyond a doubt that both specimens of granite from Richmond, as well as from the Iron Mountain are capable of enduring and resisting the combined influences of all the deteriorating gases, which may contaminate the atmosphere of our city.

Hoping that the manner in which I have treated this matter will meet with your approval, I remain most respectfully,

Your obedient servant,

[Signed] ENNO SANDER.

NAMES OF THE MEN WHO WERE EMPLOYED IN THE CAISSON OF THE EAST PIER, FROM THE TIME IT ENTERED THE BED OF THE RIVER UNTIL IT WAS FILLED WITH CONCRETE.

FOREMEN:

JAS. DONNELLY,
B. O'KEEFE,
PETER WHITE,
C. W. BROWN,
FRANK JORDAN,
JAMES LOVE.

MACHINISTS IN CHARGE OF THE PUMPS:

PATRICK GLINN,
C. MALBIN.

LOCK-TENDERS:

H. J. HARVEY,
THOS. CAVANAUGH.

WORKMEN:

W. BURNES,
JAS. LYONS,
W. S. HAWKINS,
P. McPIKE,
P. PETERSON,
JNO. FLINN,
WM. McKENNA,
CHAS. WAGNER,
HENRY COOPER,
AUG. DONKA,
P. DUMAS.
P. GALLAGHER,
WM. FOSTER,
J. McDONALD,
W. McCARTNEY,
DENNIS McCARTY,
P. FORD,
ANDREW COOPER,
JAS. SHEEHAN,
JOHN WILEY
WM. LOOMIS,
JOSEPH BOWERS,
ED. RAND,
M. IRWIN,
WM. LAFFERTY,
M. O'KEEFE,
FRANK SANFORD,
M. MEYERS,
WM. MURPHY,
M. McDERMOTT,
D. FORD,
F. FORD,
D. BRADLEY,
LOUIS GIBELER,
A. DEFORNEY,
N. NICHOLS,
CHAS. SHAFER.
WM. CONNERS.

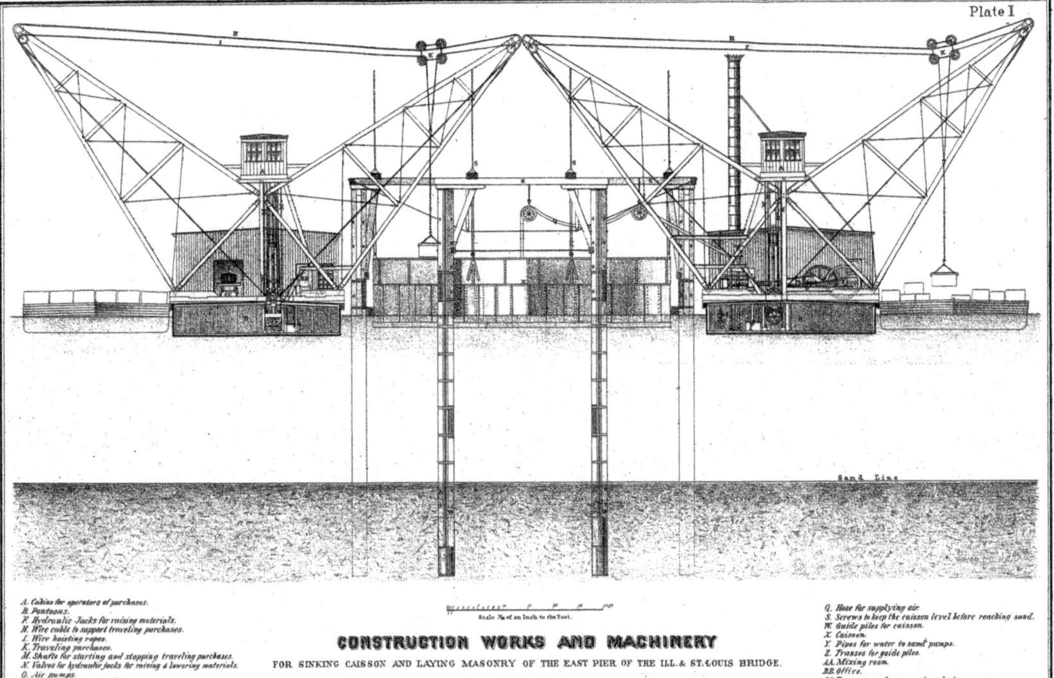

CONSTRUCTION WORKS AND MACHINERY

FOR SINKING CAISSON AND LAYING MASONRY OF THE EAST PIER OF THE ILL. & ST. LOUIS BRIDGE.

James B. Eads Engineer.

A. Cabins for operators of purchases.
B. Pontoons.
F. Hydraulic Jacks for raising materials.
H. Wire cable to support traveling purchases.
I. Wire hoisting ropes.
K. Traveling purchases.
M. Shafts for starting and stopping traveling purchases.
N. Valves for hydraulic jacks for raising & lowering materials.
O. Air pumps.
P. Engines to drive air pumps.
Q. Hose for supplying air.
S. Screws to keep the caisson level before reaching sand.
W. Guide piles for caisson.
X. Caisson.
Y. Pipes for water to sand pumps.
Z. Trusses for guide piles.
AA. Mixing room.
BB. Office.
CC. Tram ways for cement and stone cars.

Plate II.

SECTION OF EAST PIER AND CAISSON

ON LINE M. N. PLATE II a.

SHOWING THE INTERIOR OF THE MAIN ENTRANCE SHAFT AND AIRCHAMBER AND THE WORKING OF ONE OF THE SAND PUMPS.

ILLINOIS AND SAINT LOUIS BRIDGE.

JAMES B. EADS, Chief Engineer.

A. Airlocks
B. Airchamber
C. Timbergirder
D. Discharge of Sandpump
E. Sandpumps
F. Main Entrance Shaft
G. Side Shafts
H. Iron Envelope
I. Bracing for Shell

Extreme Highwater of 1844
City Directrix
Ordinary Waterline
Lowwaterline
Upperline of Sandbed
D
G
G
H
H
H
H
C
A
A
BEDROCK OF RIVER

C. Gayler del.
A. Gast & Co. Cor 3d & Walnut, St. Louis, Mo.
L. Gast lith.

Scale:
10 5 0 10 20 30 40 Feet

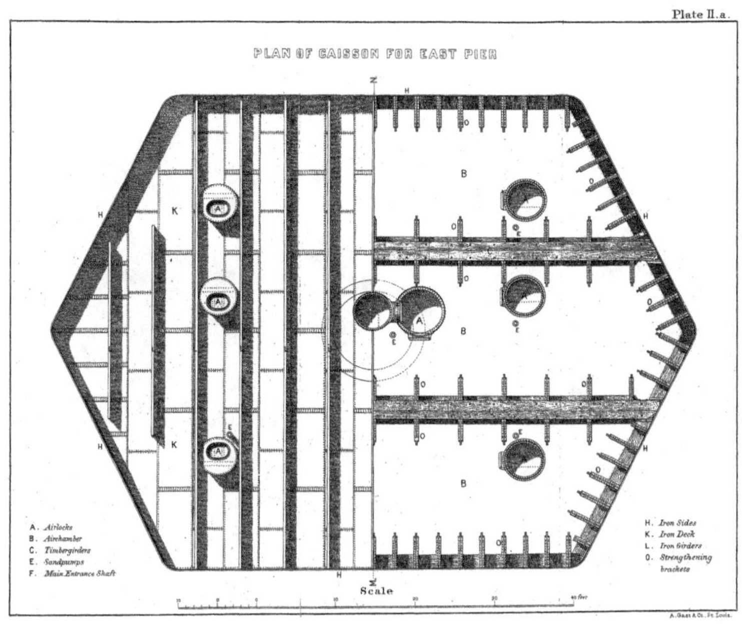
PLAN OF CAISSON FOR EAST PIER
A. Airlocks
B. Airchamber
C. Timbergirders
E. Sandpumps
F. Main Entrance Shaft
H. Iron Sides
K. Iron Deck
L. Iron Girders
O. Strengthening brackets
Scale
10 5 0 10 20 30 40 feet
A. Gast & Co., St. Louis.

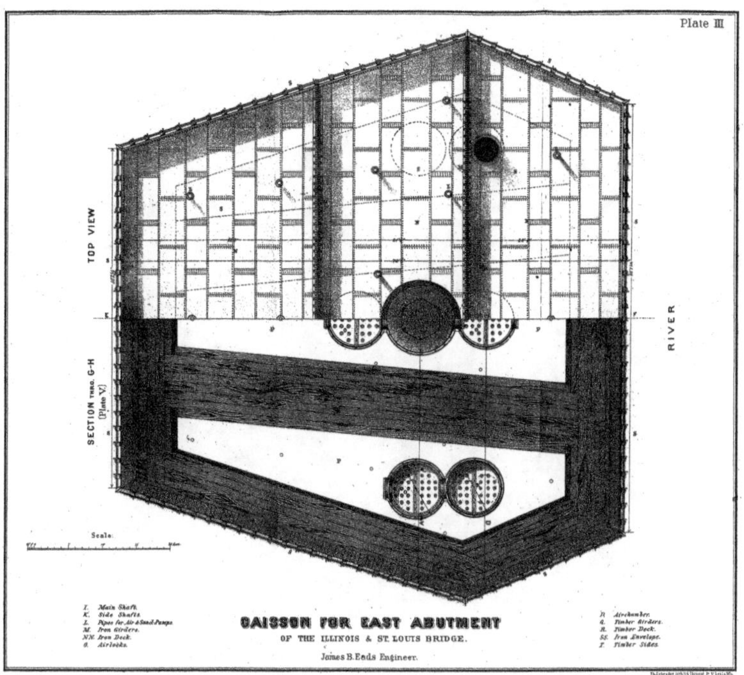

CAISSON FOR EAST ABUTMENT
OF THE ILLINOIS & ST. LOUIS BRIDGE.
James B. Eads Engineer.

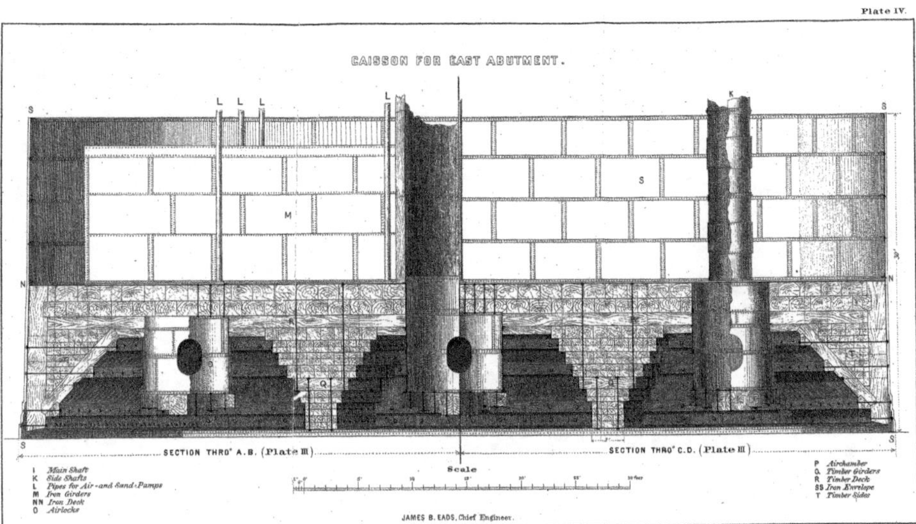
Plate IV.
CAISSON FOR EAST ABUTMENT.
SECTION THRO' A.B. (Plate III)
SECTION THRO' C.D. (Plate III)
Scale
I Main Shaft
K Side Shafts
L Pipes for Air- and Sand-Pumps
M Iron Girders
NN Iron Deck
O Airlocks
P Airchamber
Q Timber Girders
R Timber Deck
SS Iron Envelope
T Timber Sides
JAMES B. EADS, Chief Engineer.
August Gast & Co., St. Louis.

Plate V.

CAISSON FOR EAST ABUTMENT
SECTION THRO' E.F. (Plate III)
I Main Shaft
K Side Shafts
L Pipes for Air- and Sand-Pumps
M Iron Girders
NN Iron Deck
O Airlocks
Scale
P Airchamber
Q Timber Girders
R Timber Deck
SS Iron Envelope
T Timber Sides
JAMES B. EADS, Chief Engineer.
August Gast & Co. St. Louis.

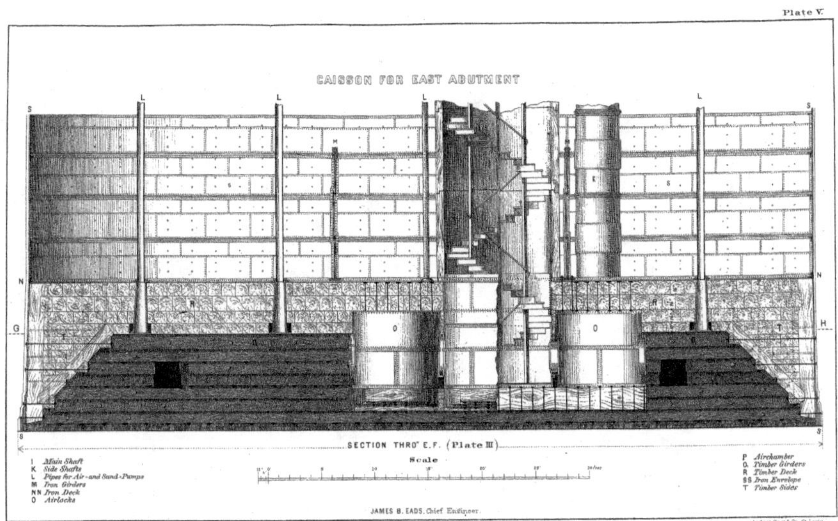

ILLINOIS AND ST. LOUIS BRIDGE COMPANY.

REPORT

OF THE

CHIEF ENGINEER.

OCTOBER, 1871.

ST. LOUIS:
MISSOURI DEMOCRAT BOOK AND JOB PRINTING HOUSE.
1871.

CHIEF ENGINEER'S REPORT.

ST. LOUIS, *October 1, 1871.*

To the President and Directors of the
Illinois and St. Louis Bridge Company:

GENTLEMEN—I have the honor to make the following report:

MASONRY.

The total amount of masonry of every kind, including brick-work, laid up to this date is sixty-eight thousand seven hundred and thirteen cubic yards. There remain yet to be laid thirty-three thousand nine hundred and two cubic yards.

EAST APPROACH.

The foundations of the five piers and towers of this approach have all been built, and are now completed ready to receive the sandstone, excepting pier No. 2, the red granite being laid up, including the wash-course, on all of them with this exception.

These approach piers (excepting No. 5, to which the towers are attached) were all sunk by the same process used in sinking the large ones. This was believed to be more certain and economical than by coffer-dams, the method used on the west approach. The result has fully confirmed this opinion. With pier No. 2 the coffer-dam would have proved very expensive, as this pier encountered in its descent the hulk of an old and strongly-built ferryboat. Its planks were three inches thick, and floor-timbers four by eight inches square. This huik had to be cut away to permit the descent of the pier, which has gone directly through it, the kelson of the wreck having been intersected by the caisson. This not altogether unexpected difficulty has delayed the completion of this pier about three weeks. It has now passed this obstruction, and needs to be sunk only one foot more to reach its final destination.

It has not been deemed necessary to sink the foundations of the first four piers of this approach deeper than twelve feet below extreme low-water mark. The caissons used are made wholly of oak timber, excepting only the air-locks and the spikes and bolts used in fastening the timbers together. They are ten feet high, consequently they are entirely below low-water line, while the masonry extends only down to that line. The surface of the wharf will be about nineteen feet above the bottom of the foundation of No. 1, and about thirty-two feet above that of No. 4.

The towers and pier No. 5 are laid on a foundation of concrete six feet deep, under which a system of piles was first driven to an average depth of twenty-five feet. The concrete is based, fifteen feet above low-water line.

The east abutment pier, resting on the rock at the depth of 136 feet below high-water mark, and standing between these approach piers and the river; and the wharf pavement covering the river shore, will, I think, be amply sufficient to prevent the current of the stream from ever affecting the foundations of these small piers.

From the towers eastward the upper roadway of the Bridge will be carried by trestling to Fourth street in East St. Louis, with a grade of four feet to the 100 feet. The railways will curve out to the north from under the upper roadway, immediately east of the towers, and will be of such grade and construction as shall be determined upon by the railroad companies who have contracted to use the Bridge, and who will pay for these railways. A sixty-eight foot grade will bring the railways down to the level of the present tracks in East St. Louis, within a distance of about 3,000 feet.

EAST ABUTMENT.

This pier has had no work done upon it during the last four months. It is completed on the river front to within two courses of the wash-course. The wash-course is the one immediately below the lower tier of skewbacks.

On the **T** wall the red granite is now being laid, four courses being required to finish it ready for the sandstone. The sandstone commences upon the wash-course, which course in the **T** wall is of red granite, and corresponds in height with the wash-courses of the approach piers on each shore.

EAST PIER.

The masonry of this pier lacks two courses of being high enough to set the lower tier of skewback-plates. These will be laid while the contractors are setting the plates on the west pier; there being but one outfit of hoisting apparatus for carrying up the masonry of these two piers, it is alternately used at each. At present no work is being done on this pier. It will, however, be finished considerably in advance of the wants of the contractors for superstructure.

WEST PIER.

The masonry of this pier has been carried up high enough to receive the lower tiers of skewback-plates, where it must rest until these are fixed against it. The stone-cutters are now engaged in making the necessary recesses in the granite to receive the plates, and so soon as this shall have been completed, these plates will be set. This pier will be completed about the first of February next. The necessary steel and iron work for it are in such a state of forwardness that no further delay need be feared in its completion.

WEST ABUTMENT.

The masonry has been carried upon the **T** wall or western face of this abutment to a level, four courses below the springing of the first stone arch over the St. Louis wharf. This portion of the masonry (the **T** wall) is of sandstone. On the river front of the pier the masonry is finished to a level five courses lower than the **T** wall, and is now ready to receive the lower tier of the skewback-plates. These four plates are now ready and will immediately be set by the contractors for the superstructure. So soon as this shall have been done the masonry of this side of the pier will be carried up to receive the second tier of skewback-plates.

These skewback-plates are seven feet by three and two-thirds feet six inches in thickness; and to insure an equal bearing against the granite throughout their entire area, iron cement will be driven in between them and the stone after they are in proper position. This work must be done before the next courses of granite are laid above the plates. These plates will sustain the entire thrust of the arches. It is against them that the skewbacks of the arches wil rest. The skewbacks are of wrought-iron, and will be firmly secured to the masonry by large anchor-bolts passing through them and the skewback-plates into the abutments, where the bolts will be fastened to cast-iron anchor-plates built in with the masonry. Into the upper and lower tiers of skewbacks the cast-steel tubes which form the upper and lower members of the arches will be inserted. The anchor-bolts are five and three-fourths inches in diameter. Some are made of steel and others of iron, according to the different degrees of strain to which they will be subjected. The lower skewbacks will each have four bolts and the upper ones three. These bolts will sustain no portion of the weight of the arches. Their object is simply to prevent any movement at the ends of the arches which would otherwise occur from extremes of temperature and excessive inequality in the distribution of load upon the arches.

When the second tier of skewback-plates are fixed upon this abutment, the remainder of the masonry of it will be rapidly completed. I see no reason now to fear any further delay in this part of the work, and think the masonry of this pier will certainly be completed by next February.

WEST APPROACH.

The piers of this approach over the St. Louis wharf are all up to the springing of the arches which they are intended to carry, except pier No. 5.

One complete sandstone arch is turned upon piers Nos. 2 and 3, and about one-fourth of an arch is turned upon the centering on each side of this completed arch. The other two arches of this approach can not be started until the T wall of the west abutment is four courses higher, and pier No. 5 is completed. This pier stands in the house-line of the wharf, and is completed from the rock to the wash-course inclusive, and is therefore ready to receive the sandstone on the red granite base-course.

The foundation of the south tower is also completed to the same extent, and sandstone is being laid now on this pier and tower. The foundation of the north tower has just been commenced.

Between the wharf and Commercial street the masonry is well advanced, piers Nos. 6, 7 and 8 being completed. On these piers is now being placed the centering for the brick arches which will surmount them, each arch having twenty-seven feet span.

Piers Nos. 8 and 9 stand on opposite sides of Commercial street, twenty-seven feet apart. Each is completed ready for the centering of the arch, which will soon be placed in position on them.

Piers Nos. 9, 10, 11 and 12, standing on the block between Commercial and Main streets, are all completed, and the three brick arches (twenty-six and a-half feet diameter) upon them are likewise completed. The spandril spaces between these arches are being filled with ballast to level up for the railway sleepers. The vaults under the arches between the wharf and Main street are inclosed by substantial masonry, and the rooms thus formed are connected by arched doorways through the piers. A large warehouse is thus created on each of these blocks, which will be available for revenue. Arched entrances are provided to these apartments through the piers on Main and Commercial streets.

The land over which the approach is carried further west, is similarly utilized for warehousing purposes as far as to the middle of the block between Second and Third streets.

Pier No. 12, now finished, forms the eastern abutment on Main street for the support of the truss which carries the roadways over that street.

Pier No. 13, on the west side of Main, is built up from the rock to the street level, and the sandstone work on it is progressing. From this point west no large piers occur, except on each side of the alley between Main and Second, and on each side of Second street, at which point abutment piers are being placed to sustain the iron trusses for carrying the roadways over these thoroughfares. The foundations for all of these abutments are built up to within one or two feet of the street levels, and sandstone work is progressing on one of them on Second street. The others are covered at present with hoisting machinery and wagon-ways for transporting materials. From Main street to the middle of the block, between Second and Third streets, the railways and roadways will be supported on strong side-walls of masonry, and two rows of brick pillars placed equidistant between these walls. These side-walls are almost entirely completed, ready for receiving the railway timbers, from Main street to the end of the approach at Third street. Between Second and Third streets they are still more advanced, being nearly completed for the upper roadway.

The brick pillars between these side-walls are well advanced, east of Second street to the alley, one tier being nearly completed to the level of the railway beams.

The entire masonry for the west approach, from the Levee to Third street, will be completed ready for the superstructure, I think, by the middle of January next.

SUPERSTRUCTURE.

CAST STEEL.

The Keystone Bridge Company, contractors for superstructure, have made but little progress in their contract, owing chiefly to delays in obtaining the proper quality of steel and iron for the work. The contract for steel was let by them to the Wm. Butcher Steel Works, near Philadelphia. Extensive additions, consisting of buildings, furnaces, rolling-mill, straightening machines, &c., were made to the works, and every indication seemed to encourage the belief that the steel would be promptly supplied. Unforeseen delays, however, occurred in getting the necessary machinery into proper working order.

The first large forgings required by the Bridge were steel anchor-bolts, five and three-quarter inches in diameter, and from twenty-two to thirty-six feet long. The first bolts, when tested, were found to be of inferior quality. Having been injured in forging, they were broken by testing. Each bolt is required to sustain, when tested, a tensile strain of 519 tons, without being permanently elongated, being twice as much as the maximum strain to which it can be subjected in the Bridge. Before this test could be applied to the defective ones, sufficiently to prove their weakness, the testing machine itself was broken twice. This involved several weeks' delay. When the defects of the machine were remedied, the inferiority in the bolts was fully discovered. New mixtures of steel had then to be tried, and greater care was used in its manipulation. Many bolts had been made before the testing machine was repaired and could reveal these defects. These were, of course, rejected when tested, and others had to be made in their stead.

In the novel operation of testing such large forgings, and in the management of the machine itself when exerting such great strains upon them, many unexpected accidents occurred, both to the machine and to the instruments required for measuring the extensions of the bolts and the amounts of strain imposed upon them. For instance, a piece of one of the bolts, which weighed over 1,000 pounds and twenty feet in length, was shot out of the machine like an arrow, when the bolt broke, and fell fifty or sixty feet distant; whilst the other end of the bolt reacted with such force upon the machine as to break the piston rod or pulling bolt by reversing the tensile strain upon it, thus driving it out of the ram at the other end of the hydrostatic cylinder, and breaking by its reactive force the fastenings by which it was secured.

The expense of testing was assumed by the Keystone Bridge Company in its contract, and it in return sub-let this part of the work, so far as it relates to the steel, to the Wm. Butcher Company. The design, construction and repairs of the necessary testing machines and appliances are, therefore, a part of the province of the contractors, they simply agreeing to subject the various materials to the requisite strains under the supervison of the Chief Engineer of the Bridge, or of his assistants, the instruments by which the strains are measured being all that is supplied by the Bridge Company.

By these various delays several months were lost before any bolts were supplied, capable of sustaining the strain above named. These difficulties were, however, fully overcome, and twenty-four bolts have been thus tested and received. Eighteen of these were sent more than three weeks ago to the Keystone Bridge Works at Pittsburg, to have screws cut upon them. Others are being made from day to day at the steel works, and I believe they will now be supplied as fast as they are needed. Twenty-six are yet to be made.

Similar difficulties and delays were experienced in other parts of the steel works. About four-fifths of the entire steel required, consists of tubes about thirteen feet long and eighteen inches in diameter. These are each composed of six staves of the length of the tube, and varying from one and one-eighth to two and one-eighth inches in thickness, and each being about nine and one-half inches wide. Several attempts were made to roll these staves before the rolls were perfectly formed to accomplish it. Each failure necessitated the removal of the rolls from the mill for alteration to the machine shop, several miles distant. Each of these rolls weighed several tons, and this usually involved a loss of two or three weeks before they were in place again and ready for trial.

An option had been given the contractors to have these staves rolled with a rib on each edge of the stave and projecting into the tube, or to roll them without these ribs. The steel company elected to roll them with the ribs. After three or four alterations of the rolls they determined to abandon the attempt to roll them with the ribs. This involved the making of an entire new set of rolls, ten or twelve in number, and when these latter were tried they had to be twice or thrice returned to the machine shop before perfect staves could be turned out with them.

In this way at least six months were consumed before a stave could be offered for testing. When this was done the steel proved inferior. Repeated changes had then to be made in mixing the steel. When a satisfactory mixture was obtained it was only then discovered that the same degree of strength was not present in all the staves made from it. This was believed to result from a want of proper care in melting and in forging the ingots, and in second heating for rolling. No doubt the difference in the the degrees of heat applied to the perfect and imperfect ones altered the proportions of carbon and iron, or their relations to each other, and thus caused a decided difference in the strength of the staves thus made from the same formula. Of the anchor-bolts about twenty or twenty-two which stood the test were carbon steel, while nearly an equal number failed under it, although many of the failing ones were made by the same formula as the good ones.

These results proved the absolute necessity of using the greatest skill and caution in the application of the requisite degrees of heat in making carbon-steel. The want of this extraordinary care has caused great loss of time and money to the Bridge Company, and has doubtless occasioned serious loss to the Butcher Steel Works. This unfortunate experience induced that company to endeavor to find some other method which would insure with less skill and caution a greater uniformity of product. With this view, experiments were commenced at the works recently in making chrome-steel under the patents of Mr. Bauer. These trials were under the direction of Mr. C. P. Haughian, Superintendent of the Chrome-Steel Company, and were attended with the most satisfactory results. An arrangement has since been made with the patentee for manufacturing this steel.

Chromium unites with iron and forms an alloy, similar in its properties to steel. Chromium is quite different from carbon in some important particulars. It is a metal, while carbon is not. It has little or no affinity for oxygen, and is not affected by excessive heating, while carbon has a great affinity for it, and by the application of heat it is liable to be burnt out of the steel.

One hundred trial staves were made last month of chrome-steel, under the directions and from the formula of Mr. Haughian. They were all beautifully and perfectly rolled, and there was no failure in any one of them to stand the test required. This steel comes from the rolls much more smoothly than the carbon-steel, and it works quite as easily, being capable of sustaining a greater degree of heat than the carbon-steel, it takes the form of the rolls more readily.

Tests made of this steel by me, before the contract was made with the Keystone Bridge Company, satisfied me that it possessed qualities eminently suited for the Bridge superstructure.

In 1869 Mr. Haughian allowed me to be made acquainted with the entire process of manufacturing chrome-steel. Commodore J. W. King, of the Engineer Corps of the Navy, now Chief of the Bureau of Steam Engineering, kindly volunteered to investigate the subject for me, and on my personal pledge that Mr. Haughian's trade secrets should not be revealed, Commodore King and my chief assistant, Colonel Flad, were allowed to pass forty-eight hours in the closest inspection of the works, during which time they weighed out the proper mixtures, placed them in the crucibles, melted them, cast the ingots, and had the steel finished by the hammer, all being under their immediate supervision. An elaborate confidential report was afterwards made by them to me of their observations and experience.

As it it was however, a patented manufacture, and made by but one establishment, to have required it to be furnished by my specifications would have been equivalent to compelling the Keystone Bridge Company (whose contract with your company was made before my specifications were complete) to forego all competition in obtaining the steel; and as several other makers expressed the fullest confidence in their ability to furnish an equally reliable steel, it seemed but fair to state the necessary qualities which the steel should possess, without prescribing any special formula that would restrict competition.

I did not feel justified in assuming that crucible carbon-steel of the qualities and forms required, could not be readily made, when I was assured of the contrary by some of the most eminent steel-makers in America. I was so fortunate as to be permitted to make a careful personal examination of Mr. Krupp's great works in Prussia, and also the mammoth works of Messrs. Petin Godet & Co. in France, and was also assured by the managers of both of them that our requirements were entirely practicable with carbon-steel. I did not, however, hesitate at any time to express my belief that the chrome-steel was most likely to meet the requirements of the Bridge; nor am I justified now perhaps, even with the experience developed at the Butcher Steel Works, in asserting more than my opinion that carbon-steel can not be made with as equal regularity and uniformity as the chrome-steel.

I think the sequel has proved that it was unfortunate for your interests that a contract for chrome-steel was not made at first, for the unsuccessful attempt to supply the carbon-steel for the Bridge by the Wm. Butcher Works has seriously delayed its completion.

While this disappointment has resulted in great loss to you by the delay it has involved, it must have inflicted serious damage upon the Wm. Butcher Company. The honorable disposition shown by the latter company to discharge the obligations of their contract with the Keystone Bridge Company, and furnish a quality of steel fully equal to their agreement, notwithstanding their many unexpected losses and disappointments, certainly merits your considerate notice. The President of the company, Mr. Samuel Huston, has repeatedly assured me of the determination of himself and associates to supply the Bridge steel as promptly as possible; and that they asked no abatement in its quality, but were resolved to make it fully equal to the requirements of the contract, cost what it would.

Acting upon this commendable determination, that establishment has contracted to pay Mr. Haughian a royalty of $15,000 for the right to make chrome-steel for your Bridge; and I have been assured by Mr. Huston that henceforth no other kind of steel but this would be made for it.

From what I know of the manufacture of chrome-steel, and from the tests of anchor-bolts, staves, and envelope plate-steel, already made at the Wm. Butcher Works, from the formulas of Mr. Haughian, I feel every assurance that the difficulties in the way of supplying the steel for your Bridge are now surmounted. The steel we are now testing is of a quality entirely satisfactory, and the workmanship is unexceptionable. The tests made of its ultimate tensile strength are considerably in excess of the specifications. In compression almost any degree of resistance can be obtained by the addition of chrome. To avoid unusual difficulty however, in finishing the steel in the lathes, it is only made sufficiently hard to meet the requirements of the specifications.

IRON-WORK.

I regret to state that our iron-work is not being prosecuted by the contractors with due diligence.

The Keystone Bridge Company contracted with other parties (as I am informed by Mr. Linville, President) to make the main braces which connect the upper and lower members of the arches together. These members are scarcely second in importance to the steel tubes which compose the arches. They are to be made of iron, and I was informed by Mr. Linville that my specifications form part of his contract with the sub-contractors. These specifications distinctly state how the iron shall be tested, and that it shall bear an ultimate tensile strain of 60,000 pounds per square inch. None of the iron yet offered by the sub-contractors has proved capable of bearing over 54,000 pounds, and very few samples have exceeded 50,000 pounds, and much of it only about 48,000 pounds. I have recently been assured, however, by Mr. Linville that the sub-contractors will supply the iron without any further delay, fully up to the standard required. As several other parties have offered to furnish the requisite quality, and have proved their ability to do so by the tests already made of their iron, we have reason to believe that the Keystone Bridge Company will not be longer delayed in obtaining it from the parties with whom they have contracted, or from other makers.

FINANCIAL.

Statement No. 1 in the appendix gives the amount of money yet needed to complete the Bridge. Statement No. 2 exhibits the amount charged to construction by the Auditor up to the first of September, 1871.

From these two tables it will be seen that the cost of the Bridge will exceed the original estimate $1,479,582.72.

Justice to myself as well as to you, demands an explanation of the causes which have led to this difference in cost. For this purpose Statement No. 3 in the appendix has been prepared. It is based upon the actual expenditures to September 1, 1871, and the estimated cost of the work yet to be done. An examination of it will show the various items of cost of the work over and above that contained in the original estimate.

In my report of last October (pages 8 and 36) I referred to the fact of a scour of fifty-five feet in vertical depth having occurred in the river bottom alongside of the east pier, and of the proofs that were met with in sinking that pier, that the scour at times extended even to the rock itself. It was generally assumed by others who had studied the peculiarities of the river that the scour never extended deeper than thirty feet below-low water mark. Although I believed it extended much deeper, and that there would be no assurance of stability for the *channel* piers unless founded on the rock, I believed, when designing the Bridge, that the abutment on the Illinois shore could be made safe on a pile foundation. The original estimates, therefore, only contemplated a foundation of this kind, with the base of the masonry starting from a level seventy feet above the bed-rock. The possibility of founding this abutment on the rock having been demonstrated by sinking the east channel pier, and the proofs of scour of the river bed to such extraordinary depths being perfectly conclusive, the Board expressed the unanimous desire that this abutment should be founded on the rock. By an examination of the appendix it will be seen that the cost of this extra work was $232,626.64, no part of which was in the original estimate.

The original design of the Bridge contemplated an upper roadway wholly of wood. The sub-structure of this roadway was designed to act as a truss to resist the action of hurricanes upon this part of the Bridge. As now designed, this sub-structure or wind-truss will be in the form of a flat or horizontal girder fifty-four feet wide extending from pier to pier, and formed entirely of plate-iron, thus giving much greater security against wind, and furnishing a fire-proof defense for the upper roadway against the sparks and heat from the engines when passing on the railways below. The wonderful force exerted by the tornado last March, which was so destructive in its effects upon the construction works of the Bridge Company, leaves no question as to the propriety of this change. Nothing equaling the power of this storm is believed to be on record. A locomotive of over twenty-five tons weight was actually hurled from the rails by it, and was thrown over on its side twenty-five or thirty feet from the track, on ground only four or five feet lower than the rails. No evidence of the engine disturbing the rails, or of touching the earth within twelve or fifteen feet of the track, could be discovered. These facts were reported to me by my Chief Assistant, Col. Henry Flad, who personally inspected the spot immediately after the storm.

From calculations based upon the data furnished by this tornado, I feel confident in asserting that the arches of the Bridge will be capable of resisting an equally powerful tempest. The extra cost involved in substituting this plate-iron wind-truss for the wooden one will be $80,000.

The destruction of machinery, scaffolding, etc., caused by the tornado, with incidental expenses caused by it, cost the Company fully $50,000.

In my report last October, I stated the fact that the Company had incurred serious losses, caused by the failure of the first contractor for granite. I then explained how these losses ensued, and stated their total amount to be fully $50,000.

From July, 1869, to May, 1870, owing to financial embarrassment, little or nothing was done in the construction of the Bridge. The official and other expenses throughout this period of inaction, not calculated for in my original estimate, were not less than $35,000.

The original estimate contemplated granite ashlar on the piers and abutments, from two feet below low-water line to high-water mark. It was afterwards determined to encase the four main piers with granite to their tops. This extra quantity of granite cost $73,476.

The items of granite masonry were originally estimated at $32 per cubic yard. The price paid was from $14.94 to $20.76 in excess of this. After the failure of our first granite contractor, although the entire granite quarries of the East were canvassed, we were compelled to pay these higher rates to the subsequent contractors. The excess of cost in this item over the original estimate is $94,149.

The original estimate contemplated an extreme width of fifty feet for the Bridge. This has been increased to fifty-four feet two inches. Several reasons made this change desirable, if not absolutely necessary. By the increased width twelve inches of additional space between the arches are obtained for each railway track. This is believed to be an important improvement, and one which was rendered desirable from the increased width given to the Pullman palace cars since the original design of the Bridge was made, in 1867.

On the upper roadway the local traffic will be more conveniently accommodated by this change. Two lines of horse railway cars are provided for on it, with room on either side of them for the largest transfer wagons. The sidewalks will be nine feet wide instead of eight. In addition to these desirable advantages, the general appearance of the structure will be considerably improved. The most important consideration, however, in determining upon this modification in design, was the increased security afforded by it against violent winds.

The extra cost of widening the Bridge four feet and two inches is estimated at $127,652, and the additional land damages at $30,000.

The cost of tramways for street or horse cars was not included in the original estimate. This item amounts to $19,113.29.

The original estimate contemplated arches eight feet in depth, with the railway tracks below the central part of the arches. The depth of the arches has been increased to twelve feet, and the railways raised up flush with the lower part of the arches at their centers. The change in the grade of the approaches caused by this alteration will cost $33,257.

The original design contemplated only two railway tracks on the approach between the Levee and Third street in St. Louis. The side-walls of this part of the approach have been widened, and an extra tier of brick pillars will be built in it, by which three tracks will be located there instead of two. The cost in masonry, iron, etc., by this change will be $10,300. This alteration will very materially increase the railway facilities of the Bridge.

The cost of widening the iron bridges over the streets and alley to accommodate this third track will be $6,000. The switches required to connect these three railway tracks together in this approach prevent the use of posts to support the upper roadway where they occur, and involve the necessity of using iron girders at an extra cost of $19,800.

The four towers of cut sandstone at the ends of the Bridge, in which the stairways will be placed, will cost $30,000 over the original estimate.

The grade of the upper roadway trestling in East St. Louis has been altered from five to four feet in 100. This increases the length of it 476 feet and the cost $28,000.

In consequence of unforeseen and unavoidable delay on the part of the contractor in getting the three caissons for the east abutment and channel piers ready early in the season, the sinking of each of these piers had to be done chiefly in the winter. This involved the absolute necessity of protecting them from the ice by putting ice-breakers in the channel above each one of these piers. This was an unforeseen expense amounting—

At the east pier to	$31,346 53
" west "	33,088 33
" east abutment	11,090 61
Total	$75,525 47

The cost of sinking the east pier is found to exceed the original estimates by $70,990.66.

The cost of sinking the west pier exceeds the estimated cost $35,442.29. The cost of sinking the west abutment, owing to several steamboat wrecks which were found embedded in the wharf extension at the site of this pier, exceeded the original estimates $47,770.80.

The original contract for superstructure was made with the Keystone Bridge Company before the detail drawings and specifications for the work were fully completed. The reasons for this unusual proceeding were deemed of sufficient moment by the Directory to justify it, but it caused several misunderstandings between the contracting parties, and resulted in the making of a supplementary contract in which, among other concessions made to the contractors, was one in the item of forty-eight wrought-iron skewbacks. The Keystone Bridge Company asserted that they made the agreement under the misapprehension that these forgings were to be of cast-iron. Your Company consented to exclude these members from the contract and to pay actual cost for them. By this concession the cost of the superstructure is estimated in Statement No. 2 to be increased fully $30,000.

It will be seen by aggregating these various items that $1,179-097.15 of the $1,479,582.72 of excess over the original estimates are accounted for by them, leaving $300,055.16, which has been expended, according to the accounts of the Auditor, in extra

2

cost of machinery and various other incidental and contingent expenses, in excess of the original estimates.

I have no additional explanation to submit in accounting for this difference between the original and the present estimated cost of the work, except to say that in computing the amount of contingencies liable to be met with in sinking foundations of such unusual dimensions, to such unexplored depths, and under conditions so very novel, I evidently under-estimated them, and have therefore, much to my regret, misled you. While I feel constrained, therefore, to ask your indulgence, I beg to call your attention to the difficulty of foreseeing or preventing such incidental expenses as some of those which are charged to constrution account and which go to swell up this deficiency—such, for instance, as "Hospital, medical attendance, and compromising suits, $9,569.21; law-suits in Illinois, $17,087.66; legislation and similar expenses, $9,800."

Some compensation for the disappointment that must necessarily result from the delay in completing the structure, and from its increased cost over the original estimates, may be found in the fact that the estimated amounts of traffic upon which the revenues of the Bridge were predicated in 1868, have been ascertained after a careful examination of actual facts and figures in 1870, by Mr. Wm. Taussig, Chairman of the Executive Committee, to be greatly under-estimated. It is confidently believed, from facts developed by this examination, that the income of the Bridge will be very largely in excess of the amount estimated in 1868.

With respect to the work remaining to be done, I do not think there can be a possibility of the actual cost differing materially from the estimates henceforth. It is all under contract, and the weights and amounts have been very carefully verified. I feel quite confident that the delay in the superstructure, which has retarded the entire work, and added very considerably to the expenses already incurred, is fast drawing to a close, and that before many more weeks we will see some of it in the course of erection.

The character of the work, as far as it is finished, is unsurpassed in excellence and solidity by anything in this or any other country. When finally completed, I feel confident that the magnitude of the structure, the superiority of workmanship, and the quality of materials used, will fully justify the total cost of its erection, and that its revenues will amply compensate for the investment.

When all of the many difficulties that have retarded this great work shall have at last been surmounted, and the Bridge becomes an accomplished fact, it will be found unequalled in the important qualities of strength, durability, capacity and magnitude, by any similar structure in the world. Its great usefulness, undoubted safety, and beautiful proportions will constitute it a national pride, entitling those through whose individual wealth it has been created to the respect of their fellow-men; while its imperishable construction will convey to future ages a noble record of the enterprise and intelligence which mark the present times.

JAMES B. EADS,

Chief Engineer.

APPENDIX.

STATEMENT No. 1.

Estimate of funds needed to complete the Bridge, September 1, 1871.

Trestling in East St. Louis		$71,880 00
Pier No. 5 and toll-houses in East St. Louis		24,060 00
East St. Louis approach over Levee		84,020 46
Channel piers and main abutments		143,909 22
Approach over St. Louis Levee		64,103 34
Towers on St. Louis Levee		25,897 00
Approach from St. Louis Levee to Main street		52,742 64
Bridges over Main and Second streets and alley		18,197 84
Approach between Main and Second streets		38,004 56
Approach between Second and Third streets		37,023 30
Ballast and ties in approaches		11,000 00
Rails on approaches		6,500 00
Superstructure		1,528,153 21
Tram-rails on approaches		11,352 60
Engineering, etc		60,000 00
		$2,176,844 17
Less proceeds of sales of boats, barges, machinery, materials, etc., at 40 per cent. off cost	$216,347 00	
Railroad iron	11,000 00	
		227,347 00
		$1,949,497 17

STATEMENT No. 2.

Expenditures for construction to September 1, 1871, according to the books of the Auditor.

West abutment	$228,355 30
West approaches	168,952 19
East abutment	354,723 16
East abutment caisson	139,697 62
East pier	409,175 46
East pier caisson	111,056 63
Amount carried forward	$1,411,960 36

Amount brought forward	$1,411,960 36
West pier	309,330 28
West pier caisson	62,437 22
Tools and machinery	387,119 81
Boats and barges	118,012 68
Materials on hand	283,428 65
Repairs	76,467 06
Horses and expenses	15,150 00
East approaches	47,900 79
Superstructure	14,889 41
Cement account	4,957 11
Blacksmithing	6,912 53
Wooden buildings	30,085 16
Expense account	97,633 73
Contingent account	137,608 15
Engineering account	176,080 74
	$3,179,973 68
For land damages	436,587 31
Total	$3,616,560 99
Add amount required to complete the Bridge	1,949,497 17
	$5,566,058 16
Original estimate, including land damages	4,086,475 44
Excess of cost over original estimate	$1,479,582 72

STATEMENT No. 3.

Extraordinary expenses of construction incurred and to be incurred, not contemplated in original estimates of May, 1868.

Sinking east abutment pier to the rock—		
Masonry, extra	$69,796 00	
Caisson	139,697 62	
Labor, sinking, concreting, &c	71,127 02	
	$280,620 64	
Less estimate for coffer-dam, pumping, &c., May, 1868	48,000 00	
Total extra cost of east abutment		$232,620 64
Estimated cost of upper roadway and iron wind-truss over original estimate		80,000 00
Loss by the tornado last March		50,000 00
Loss ensuing from the failure of the first granite contractors, as stated in October, 1870		50,000 00
Official and incidental expenses incurred from July, 1869, to May, 1870		35,000 00
Amount carried forward		$447,620 64

Amount brought forward		$447,620 64
Additional granite, over and above that specified in the original estimate provided for the channel piers and abutment, from the upper roadway to high-water mark		73,476 00
Excess of cost of granite over the original estimate,		$ 94,149 00
Cost of increased width of Bridge, four feet two inches		127,652 00
Additional amount of land damages for four feet two inches extra width of Bridge		30,000 00
Cost of tram-rails for street cars and vehicles		19,113 29
Change in the grade of the approaches, caused by alteration in depth of the arches		33,257 00
Extra masonry, iron, etc., required for third railway track in west approach		10,300 00
The cost of widening the iron bridges over the streets and alley to accommodate third track		6,000 00
Iron girders required by use of the third railway track above named		19,800 00
Extra cost of the four towers for stairways at the end of the Bridge		30,000 00
Alteration in the grade of the upper roadway trestling in East St. Louis		28,000 00
Ice-breaker at the east pier	31,346 53	
Ice-breaker at the west pier	33,088 33	
Ice-breaker at the east abutment	11,090 61	
		75,525 47
Cost of sinking the east pier—		
Cost of caisson	$111,056 63	
Labor in sinking, &c	77,812 42	
Guide piles, &c	8,796 97	
Piles and pile-drivers	10,481 78	
Fuel	5,616 88	
Coffer-dam	7,329 34	
Materials, supplies, &c	29,896 64	
	$250,990 66	
Less estimated cost	180,000 00	
Excess over original estimate		70,990 66
Extra cost of sinking west pier, over original estimate		35,442 29
Extra cost of putting in the west abutment foundation, over original estimate		47,770 80
Extra cost of skewbacks		30,000 00
		$1,179,097 15

STATEMENT *of Masonry, in cubic yards, completed up to October 1, 1871, and amount yet to be done.*

	GRANITE.		Sand Stone.	GRAFTON LIMESTONE.			Rip-rap.	Brick.	CONCRETE.			Total laid.	Total to be laid.	Grand total.
	Gray.	Red.		Cut Stone.	Rubble.	Backing.			In shafts.	In air-chamber.	In foundation.			
NEW CONTRACT.														
Between 3d and 2nd streets...	......	......	......	......	2,055.0	......	......	......	......	......	......	2,055.0	......	......
Between 2nd and Main streets	......	......	52.7	......	1,021.1	......	......	55.3	......	......	......	2,129.1	. ....	......
Bet. Main street and Commercial Alley..................	......	......	171.7	......	1,148.0	......	......	589.6	......	......	. ....	1,909.3	......	......
Commercial Alley & Front st.	......	......	72.5	......	1,234.2	......	......	22.7	......	......	......	1,329.4	......	......
West Towers....................	......	44.2	......	......	191.0	......	......	......	......	... ..	......	235.2	......	......
East Approach, Pier No. 5, and Towers....................	......	111.6	......	......	660.9	......	......	......	......	......	......	772.5	......	......
Total of New Contract...	......	155.8	296.9	......	7,310.2	......	......	667.6	......	......	......	8,430.5	7,869.5	16,300.0
OLD CONTRACT.														
West Approach, Piers from 5 to 1........................	......	439.3	1,573.8	......	......	2,453.8	......	......	......	......	......	4,466.9	4,343.1	8,810.0
West Abutment.................	540.7	124.6	166.6	145	......	7,371.0	......	......	......	......	......	8,347.9	3,112.1	11,460.0
West Pier........................	1,026.7	......	30	130	......	7,922.5	......	262.0	219.0	1,120.0	......	10,710.2	3,360.8	14,071.0
East Pier.........................	985.5	......	......	......	......	10,535.8	......	489.0	573.0	1,340.0	......	13,923.3	3,793.7	17,717.0
East Abutment..................	260	68.7	......	......	......	16,395.9	411	......	422.0	82.0	......	17,639.6	5,752.4	23,392.0
East Approach, Piers from 1 to 5.........................	......	317.7	......	......	......	2,939.3	......	......	......	141.0	669.	4,067.0	5,670.0	9,737.0
Total of Old Contract....	2,812.9	950.3	1,770.4	275	......	47,618.3	411	751.0	1,214.0	2,683.0	669.	59,154.9	26,032.1	85,187.0
EXTRA WORK BY														
The Company...........	......	......	......	......	......	......	......	18.0	......	......	......	18.0	......	......
Mr. Andrews.....................	......	......	......	......	528.8	......	......	......	......	......	......	528.8	......	......
Messrs. Hennessey & Yowel.	......	......	......	......	......	......	......	581.2	......	......	......	581.2	......	.... .
GRAND TOTAL...............	2,812.9	1,106.1	2,067.3	275	7,839.0	47,618.3	411.0	2,017.8	1,214.0	2,683.0	669.	68,713.4	33,901.6	102,615.0

AMERICAN SOCIETY OF CIVIL ENGINEERS.

INCORPORATED 1852.

TRANSACTIONS.

NOTE.—This Society is not responsible, as a body, for the facts and opinions advanced in any of its publications.

DISCUSSIONS OF SUBJECTS PRESENTED AT THE EIGHTH ANNUAL CONVENTION.*

ON LEVEES.†

MR. CALEB G. FORSHEY.—The paper under discussion has much merit; especially in the history of this phase of hydrologic science. The "Mississippi levees" have been treated with more or less detail by all writers on the history or physics of this great river; Pitman, Stodart, Martin, Flint, Monette, Forshey,‡ Thomassy, by Humphreys and Abbot, and now by Bayley. It may be considered as well recorded in the pages of hydrographic literature. Referring to the paper, attention is first called to—

EFFECT OF LEVEES UPON THE FLOOD LINE.—The writer undoubtedly places that question beyond cavil, if anything was before needed. Prior to levees, every bend gave an outlet of 3 or 4 feet over the banks, for 2 or 3 miles of current. The sum total of this outlet capacity was much greater than any crevasses that in recent times inundated the country. "There are many banks on the river front where the natural surface of the ground has never been overflowed in the memory of man." This is termed a fallacy by the learned authors of "Physics and Hydraulics of the Mississippi river," chiefly because "there have been crevasses more or less, every flood." I respectfully dissent, and allege that if the waters before levees existed were high enough to deposit these banks, they were higher than at present under the influence of levees.

* Continued from page 298. † Referring to—CXXI, Levees as a System for Reclaiming low Lands, G. W. R. Bayley; page 115. ‡ Delta of the Mississippi, and Physics of the River, Control of its Floods and Redemption of the Alluvion, a paper read before the American Association for the Advance of Science, 1872. The Levees of the Mississippi River, Transactions, Vol. III, page 267.

The levees were built from below; and the gradual manner of their application enabled the river's bed to adapt itself to the new servitudes. We are forced to the conclusion that the river's bed has greatly enlarged. In addition to the sections measured by me, as stated,* I have since assisted Lieut. Davis in a very careful remeasurement of Sections 5 and 6 of the prime base of the Delta survey, as measured by me in 1851 for Gen. Humphreys, chief of that survey. The remeasurement of these sections shows a total enlargement of 13 646 square feet of the sections sounded by the Delta survey above the prime base, and within 2 miles above Carrolton I have resounded 4 sections, and Mr. W. H. Williams has re-computed them with care and precision.

They correspond to sections of Delta survey, thus:

	Square Feet.		
Section.	1851.	1872.	Difference.
56	226 267	233 193	+ 6 926
58	227 458	226 877	— 581
69	209 241	229 325	+ 20 084
78	189 128	194 945	+ 5 817

These illustrate the allegation of an increase of channel capacity.

The facts, of the shifting banks of the river and the levees preventing the deposit of materials upon the ground formerly visited by the river, are of some importance to record, while they are remembered; the localities where this testimony is furnished proving the early floods as great as more recent ones. I would, therefore, refer to a series of points not changed, where the water has never been *a foot* above the banks since the application of levees. This kind of testimony is now rare, and the persons who remember the localities are much rarer.

Beginning below New Orleans and ascending, they are:

1. The upper extreme of Point La Hache, 40 miles below. L.†
2. Deer Range, above landing, 36 miles below. R.
3. Concord plantation, upper end, 25 miles below. L.
4. Fort St. Leon, 17 miles below. R.
5. Becka plantation, 13 miles below. R.
6. Belleville Foundry, opposite lower portion of the city. R.
7. Friendship, Labarre's place, 2 miles above Carlton. L.
8. Union, Dussieux plantation, at lower end, 13 miles above. R.
9. Red Church, 26 miles above. L.
10. Bonnet Carre Point, Glendale, Ferry landing, R.

* Page 137. † L for left, and R for right bank.

11. College Point, 60 miles above. L.
12. Australia, lower line, 115 miles above. R.
13. Glennons, 160 miles above. R.
14. Bayou Sara, below opposite 168. R.
15. Home Place, 235 miles above New Orleans, 30 above Red river. R.
16. Ellis Cliffs, be ow opposite, 252 miles above. R.
17. Goodman's plantation, 310 miles above New Orleans, 3 miles above Waterproof. R.
18. Perkins, above mouth of Vidal Bayou, 360 miles above. R.
19. Wilkinson's Point (T 15, R XIV lower side). R.
20. Hendersons, lower part, T 19, R XIV, 412 miles above. R.
21. Pilcher's Point, upper end, Bunch's Bend, 460 miles above. R.

At each of these points, there was in 1872, testimony of adequate kind, that the highest flood mark was not higher now than when the land behind the levee was deposited. The levee was small, less than 2 feet high, in many cases not 1 foot, and the flood mark often less than 6 inches. The water depositing the land must have been 1 foot deep.

TENDENCY OF SOUTHWARD FLOWING WATERS TO IMPINGE AGAINST THE WEST BANK.—Reclus is well sustained in his remark upon the Mississippi as not confirming "the law of displacement of running waters." I however, dissent from the doctrine as alleged by him and affirmed by Mr. Bayley, although it appears to be sustained by illustration. The laws of physics forbid it. The earth in its rotation revolves as a whole, water and all; and there is no appreciable tendency of water rather than of solids, to incline to the West. The rate of velocity, 3 miles per hour against 900, would be inappreciable in the revolution of the earth.* The weight of evidence is on the other side.

The Mississippi river hugs the bluffs of the eastern bank from Cape Girardeau to Lat. 35°, below Memphis, a distance of 300 miles. From thence to Vicksburg, it bisects the alluvial area 380 miles, inclining to neither side. From Vicksburg to Baton Rouge, a distance of 250 miles, it hugs the eastern bluffs again, and thence to the mouths it inclines to the South East for 240 miles. In its whole distance of 1200 miles it touches but once the western bluffs at Helena, when as free as air to choose its course. And when the mouth is reached, and it divides in three, and ultimately into about seventeen mouths, it sends one-third to the South Pass and two-thirds to the other directions, as moved above, southeastward. And again; the deposit of sediment on the west side,

* I take exception to Reclus' doctrine of the westward tendency of rivers emptying southward; and chiefly because of the disproportion between the velocities. I quote the velocity of the Mississippi river at 3 miles per hour; this is the rate of channel movement, and not the movement in latitude, which is much less. The movement southward, of the Mississippi's water is as one to two compared with the channel movement. The rate compared with the movement of the earth upon its axis is then as 1.5 miles to 900 miles, and is, therefore, for a stronger reason than the one assigned, inappreciable.

thus fending off the river, is in proof that all rivers with alluvion should be driven to the eastward rather than toward the western shore.

The Mississippi river in its whole alluvial length is in singular defiance of this hypothesis. An examination of the chief rivers of the American continent, where they are larger than elsewhere, will be found to contravene the allegation of any appreciable influence. The Mississippi, Pearl, Pascagoula, Mobile, Apalachicola, Savannah, Santee, Cape Fear, Neuse, Roanoke, Pamlico, Chowan, James, Potomac, Delaware, Susquehanna, Hudson, Housatonic, Connecticut, Androscoggin, Penobscot, St. Croix, Sabine, Trinity, Brasos and Corao, with a singular uniformity contradict the assertion of westward tendency, leaving only, some small unimportant rivers on the whole North American continent apparently sustaining the hypothesis.

In South America, the direction of flow of the Orinoco, the Amazon and all smaller rivers to St. Roque, is coincident with the alleged influence, and nothing can be inferred from them. Thence all the rivers down to the La Plata run normal to the ocean beach, and do not sustain the hypothesis.

The rivers of Western Europe running south are all small, except the Rhone, Guadiana, Guadalquiver and Ebro, which affords a striking contradiction. In Eastern Europe, the Dneiper and the Don, the Volga and the Ural are all wanting in testimony in its favor.

The only rivers of any magnitude in Asia, that flow southwardly, are the Euphrates, the Indus and the Ganges, and we look in vain to these for testimony that their waters have a westward tendency in their flow.

The hypothesis would require that all rivers flowing southward, in their approach to the mouth, should hug the uplands till they reach the alluvion and then have a westward flexure in their discharge; whereas the cumulative evidence is indefinitely great that no such influence is appreciable. I have been thus elaborate, because of the high authority of Reclus, sustained by Mr. Bayley, and because of the necessity of being right in the establishment the physics and projecting the works, of a river, to which the attention of the engineering world is now drawn.

CUT-OFFS.—The cut-offs of the Mississippi have been too numerous, since its navigation by steamboats and occupation by man, to permit the return to a previous regimen, from natural causes. The assumption that it will maintain the same length, in any long period, is too violent, in recent times, whatever may have been the truth prior to the settlement of its hydrographic basin. The number of cut-offs by artificial means has outstripped the tendency to lengthen itself, and the plane of discharge has been greatly increased in the present century. Every cut-off that has occurred has been largely assisted by artificial means. No less than seven have taken place below the mouth of Arkansas, within a half century. Probably not more that two or three of these would have occurred without aid. They have abridged the length of the river by about 106 miles, and it has lengthened itself less than 20 miles, by increased caving in the concave bends ; all of which have travelled downward. The 618 miles as now measured, should be 724 miles or 17 per cent. more; the velocity of 3 miles per hour has increased to 3.4 miles ; and the abrasions have been in proportion. The confinement of thé water to the channel by levees, has increased the servitude without sensibly increasing the velocity. They have assisted to increase the capacity of the channel by widening and deepening, as shown by Mr. Bayley. The cut-offs, however, have increased the steepness of the plane of discharge, and hence the ravages upon the banks. They are most disastrous in their effects, and should be prevented by all the means that law and watchfulness can devise.*

OUTLETS OR WASTE WEIRS.—The effects of these are well elaborated by Mr. Bayley, in his proofs that a bar will form almost immediately across the stream, directly below the weir or outlet. This is amply shown in my report upon Bonnet Carré in 1850.† Soundings in the fall of 1850, showed section below to be contracted 75 613 square feet as compared with section at upper end of crevasse. Soundings made during high water of 1851, the crevasse having been closed, proved that the great bar thrown across the river channel by weakening its transporting forces, in the discharge of water through the crevasse, was entirely carried away again, when the river was confined by the new levee. The difference was 23 000 feet in section.‡

This paper of Mr. Bayley, is full of suggestion and a valuable contribution to the annals of the Society.§

* I herewith submit a paper on "Cut-Offs on the Mississippi River, their Effects on the Channel above and below ;" wherein the subject is discussed more at length. It will be found mainly in harmony with the paper under discussion.

† Published in Public Documents, Louisiana Senate, 1851.

‡ As I was first to announce this fact in the physics of the river, and it has given rise to much discussion since, I deem it worth re-claiming, as a great practical principle in the treatment of the river.

§ Although the writer has given frequent references to authorities, one omission is to be noted. The statistics in the remarks on Tones Bayou are furnished by a survey of Gen. Jeff. Thompson and myself, one of the most rapid and exposed expeditions, and most fruitful in the number and value of results, to be found in American engineering; see Report of Commission of Levee Engineers, January 1st, 1873.

Mr. Gouverneur K. Warren.*—My ideas on this subject, in relation to the Mississippi, are set forth in the report of the Commission on the reclamation of the alluvial lands of the Mississippi,† of which Commission I was appointed President. This Commission was composed of five members appointed by the President of the United States, under an Act of Congress, which provided that two of them should be "civil engineers eminent in their profession," and three of them, officers of the Corps of Engineers. After a thorough consideration of the subject, with the most recent data carefully collected and studied, that Commission made an unanimous report. One of the members, Gen. Abbot, of the Engineer Corps, had shared with Gen. Humphreys, the laborious investigations in regard to the subject of levees on the Mississippi river, and also the honor and credit which their contribution, known as the "Physics and Hydraulics of the Mississippi River," has received.

In transmitting the report of the Commission through the Chief of Engineers, Gen. Humphreys, to the President, a common sense of justice caused me to say: "The foundation of the report of the Commission rests upon your invaluable surveys and investigations, which, begun in 1850 and continued until 1861, are published in the great work 'The Physics and Hydraulics of the Mississippi River, and upon the protection of the alluvial region against overflow,' &c., and upon the further contributions to these subjects contained in your published official reports in 1866 and 1869." I continued; "the Commission has obtained additional data upon subsequent floods and the results of the more recent experience in building and re-building levees, as far as they are attainable, so that their report is in a great measure exhaustive of the subject, and the conclusions reached may be considered entitled to confidence."

I wish it to be known that this letter of transmittal was written and signed by myself only, just as the printed report shows, and this expression of confidence was but an individual opinion. The report, signed by all the members, gives the foundation for that confidence, and is expressed in facts and reasons. To the report itself, I therefore invite attention of those who wish to become informed of my views on the subject of levees.‡

* Presented June 15th, 1876.

† Report of the Commission of Engineers appointed to investigate and report a permanent Plan for the Reclamation of the alluvial Basin of the Mississippi River subject to Inundation. Washington. 1875.

‡ I will endeavor to furnish a copy, to every one who will apply to me for it, giving his address.

To show what these conclusions were, I will here quote them.

1°. *Cut-offs.*—" So far from artificially aiding in their recurrence, it is therefore the emphatic opinion of this Commission, that in every case they should be prevented, or at least retarded, if this can be done at any reasonable cost."

2°. *Diversion of Tributaries.*—" No such works are practicable except at enormous expense, and the injury to navigation which would be sure to result, would in any event forbid their execution."

4°. *Outlets.*—" This Commission is forced unwillingly to the conclusion that no assistance in reclaiming the alluvial region from overflow can judiciously be anticipated from artificial outlets. They are correct in theory, but no advantageous sites for their construction exist."

5°. *Levees.*—" There are certain theoretical views concerning the effects of levee system which are raised again and again in discussing the subject." * * " It is claimed, since the effect of embanking a river is to confine its sedimentary matter to the channel, that the deposit formerly made on the banks must settle on the bottom, and thus ultimately raise the bed and with it, the high water mark." * * " No change of the kind attributable to levees can be shown to have occurred in any river, and the theory is therefore without any foundation in fact. Diametrically opposed to this is another theory, which, for the Mississippi, is equally erroneous, * * that the increased velocity resulting from the confinement of its flood volume between levees will rapidly excavate to a correspondingly greater depth, thus avoiding any permanent increase in the high water mark. This reasoning, if true, would establish conditions singularly fortunate for the levee system; but unluckily the wish has been father to the thought. Uncompromising facts show that the premises and conclusions are both erroneous for the lower Mississippi. Very numerous soundings with leads adapted to bring up samples of the bottom were made by the Mississippi Delta Survey* throughout the whole region between Cairo and the Gulf. They show conclusively that the *real bed* upon which rests the shifting sand bars and mud banks made by the present river is always found in a stratum of hard blue clay, quite unlike the present deposits of the river. It is similar to that forming the bed of the Atchafalaya at its efflux, and is well known to resist the action of the strong current almost like marble. Clearly then the bed of the Mississippi cannot yield, and if the velocity be increased sufficiently to

* Humphreys and Abbot.

compel an enlargement of the channel, it must be made by an increased caving of the banks, an effect which is not quite so agreeable to contemplate."

I will here interrupt the quotation to allude to the reference to this clay bed of the Mississippi, made by Mr. G. W. R. Bayley.* He says,† "It is claimed on high authority that the clay bed of the Mississippi resists the action of the strong current like marble, also that the bed of the Mississippi cannot yield." In a foot note, Mr. Bayley says, the "high authority" is "Humphreys and Abbot." This reference, I think, is a mistake. I have looked the work of Humphreys and Abbot through without finding it. It seems probable that Mr. Bayley's quotation is derived from the report of the Commission, from that part I have just quoted. But attention is asked to the fact, of his having omitted the word "almost," so that he makes the quotation read—the clay bed "resists like marble," whereas it should read—"resists almost like marble." Even in this last form, it is perhaps too strong an expression and might better have been omitted altogether. Nothing in the report of the Commission depends upon it.

To say the clay bed resists the action of strong currents, as clay is known to do, where the current can act upon the bars and banks, which are largely composed of sand, is all that is claimed. I will return to this subject of enlargement of the channel after I have finished quoting from the report of the Commission, which I will now resume. "In truth, no marked effect of the kind is to be anticipated, owing to the comparatively short duration of the increased discharge ; for evidently the levees can produce no effect upon the regimen of the river where the water does not stand over the natural banks." I will again interrupt the quotations from the report of the Commission, to state that the data showing the number of days the river water is against the levees, is given for several floods from Carrollton to Columbus, in "Physics and Hydraulics of the Mississippi."‡ At Carrollton, this period is, on an average, 100 days in a year ; at Donaldsonville, 50 days. The number of days rapidly decreases as we ascend the river.

I will resume the quotations. "Hence really the practical effect of the levees will be limited to raising the high water mark, and to slightly increase the caving. Since the absolute amount of the increased flood-

---

* One of the most eminent engineers of the delta region, in his interesting paper "Levees as a System of Reclaiming Low Lands," page 115. † Page 138. ‡ Page 411.

height does not carry the cost beyond the limits of a remunerative investment, it is the part of wisdom to steadily continue work without indulging in groundless fears that the river bed will rise, or in the equally groundless hopes that it will be sensibly depressed. * *

"The prolongation of the delta into the Gulf by the aggregation of sedimentary matter is also assigned as a cause for the ultimate rise of the bed, and hence a future necessary increase to the height of the levees. A possible secular change of this nature is quite too remote in its effects to merit attention from practical men of the present day, Simple calculation will show that hundreds of years will be required to raise the flood-height at New Orleans, an inch from this cause. In fine, then, we are to conclude that there is no mysterious agency, either favorable or injurious, which may be expected to exert a controlling influence upon the levee system. * * It being certain that the alluvial regions of the Mississippi can only be reclaimed by levees, it remains to consider what experience has taught respecting them. The existing system was begun a century and a half ago near New Orleans, and has gradually extended upward until there are but few points on the river at which it has not been tried. * * The faults" (of the system) "are only too apparent. They are—

"*First.*—Vicious levee organization."

"*Second.*—Insufficient height, in adjusting which, only existing high water marks have been considered, without remembering that there has never yet been a great flood in the river in which the water has not been greatly lowered by immense crevasses which occur with absolute certainty."

"*Third.*—Injudicious cross seetions and constructions, which alone would be sufficient to explain many of the frequent breaks, under the combined influences of pressure, seepage, burrowing of crawfish, &c."

"*Fourth.*—Inadequate arrangements for inspecting and guarding."

"*Fifth.*—Faulty location of the embankments, which are often placed so near caving banks as to insure an early destruction. Each of the causes of this failure will be considered in turn."

I will not quote this,* but will invite every one interested in the subject, to consult the report of the Commission and see how these matters are there treated.

---

* As it occupies 11 octavo pages.

The report of the Commission ends with recommending a plan for protecting the alluvial region of the Mississippi from overflow, premising it with the remark that in their judgment "no practical aid can be derived from any diversion of the tributaries or making artificial reservoirs, that cut-offs are very pernicious, and that artificial outlets, although correct in theory, find no useful application to the Mississippi. The plan consists; *first*, in keeping open the Atchafalaya, and the La Fourche, and if borings shall show it to be safe, in re-opening the Plaquemine; *second*, in a general levee system, extending from the head of the alluvial region to the Gulf, including the valleys of the tributary streams. The requisite laws to be enacted by the several riparian States to give the right of way, to confer the authority to make borrow pits and bench marks, to secure the levee from injury from cattle and hogs running at large, and to order out in times of danger, under suitable penalties for non-compliance, the population residing within a reasonable distance from the levees. The main line of levee to be of sufficient height (as already computed) to restrain the floods, and of the requisite cross section to resist the action of the water. Where reasonable security against caving requires large areas of front lands to be thrown out, protection against ordinary high waters is to be given by low front levees closely following the bends, suitable sluices and gates in such cases to be provided in the front and main levees for the rain-water drainage."

This quotation comprises the engineering features of the plan. The report also gives an outline of the administration of the work, its division into districts, and the manner of regulating each by itself and also as a part of the whole. The report expresses no opinion as to whether corporations, States or general government could best carry on the work, leaving that matter to the legislative body that instituted the Commission.

It should be observed that the report of the Commission presents a practical plan for the whole alluvial region, which is based on plain facts, freed from hypothesis. It is applicable to the whole region at once. Were there money enough, it might all be built in a very short space of time. It accepts an increase of the flood heights under what seems to be the most unfavorable conditions, the ascertainment of which was one of the important contributions of Humphreys and Abbot.

The people in Missouri, Arkansas and Mississippi can go to work under the proposed plan without waiting for a proper beginning in

Louisiana. No plan of protection from overflow, however theoretically perfect, would be acceptable to the people of the Mississippi valley, which had to begin at the mouth and be carried upward.

I will return to the question of the enlargement of the natural waterway in consequence of confining to it all the water which now escapes over the banks. I will waive the question whether the enlargement is to take place by scouring out the clay bed or by the increased width due to caving banks, for the practical end would be the same, the enlarged bed would carry off the increased volume of the water without raising the flood height as well in one case as the other. But obviously, we cannot get the increased scour until we build the levees and close the outlets, so as to confine the escaping flood water. I will take as an example of what must be done, the case of a levee at Natchez, a midway place of the alluvial region. There the river on March 6th, 1851, was level with the natural banks, and on March 31st, was 4 feet above them. This gives a fair idea of the sudden nature of the rises even at high stages, with the river imperfectly leveed. Had the river been perfectly leveed, so that the floods which inundate the whole region 25 to 60 miles wide, were confined to the main channel, the rise would have been more rapid and higher. This is the view held in the report of the Commission. But the theory of an enlarging channel says *no*, the channel would have increased so as to prevent this increase of flood height. Granting everything to this hypothesis of an enlarging channel that can be claimed for it, does any one believe that this enlargement could take place throughout the length of the river between Natchez and the mouth, in the short space of 25 days? Think of, or compute the amount of material that would thus have to be carried away by the river in a few days and thrust out into the Gulf, to keep down a rise of a few inches, if adequate levees were built for the whole region. It must not be forgotten nor kept out of sight, that it is the *whole* alluvial region we are considering. It does not seem reasonable that the enlargement could, even under the most favorable conditions, keep pace with the increasing volume. Does it not seem more probable that the levees *at first* would have to be as high as if the bed was unchangeable, even though, when once the water was actually confined to the channel, the flood heights should afterwards, through many years of erosion, gradually diminish?

Common experience, and all accurate measurements, show that in a rising stage of a stream, as the volume is increased the surface of the water in the stream rises, and it cannot make any difference where the increase of volume comes from. The increase of volume in the Mississippi below, by closing the Atchafalaya, is just the same as if the volume of water before carried off by it came from a new affluent of the same capacity; or more exactly to indicate what I mean, suppose at a flood stage in the Mississippi, the Atchafalaya just carried off the water brought in by Red River, then the closing of the Atchafalaya would practically add the volume of the Red River to the Mississippi, and cause it to rise. Increased levee heights would then necessarily be needed on the Mississippi below it, unless we can suppose the bed of the Mississippi to accommodate this increased volume.

A belief in such sudden enlargement is not generally held by engineers. Very valuable experience on this point has been gained in the attempts to confine the Red river to one channel, a smaller stream, and therefore more in our control. Some of the results of this experience on this river are given in the report of Mr. C. M. Fauntelroy,* where he states the views he obtained from Mr. W. C. Melvin, C. E., Asst. State Engineer. Mr. Melvin says: "As it would hardly be possible to carry on the work of leveeing both sides (of the Red River) at the same time, it is obvious where the work should be first entered upon. Time and assistance must be given to the river to scour its bed to a greater depth, and for its banks to cave. For this purpose, all the growing timber of every description that is standing within 60 feet of the crest of the banks should be cut away; roots and stumps loosened; in short, everything done to facilitate the caving and scouring process."

It is held by some, this view that more water makes the stream rise, is an hypothesis; disregarding all the experience of mankind, they point to the one fact that the closing of Bayou Plaquemine has not increased the flood height at New Orleans, entirely ignoring the well known fact that there has never been a flood since it was closed that has not caused large crevasses in the Mississippi between the Plaquemine and New Orleans, which crevasses have prevented the effect of the closure ever being felt at New Orleans as an increased flood-height, or as an increase of scouring power.

There is no doubt that closing the Plaquemine was a benefit to planters along that bayou, and it was probably at the expense of the planters on the Mississippi. A similar result will probably attend the closing of the La Fourche, if it is ever permitted.

---

* Secretary to the Commission of Engineers, &c.

There is a moral point of view to this subject as well as an engineering one, and that engineering is always to be received with caution which benefits its advocates at the expense of, or injury to others or the public. Of such is the engineering of the bridges needlessly obstructing navigation, and the flimsy structures of many kinds by which human life is sacrificed to avarice.

In closing, I would earnestly urge those who would wish to be well informed on the subject of levees on the Mississippi to *study* thoroughly the "Physics and Hydraulics" of that river by Humphreys and Abbot. The question is one too vast to be developed in the limits of an ordinary discussion.

The report of the Commission treats of several points briefly, because they are so fully elaborated and disposed of by Humphreys and Abbot, whose conclusions have been generally accepted.*

Mr. George W. R. Bayley.†—I fully recognize and freely admit the fact that "cut-offs" lower the flood-line of a sedimentary river, although the temporary effect is to elevate it below. The first effect of the recent Vicksburg cut-off was an increased rise below, but it soon ceased, and a reduction will follow. The flood-line at Vicksburg and above and below that point, has been reduced several feet by the Terrapin Neck and Palmyra Bend cut-offs of 1866 and 1867, and this reduction extends as far down as Natchez. The lengthening of the river channel by the caving in of its banks in the bends tends to lower the high water slope, and because the velocity required for the discharge of the flood waters or maximum quantity requires a greater slope, the surface rises until the increased slope is obtained. As the length of the river increases, therefore, the flood line rises. On the other hand, a cut-off shortens the river's length, and the slope, for the time being, becomes too great. It can only be reduced to what the quantity and velocity require by excavating its bed and depressing its surface. This always happens. As the river lengthens itself, the flood-rises; when a cut-off shortens it, the flood-line falls.

The quantity of water flowing, its mean velocity and slopes of bed and surface, are reciprocally dependent and proportional. The resulting effect, however, of excavating the river bed after a cut-off is to

* The "Report of the Commission of Engineers appointed to investigate and report on a permanent Plan for the Reclamation of the alluvial Basin of the Mississippi River subject to Inundation," from which, frequent and full quotations have been made, was officially published as part of the Annual Report of the Chief of Engineers for 1875-6, pages 536-678 (Appendix, O). † Presented May 25th, 1876.

increase the rate of caving in of the river banks and of the higher cultivable lands near its margins; the lengthening of the river goes on, then, with renewed energy until another cut-off occurs, and so the flood-line rises and falls. If it is financially practicable to protect the river banks from being undermined and from caving in, great good can be realized by making cut-offs and shortening the river's length. In the case of the Rhine, which is comparatively a shallow river, this has been done. Can it be as successfully applied to the Mississippi river? When the river, by becoming too long, elevates its flood-line too much, a cut-off becomes necessary to reduce it, but none are practicable for 200 miles above its mouth.

In the case of Red river, next above and below the city of Shreveport, and down to Loggy Bayou (the outlet of Lake Bisteneau), I am decidedly of opinion that the plan of cut-offs can be applied to very great advantage, and that it should be utilized there. By means of it, the flood-line can be very much lowered, its bordering lands reclaimed, levees in great part dispensed with and navigation very much improved there. Three cut-offs can be advantageously made above Shreveport, and eleven or more others below, above Loggy Bayou.* I recommend the application of the plan of cut-offs to Red river, above Grand Ecore, most earnestly, and advise our Society to advocate it.

I have said that the lengthening of a sedimentary river, by reducing its slope or prolonging it, causes a rise of its flood-line in the effort to maintain its slope of surface. The advance of the river's mouth into the sea has the same effect, and I wish to add a few remarks on this point.

In Louisiana, there are many old outlets of the Mississippi, and secondary outlets from these, which were filled up and cut-off from the river in times long past. I will name a few of them only, for they are numerous. Below New Orleans, left bank, the Bayou Terre Aux Bœuf had a course 30 or more miles in length. It is now but a stagnant ditch or coulé, bordered by old sugar plantations for many miles below its former head, 12 miles below this city. Thence to the Gulf its alluvial banks become more and more narrow, the swamps and marsh lands back approaching nearer and nearer to its margins, until only sea marsh is found. The Metairie and Gentilly bayous, back of New Orleans, have their delta ridges formed in like manner. The Terre-Bonne and Bayou

* See lithograph map, herewith (on file at Rooms of the Society).

Black, right banks, were old outlets of the Bayou Lafourche, or secondary channels, and the Little and Big Caillon's and Chacahonla mere outlets of the Terre-Bonne and Black. Each and all have their deltas, which are high, dry, cultivated lands now, and all were formed by overflow deposits ; all were old outlets or "passes."

In each, as its slope was prolonged and so reduced by the advance of its debouchure, the flood line was gradually raised and the banks were elevated and extended laterally. When the prolongation of the main channel became too great for the quantity flowing, and for the maintenance of the velocity of current necessary for its discharge, then the mouth widened, shoaled and divided; a division of channels occurred, and new and steeper slopes more nearly such as the quantity in the secondary channels required. The beds and banks of the new channels were elevated by deposits, and this process backed the water up in the old main channel, and caused further deposits in its channel, and flattened, by elevating, its high water slope. Lateral overflows and outlets then caused a rise of its banks. These still further reduced the quantity flowing in the main channel, added to the shoaling and the rise of the flood line. In this way and by this process, the elevation of the bed and banks went on, further and further up stream, until it reached the parent river or the primary outlet and nothing more than a portion of the high flood waters during inundations escaped into these silted-up outlets. After the settlement of Louisiana, even this supply was cut off by means of levees built across the heads of the old outlets, and they became stagnant pools or rainfall drains.

The Bayou Lafourche is now, and has for many years, been going through this very same process, but it has been modified and prolonged by the maintenance of levees above where the lands are too narrow and too often overflowed to be worth reclamation. Sixty miles below its head, where levees 2 feet high were sufficient fifty years ago, levees of 12 feet high are insufficient now unless crevasses occur through them in some places, annually, to relieve, for that year, the flood in the gorged channel. But each relieving crevasse adds to the difficulty year by year, and the flood line rises in the effort to obtain that slope which the quantity admitted into the bayou at its head requires. The head level cannot be raised, for that is the surface level of the Mississippi river itself. There is no remedy but the closure of the outlet next the river by a dyke, and the substitution of slack water navigation by means of a lock in it; for this contest against nature's laws cannot be prolonged indefinitely. The length of the outlet is too great, and its slope too little, for the quantity of water passing into it at its head.

I now come to the case of the Mississippi river itself, at its mouth. Before the era of levees a large proportion of the flood waters of the great river were lost through outlets and over its banks below its last tributary, Red river, and, probably, considerably less reached the sea through its mouth than now. Even now less passes New Orleans, at high flood, than Columbus, Kentucky; the Atchafalaya carries off the difference, less the quantity lost by evaporation.

Before the settlement of Louisiana, some centuries at least, the prolongation of the river into the Gulf below the present forts (21 miles above the Head of the Passes), had reduced its slope to less than what the quantity flowing required, and the quantity passing to sea was further checked by tidal action. The river widened its section from less than half a mile (opposite the present Forts) to three times that width, and correspondingly reduced its depth. It then divided, right and left, into two main channels, with one lesser channel between. Here, gradually, the surface level at flood time was elevated so as to give steeper slopes to the divided channels. Now, the flood line of the river at the Head of the Passes is nearly 3 feet above the mean level of the Gulf of Mexico. As the distance to sea, southwest and eastwards, is nearly 18 miles, and by South Pass, in a south-southeast direction, 12 miles, the flood line slopes are about 2 and 3 inches per mile respectively, east, southwest and south-southeast. Between the Head of the Passes and the Forts, 21 miles, the average slope of the main river is but 1⅓ inches per mile (the lower portion still less, not more than 1 inch), and from the Forts to New Orleans about 1½ inches per mile.

Now, it is certain that before the division of the waters of the Mississippi at the present Head of the Passes, the mouth of the river was at tide level, and the river surface slope below New Orleans was greater than it now is. As it discharged less water then than now (because depleted by outlets above), its slope needed to be greater. The increase of quantity and of current velocity, since the leveeing up of the outlet channels below Red river and down to the Forts, has enabled the channel to discharge a greater quantity with a less slope than before ; therefore, the closure of outlets under the levee system has had a very beneficial effect and every outlet should be kept closed.

About one-third of the river's volume is discharged through the Southwest Pass, but its slope was becoming too flat, by prolongation, for this quantity ; a tendency to widen and divide at its mouth is manifest. Its discharge needs to be increased to compensate for its reduced slope.

About 55 per cent. of the river's discharge has been passing out to the eastward through Pass a l'Outre, Southeast, Northeast and Balize Bayou Passes and their subdivisions, the discharge through which has been checked and their division hastened by the prevalent easterly winds and storms. The repeated division of the waters flowing to the eastward, and the consequent tendency to increase the slopes of the divided channels by elevations of bed and surface, has retarded the flow into them and favored and increased flow down Southwest Pass, because of its having but a single channel, and down the South Pass because of its steep slope, directness, and short length. The Head of Pass dyke or jetty, built out into the edge of Pass a l'Outre, up stream from the east side of the head of South Pass, diminishes the flow down Pass a l'Outre, and adds to it down South and Southwest Passes, probably more down the latter at present than down South Pass, thus increasing their currents and channel-making power and compensating for extension. By encroaching, gradually, still further upon Pass a l'Outre, and diverting still more of its water westward—the navigable channels to the eastward are useless now—both the Southwest and South Passes may be improved. The effect of the east dyke is to prolong, further up stream, the 2-inch per mile slope of Southwest Pass, but the 3-inch per mile slope of South Pass cannot be extended, obviously, so far up. Hence the South Pass slope should and must be extended into or to a junction with the Southwest Pass slope, below its head, for on that side the fall is greatest, because the distance (and from deep water to deep water as well) is least. Flowing water will always seek the shortest route, if it can, where the fall is greatest. I, therefore, conclude that, at the head of South Pass, the best channel into it is and will be found on the west side of the island in the head of the pass, and that the east channel should be entirely closed by a dyke across to the island. Better water can be maintained in one channel than in two, and one of them should be closed for that reason. Because the shortest distance from deep water to deep water, and therefore the most rapid slope exists on the west side, that side is the best for developing a channel into the South Pass. If we work in accordance with natural laws, we cannot go astray.

Again, South Pass loses 23 per cent. of its water through Grand Bayou, about half way down from its head, hence the surface slope of South Pass must be more rapid below than above Grand Bayou. We have, by perfecting the prolongation of South Pass about 2 miles seaward by jetties, extended (it was partially extended by side shoals and reefs previously), and thereby flattened its slope. To compensate for this, we should increase the quantity of water flowing to sea between the jetties by closing Grand Bayou, and so provide for the prolongation. I also think that the width between the outer jetty ends should be less than above, in order to concentrate the discharge there, and excavate thereby a deeper channel in the outlet to sea. By reducing the width we will gain in depth, and maintain the current velocity further out into the Gulf.

Because the great outlets, the "Jump," 11 miles above the Head of the Passes, and "Cubitt's Gap," 4 miles above, lessen the quantity of water in the main river, above the passes, and thereby reduce the velocity of current and channel-making power (as is evidenced by the shoaling above the Head of the Passes, from 10 to 12 feet across the whole river since 1838), these should be closed, and for the same reason, the great Morganza and Bonnet Carre outlets, between the mouth of Red river and New Orleans, should also be closed. Every cubic foot of water which passes the mouth of Red river, or enters the Mississippi there, should by all means be confined to the river channel until it reaches the sea through the river mouths proper; none should be diverted.

The greater the quantity flowing, the greater the velocity, the deeper the section, the less the frictional resistance to motion, and the less the surface slope required for the discharge of a given quantity in the same period of time.

CXXVI.

CUT-OFFS ON THE MISSISSIPPI RIVER.

THEIR EFFECT ON THE CHANNEL ABOVE AND BELOW.

By Caleb G. Forshey, C.E., Member of the Society.

Presented June 17th, 1876.

Of the several problems that have presented themselves for the solution of the practical engineer, in the treatment of the physics of the Mississippi river, none have been more obscure than the effect of cut-offs. Their application to the great desideratum—the redemption of the alluvial lands from overflows—has been, and is yet advocated, by those who believe the straightening of the river would prove beneficial. Fortunately they are few and newly acquainted with these grave questions.

The first cut-off was that known as Shreve's, at the mouth of Red river. It seems to have been made in the interest of navigation, and very little importance attached to the work, in respect to its influence upon the regimen of the river. But from that time forth—1832—there has been a discussion upon this method of redeeming the lands from inundation. As one of its advocates, I made a series of measurements and observations upon the results, to influence the Legislature to effect the cut-off at Racourci. The facts are of record and I re-state them here.

Just below Lat. 31° North, the river made a bend, northward and westward; at about 8 miles it received Red river, at the fenders of the bend, and sweeping around southwardly 3½ miles, sent off the Atchafalaya; thence it returned nearly to the place of departure, after a circuit of about 18 miles. The neck was very narrow, not more than 800 feet across. Capt. Shreve, under authority of the United States, by a little trench guided the water through, and in a short time the cut-off was accomplished. The river established its new channel by the shorter route.

As soon as the river had time to accommodate itself to the new channel and assume a new and permanent regimen, in 1844, I measured the water marks, and ascertained the levels of a flood approaching that of 1828, which, it will be remembered, was higher than any other recorded in river annals. Then the next in height was that of 1844. In the 16 years of interval the river had time to assume the supposed new regimen.

SHREVE'S OR RED RIVER CUT-OFF.—At the mouth of Red river the fall was 3 feet, by the marks, both of which were very plain upon the trees. At Vidalia, 65 miles above, the fall was 8 inches, on a locust tree upon the batture. It was 3 inches at Waterproof, 105 miles above the cut-off. There was no mark above this point, but I assume that the two floods reached the same elevation at St. Joseph, 120 miles above Red river.

Then below the cut-off, at Morgan's Point, 28 miles below, the depression was 18 inches, by the testimony of Col. Morgan himself; and at Bayou Sara, 40 miles, by my own observation, the mark of 1844 was 3 inches below that of 1828. Beyond that point I had not any bench-mark or testimony, but presume that it expired at Profit's Island, 60 miles below the cut-off.

RACOURCI CUT-OFF was made by the State Engineer in 1848–9. It abridged the channel distance by 24 miles. Its location was but 3 miles below Shreve's cut-off. A canal, some 20 feet in width and 1 mile long, was made in 1848; but the drift wood floated in it, and the river failed to go through. In 1849, the woods were cleared away for 100 feet on each side, the canal was dug deeper to the sand, below the blue clay; some gunpowder was used in blasting, and ultimately, when the water ran through the canal freely, a flat-boat was fitted with a wheel that worked rapidly. This was very effective. The blasting had loosened the earth, and it commenced caving very suddenly. The scene is described as one of terrific grandeur as the widening reached the lofty forest. The falling of trees and the whirl and boil of eddies were truly sublime. In two hours' time, it was a river. The Natchez, Capt. Tom Leathers, with some degree of recklessness, put her head into the tide, steamed through the rushing current and the terrible tempest of falling cypresses. After this, the cut-off was established and the boats generally passed through the shorter channel, though it was the end of the season, before the great Mississippi lay snugly in the new bed thus prepared by the hand of man.

The observations of the Delta Survey, made in 1851, were commenced but two years after this event, and before it had effected much in its new state. Its first effect was to transform the region about the mouth of Red river into a habitable country. Its effect in lowering the water was added to that of Shreve's, making the abridgment of distance about 24 miles,* and added to the shortening effect of the previous cut-off, amounted to 42 miles. The joint effect upon depression of water was equal to 6 + feet.

The effects were felt on the force and direction of the currents upon the banks of the river. The ravages commenced immediately above and below the cut-off, and especially in the direction of the points of attack, where caving had never been experienced before.† The whole community, with one voice, cried out against such tampering with the river. The policy opposed to cut-offs was established, and since they have not been seriously advocated, except by some newly arrived engineer or planter, whose experience was not cognizant of these disasters. The policy is likely to remain, unless the councils of men newly introduced to the history and habits of the river, shall prevail to disturb it.

TERRAPIN NECK AND PALMYRA.—In 1866, nearly 17 years later, Terrapin Neck, which had threatened for many years, was, by the aid of artificial means, cut-off, and abridged the river's distance by 14 miles. It occurred at Lat. 32° 30′ North. Palmyra cut-off occurred in the following year, at Lat. 32° 10′ North; only 20′ latitude intervened between them. Palmyra abridged the channel by 20 + miles.

It will be necessary to consider these two cut-offs together and as one, because their effects were merged in each other so that they cannot be separated. They will, moreover, have to be considered with reference to a new water mark. The flood of 1828 was no longer legible upon the trees, in 1851, and no bench marks had been established. The Delta Survey, under Gen. Humphreys, had to establish an arbitrary bench, which was referred to the mark of 1828, where practicable.

The mark of 1851, which was a high water year, was established by this survey, for future reference. It was preserved and revived by the Commissioners of the Levee Company of Louisiana, in 1871, and in 1872 by the U. S. Engineers, for systematic observations.

* I do not lightly differ from Humphreys and Abbott, but this distance was uniformly called 27 miles. They call it 21 miles. I have revised, and by way of compromise, put the abridgment of steamboat distance, descending, at 24 miles.

† No analysis of the limits of influence was ever made. It is to be regretted; for the 17 years gave it ample time to distribute its effects over a long distance. Its relief was felt at Natchez above and at Baton Rouge below, but how much will never be known.

In 1874, a great flood came, and made fresh marks all over the entire Mississippi alluvion, from Memphis down; and as these two cut-offs occurred midway between the two periods, 1851 and 1867, we shall assume them as reliable, and compare the effects by the two registers. The one is carefully recorded in "Physics and Hydraulics of the Mississippi River," and the other, in the report of the U. S. Commission for reporting a plan for the reclamation of the Delta, as also by the State Engineer. We will state the several differences as shown in 1874, from the mark in 1851.

The city of Vicksburg is about midway between the cut-offs. The register at that city will be taken as the standard. The difference made here by the cut-offs of 34 miles is 72 inches; that is, the water was depressed from 51.3 to 45.3 inches. The difference at Lake Providence, 68 miles above Vicksburg, is 63 inches; that is, the water-mark is reduced from 45.6 feet on the gauge, to 40.37 feet. At Ashton, 88 miles above Vicksburg, it is reduced to 2 feet by the marks upon the trees, as compared with a previous mark, whether of 1851 or 1862 is not certain.

This is the limit of observation from below, and probably comes within the influence of the American Bend cut-off. It would have expired by proportion, at 132 miles distance above Vicksburg.

At Natchez, 84 miles below Palmyra, the greater of the two cut-offs, the depression was 1.5 feet. The slope from 6 feet was gradually observed, though not measured above Natchez. The depression was from 51.3 feet at Vicksburg to 49.8 feet at Natchez, or 1.5 feet. At Red river the effect is still greater. It was reduced from 46.4 to 44 feet, or 2.4 feet. At Baton Rouge, again, it is reversed, and instead of being raisod, it is depressed nearly 2 feet. We would place the lower end of the effect at Bayou Sara, 191 miles below Palmyra.*

Thus the cut-offs have depressed the level of discharge for more than 130 miles above and 191 miles below the point where their influence commenced. These cut-offs effected, respectively 30 and 42 inches at their source, making a whole depression of 6 feet; that is, the abridgment of the river by 34 miles, disturbs the regimen for a distance of 423 miles.

But this is not all that we observe. We shall see the ravages upon the banks. At the Terrapin neck, the first effect was to cut away the Hawes Harris plantation, and completely to occupy by the channel of the river, this fine estate. Then attacking the point below, it was carried entirely

* The effect at Ashton was only inferred from the overflow being largely reduced, which effect we put at 2 feet. The crevasse here is now 3 miles wide, and was formerly very deep. It is now so much overgrown with cottonwood that it vents comparatively little water, much less than formerly. It has been open since the war, and is filling itself up rapidly.

away on the left bank. Then crossing over to the right bank, in the Milliken's Bend, it caved in the upper portion of that plantation. It did not stop there, but continued to ravage the two next estates of lower Milliken and Mrs. Maher, and thence continuing, it made havoc of Paw-Paw island. In fact, it has disturbed every portion of the river down to the bend above Vicksburg. In a very short period the effect must be to cut off that very narrow peninsula, and leave Vicksburg entirely an inland city.*

The Palmyra cut-off has in like manner made havoc of Point Pleasant plantation, one of the noblest estates in Louisiana. Thence it crossed over to the Conger place, carrying away the best fields, then reacting upon the bend opposite, the caving commenced upon Ships Bayou and the Alligator Levee, that cost the State so largely, and, far as it was placed back from the front for safety, it is now at the very bank of the river and must be renewed. Then its effects upon Hard-Times must be to carry the river through that bend. The crevasse there this season is the legitimate effect of this cut-off, and all the ruinous consequences upon the plantations of Lake Bruin and lower Lake St. Joseph. It indirectly influences the cavings above Rodney, and the disasters of Waterproof are attributable to it ; and the Kempe estate, whose levee cost the State near $400 000, is legitimately attributable to the same cause.

In general, the effect of every cut-off is to change the points of attack of the river, and with the full force of the fall, due to the shortening of the channel, to precipitate it upon the land and levees that have been reclaimed for many years before. The points of highest improvement are doomed to new servitudes because in the normal condition, these reaches of the river have been least exposed.

Cut-offs as a means of reclaiming the lands are, for all these considerations, so injurious, so disastrous, that they should be guarded against and prevented by legislation and unceasing vigilance.

FLOODS FROM CUT-OFFS.—We should not dismiss this subject without considering the effects beyond and below the depressing of the floods in the neighborhood of the cause.

Below and beyond that influence comes the *raising* of the water, and the elevation of the *flood-line.* Though its first effects occur at the cut-off itself, there must be some limit to the depression. At that place, wherever it be, commences the congestion which produces an elevation

* Since this was written, the cut-off at Vicksburg has taken place—about April 20, 1876.

of the flood. This distance cannot be predicted, but every cut-off illustrates it and travels from it, towards the mouth of the river. In this instance it was 191 miles from the cut-off. The fact, that at Baton Rouge the river was higher than before, is not isolated. It continued the congestion so far as observed. At intermediate places down to Carrolton, in building and repairing levees, they had uniformly to be raised.

At Carrolton, where it was carefully measured, the rise was 0.7 feet where the range was 15.4 feet. At New Orleans, it was 0.7 feet, and at English Turn, 15 miles below New Orleans, it measured 6 inches. At Poverty-Point, it was raised about 6 inches. Judging from the necessity of raising the levee, and below that point, though I had much experience in the repair and renewal of levees and increasing their height, I could not state precisely what the elevation was. But down as low as Tagliaferos, 50 miles below New Orleans, I felt it necessary to raise the levees by a small fraction.

Thus, for 215 miles, the volume of water was congested in the river channel, as I verily believe, by the effect of the various cut-offs. This was doubtless the cumulated influence of all the cut-offs, probably from the Arkansas down to the Racourci; for if it had been the effect of the Racourci and the Shreve's cut-offs it would have shown itself earlier.

It may be stated, then, that the abridgment in channel of 106 miles in the past 50 years, by seven cut-offs, has had the effect to congest the waters by a small but measurable fraction in the channel for the last 260 miles of the leveed river. Its maximum effect may be stated at 2 feet, and this effect is at the upper end of the congestion.

It is believed that this will gradually disappear, as the result of accelerated velocity and enlargement of channel capacity from the confinement of levees and the lashing of steamboat waves. In what period this will occur cannot be predicted.*

* I would take this occasion to retract all the arguments used by me in 1847, to induce the Legislature to authorize the Racourci cut-off. This was done in 1850, but it had not the publicity that I desired, being buried in a public document. For the past 27 years, I have on all occasions used my voice and pen against the resort to cut-offs to prevent the overflows of the Mississippi river.

AMERICAN SOCIETY OF CIVIL ENGINEERS.

PROCEEDINGS.

MINUTES OF MEETINGS.

(Abstract of such as may be of general interest to members.)

CVIII.

THE DELTA OF THE MISSISSIPPI,

Considered in Relation to an "Open River Mouth."

A Paper by John G. Barnard, U. S. Corps Eng., Honorary Member of the Society.

Presented March 15th, 1875.

One of the most interesting problems of engineering, as well as one of the most important works of internal improvement our government has been called upon to engage in, is that of providing an adequate navigable outlet to the gulf from the Mississippi river—an outlet for the mightiest system of internal navigation and for the commercial products of the most extensive and fruitful valley of the earth.

It is well known that the mouths of the several delta arms, or "passes," of the Mississippi are obstructed by bars over which 15 feet of water is rather more than an average maximum, even for the greatest of these—the "Southwest."

A brief retrospect of the history of the question of augmenting this depth will be quoted.*

"The necessity and feasibility of deepening one or more of the passes of the Mississippi is not a new subject. It is one almost coeval with the settlement of the country itself. Yet it is only of late years that projects to accomplish this object have been seriously entertained."

"By reference to ancient charts, it would appear that the North East Pass for a period of at least 70 years, maintained a depth of 12 feet on its bar. This depth was found more and more inadequate as commerce rapidly increased after the transfer of the country to the United States, and about the year 1835 public attention was strongly attracted to the necessity of increasing the depth in this and other passes."

"With a view to this object a preliminary survey was made under the direction of Maj. W. H. Chase, Corps of Engineers, who based thereon certain projects and estimates for increasing the depth of water by closing several of the Passes and dredging the channel through the North East and South West bars."

---

* From a document (dated 1852) to be named hereafter.

"Congress appropriated for these objects the sum of $250 000; but the subject was deemed so important by the War Department that it was referred to a special board of Engineers, who, simultaneously with the experiment of dredging, ordered a new and very thorough survey of the delta, with the view of obtaining more extensive and accurate data on which to base a project, and also to furnish a standard to which engineers could in future refer in investigating the changes which are continually taking place in the channels and at the mouths of the passes."

"The survey" (since known as Capt. Talcott's) "was executed with all desirable precision and scientific skill; a powerful dredging boat and tenders were procured and the experiment of dredging commenced. Unfortunately, the survey and building of dredging machinery nearly exhausted the sum appropriated, and Congress having failed to make further appropriations, the experiment was necessarily abandoned before it had progressed sufficiently to test its efficacy. Thus the operations of this period failed to cast any light upon the important question now before the Board, viz.: 'what is the proper method of securing a depth of water over the bars adequate to the wants of commerce.'"

"As the North East Pass became more and more innavigable, it was found that the South West, which had heretofore been little used, answered sufficiently well the existing wants, and it has continued to answer them, without material inconvenience, till a recent date."

"During the past year, however, public attention has again been attracted to this subject. Vessels carrying large and valuable cargoes have been detained for weeks and even months on the bar, and it has been stated that the South West Pass has, in its turn, commenced shoaling while the Pass á Loutre has commenced deepening."

"The Board does not find evidence to confirm the opinion that any deterioration has taken place at the South West bar. * * *

"But the Board, though having little fear of a sensible or rapid deterioration of this pass, is nevertheless of opinion that it is not adequate to the existing and prospective wants of commerce, and it is this inadequacy and not its deterioration which has now made it necessary to look for some efficient means of deepening this or other passes."

The facts recorded in the above quotation had caused an appropriation to be made by Congress in the year 1852, in words as follows: "for opening a ship channel of sufficient capacity to accommodate the wants of commerce, through the most convenient pass leading from the Mississippi river into the Gulf of Mexico, seventy-five thousand dollars. And it shall be the duty of the Secretary of War to apply said moneys to the opening of said channel by contract, and at an early day in the next session of Congress to report the progress of the work, the amount necessary to complete it and an estimate of the annual cost of keeping said channel open, and any contract made shall be limited to the amount hereby appropriated."

To carry into effect the above, a board was organized consisting of one naval officer, the late Com. W. K. Latimer, and three engineer officers, viz., Maj. W. H. Chase, (since deceased.) Maj. J. G. Barnard, and Maj. G. T. Beauregard. Com. Latimer, (at that time in command of the Navy Yard, Pensacola,) had been long on duty in the gulf waters, and was familiar with the Mississippi. Maj. Chase had served since 1820 in this region, commencing at that date the very first work, (Fort Pike,) of the modern, or third system of sea-coast defenses, which was located in the marshes of Louisiana.

It is scarcely necessary to say, that to engineers of Louisiana, the Mississippi river—its floods, its mouths, its levees, its crevasses, its encroachments, &c., are an ever-present theme, and Maj. Chase, as we have seen, not only directed the first government surveys, but was the author of "projects and estimates" for increasing the depth of water on the bars. He was, more notably, the author of the first actual *plan** for a "ship canal," though not the first to propose one.

Maj. Beauregard and the writer (the former a native of Louisiana) had both been stationed in New Orleans, in charge of fortifications of the river and other navigable approaches. Both had had extensive experience in construction on the peculiar soil of Louisiana and of excavation therein; indeed their experience had in part been, (at Forts Jackson and St. Philip,) in the very locality where the proposed ship canal was designed to be.

The officers of 1852 were selected, therefore, for their supposed familiarity with the peculiar problems of hydraulic engineering which characterize the Mississippi. In entering upon the duty assigned them, they did not find themselves confronted with a novel—even though it were a difficult—problem. They spent several weeks on the spot in execution of their task, eight days of which were devoted to personal examinations of the bars, occupying themselves mainly with "studying the changes which had taken place between the survey of Talcott and the more recent one of Capt. Sands; the nature of the formations exhibited; the character of the bottom, particularly of the South West Pass and Pass á Loutre, and the general slope of the bottom of the gulf seaward for several miles from the Passes."

It would be foreign to the scope of this paper to follow further the report of the Board of 1852;† it enumerates as the eligible methods of

* This plan which is elsewhere alluded to by the writer as "boldly, ably yet so imperfectly sketched out," is certainly superior to any subsequently made, till the Board of 1874 presented what may be called a thorough solution of the canal problem.

† Drawn up by the present writer, and from which a quotation has already been made.

proceeding: "1st. Stirring up the mud at the bottom by suitable machinery, throwing it into the current whereby it is to be swept off. 2d. Dredging. 3d. Jetties projected from the shores to contract the current over the bar. 4th. Closing the useless passes."

But the members of the Board were limited by their instructions to devise, if possible, a work which could be executed—without reference to other appropriations—for the small sum of $75 000.

No other plan suggested itself to the Board by which this sum could be applied with hope of obtaining any important result than that of "stirring up" the bottom, and upon its recommendation a contract was entered into with the Tow-boat Association, by which a channel through the bar at South West Pass, 18 feet deep and 300 feet wide, was to be made. The execution of this contract was the very first successful application of any artificial means to deepening the channels over the bars, and it demonstrated the efficiency of dredging by that method.

But the Board could not of course be *certain* of success by this means. It further recommended: "in case the Tow-boat Association fails to perform the contract, and it should not be thought expedient to resort to dredging, the above sum, together with the available existing appropriation, should be applied to *the construction of jetties;* as the Secretary of War may direct."

"The project of *jetties* is based upon the simple fact that by confining the water which now escapes uselessly in lateral directions, to a narrow channel *over the bar*, the depth of this narrow channel must be increased; in other words, the existing bar must be cut away." * * *

"The rate of annual expenditure for extension of these *jetties* the Board is unable to estimate. The Board recommends the trial of the project, in case all efforts of stirring up the bottom, or dredging, fail."

The Board of 1852 is, therefore, not only the inaugurator of the first successful application of artificial means to deepening the channels over the bars; but it was the first to give official sanction and recommendation to the project of *jetties* for the deepening of the outlets of one or more of the passes. But though this may be the first formal expression, it was even then by no means a new or unfamiliar project. One of the members, (Maj. Beauregard,) had some years before, somewhat warmly espoused their trial.

After the appropriation of 1852 (by which a channel 300 feet wide and 18 feet deep was opened by the Tow-boat Association) no further appropriation was made till 1856, at which time, of course, that channel had become obliterated. In that year an appropriation of $330 000 was made "for opening and keeping open ship channels of sufficient capacity to accommodate the wants of commerce through the South West Pass, Pass á Loutre," &c., &c. It being further provided that the work should be done by contract, proposals were advertised for, which were submitted to a board consisting of the late Maj's Chase and Bowman and the (now) Gen's Humphreys and Wright.

This Board recommended the acceptance of the bid of the New Orleans Tow-boat Association for deepening a channel 300 feet wide through the South West Pass to 18 feet depth for $125 000, and for keeping the same open at the rate of $75 000 per annum ; that the bid of Messrs. Craig and Rightor be accepted for opening the Pass á Loutre channel for $125 000, and for keeping the same open *for five years* for $40 000 (*i. e.* $8 000 per annum). With respect to this bid the Board remarks :

"The Board have great doubts of the practicability and efficiency of this mode—of the practicability of construction and of efficiency, should the work be accomplished. But an important point will have been ascertained either by its failure or success. If failure is exhibited, future projects on this score would at once be rejected. If success is exhibited two reliable modes for future improvement will have been obtained ; the one by dredging, scraping and raking, and the other by closing passes and increasing current, or by jetties ; and one or the other, or both, maintained as the value of their several results may be determined."

The Secretary of War (Mr. Davis) decided that the bids of Craig and Rightor should be accepted for *both* of the passes, and a contract was accordingly made, (November 13th, 1856,) in which "the said Craig and Rightor contract to open, through the entire length of the bar or shoal at or near that outlet of the mouth of the Mississippi river into the Gulf of Mexico, known as the Pass á Loutre, a straight ship channel, having a well defined width throughout its whole extent of not less than 300 feet, and a depth of not less than 20 feet below the level of ordinary low water." * * *

"It is understood that the means by which the said Craig and Rightor propose to accomplish the work are by stopping the minor passes or outlets of the river, and, if necessary, by constructing jetties on or near said bar, adopting one or either or both of these alternatives, as may be found expedient, substantially after the manner explained and set forth in their proposals submitted to the Engineer Department."

Inasmuch as nothing was actually done by them in the way of "stopping the minor passes or outlets," and as the work of constructing a jetty by a patent sheet-pile construction (an invention of Craig and Rightor) was, at first, exclusively resorted to, it is to be inferred that the jetty system was the essential part of Messrs. Craig and Rightor's undertaking. The late Col. S. H. Long, U. S. Engineers, thus reports thereon April 6th, 1857 :

"The operations of Messrs. Craig and Rightor have hitherto been confined to the Southwest Pass. I visited their work on the 27th ult., and had the satisfaction to find that they had formed a line of piles, in a direction obliquely downward towards the deepest channel across the tidal bar, 1 064 feet long, the depth of water along the line varying from 4 to 8 feet. The line consists of a series of posts or piles, about one foot square, driven vertically into the bottom to the depth of about 25 feet below its surface, and at the distance of 15 feet apart. Longitudinal strings or streamers, 4 by 8 inches and 30 feet long, are spiked to the upper sides of these posts a little above the surface of the water. The strings serve as guides to the plank piling, which is composed of planks 5 inches thick at top and 2½ inches thick at bottom, rebated in the manner specified in the patent."

"The plank piles vary in width from 12 to 20 inches, are driven 10 to 15 feet into the ground, and fastened by iron spikes to the upper sides of the streamers. The spikes employed for the fastenings are about half an inch square and 9 inches long, and the timber of the structure consists of yellow pine and cypress. The line thus formed presents a substantial and well built structure, is able to withstand a current of about two miles per hour, and is quite impervious to water. On the upper side of the line, the depth of the water remains as it was before the piles were driven, while on the lower side, sedimentary deposits have been made to the depth of 3 or 4 inches, the water on this side having become nearly or quite stagnant."

"Since the date of the inspection, as above, I have been informed that the line has been prolonged more than 500 feet, making the entire length of the line about 1 600 feet. The daily progress in extending the line, the requisite materials being at hand, and the weather favorable, is about 150 feet."

On December 31st, 1857, Col. Long reported that the "pile-dam" had a length of 5 733 feet.

"At the upper or northerly extremity of the dam the water does not exceed 3 feet in depth, and as we descend along the line of the dam the depth gradually increases to about 12 feet, which is the depth at the lower end of the dam."

"Through a distance of about 1 500 feet, on the upper portion of the dam, indurated beds of sand and clay occurred at the depth of 6 to 8 feet below the water surface. On being penetrated by the piles, these beds thus disturbed resolve themselves into a sort of quicksand, too yielding to afford the requisite stability to the piles. In consequence, and on the occurrence of protracted boisterous weather, soon after this portion of the dam was built, the line of piles was ruptured in many places, and in some instances thorough breaches of greater or less extent were found in it."

"The residue of the dam being strongly fortified by substantial square piles driven on both sides of the plank piling, and at intervals of only 4 or 5 feet asunder, successfully withstood the buffetings of the storms and the surf produced thereby, and still remains erect and stable." * * *

"The materials used in the formation of the dam, exclusive of a large quantity driven away and lost in storms, amount to about 2 000 000 superficial feet of yellow pine and cypress timber, and 5 tons of iron in bolts and spikes." (The accompanying sketch shows the extent and position of this pile-dam.)

A report, dated December 10th, 1857, to Col. Long of Mr. Wm. Johnson, supervisor (under the former) of the work, gives some interesting particulars.

"The contractors have been much troubled in driving any permanent work at the north or upper end of the dam. For about 1 500 feet from the marsh, the bottom is composed of yellow sand indurated with clay, and in some spots, of sand alone. The driving of the piles in these places is a matter of great difficulty, and when driven they have a tendency to work up and out of place, and upon the smallest aperture or opening being developed, the current immediately commences to wash away the surrounding sand, and in an incredibly short space of time it will excavate below the bottom of the piles in the immediate vicinity of the old cranny, and the work thus affected will, during the first gale thereafter, wash up and be drifted out to sea."

"In this section of the work I have known the current at one of these apertures to excavate from 2 to 16 feet in 48 hours."

"Several breaches of this character have occurred during the last six months—have been as often repaired, and in spite of every precaution still continue to break out anew. With the exception of this division of the line, the balance of the dam, over 4 000 feet (the whole length of the dam being 5 733 feet) is driven in a blue clay bottom, with a depth of from 7 to 15 feet, below which an indurated bed of white sand is found, with an average thickness of some 10 feet, below which again lies a stratum of yellow clay to an indefinite depth. The work driven in this bottom is now standing in perfect order; has remained so since the date of its construction; is unshaken, and, in my opinion, is unshakable, except by the power of some irresistible tornado, or the more insidious effect of the Gulf worm. I am happy to inform you, however, that I have in vain sought for some trace of this animal in wood planted in the water last February, and which has been submerged ever since up to this date."

A year later (December 22d, 1858), Mr. C. A. Fuller, who had succeeded Mr. Johnson as supervisor, reports:

"Since that date (May 28th) a portion of the pile-dam near its upper end has been swept away, leaving a clear and continuous breach of about 900 feet in length. The remaining portion of the dam, with the exception of several breaches which are not of recent formation, appeared to stand well. In examining this dam in a light skiff I was obliged to keep

MOUTH OF S. W. PASS,
reduced from
map of Col. Long's surveys in 1857,
to exhibit the localities of the
Current Observations
of the
Delta Survey.
and showing the portion of "pile-dam" jetty made in 1857
Scale
0 ¼ ½ ¾ 1 mile.
SOUTHWEST PASS
var. 8° 15' E.
Pilot Station
Telegraph Station
Light H.
Length of Dam 5725 ft.
Can Buoy
Stake Isd.
Upper Bush Buoy
Lower Bush Buoy
Basket Buoy
East Breaker
Outer Can Buoy
GULF OF MEXICO

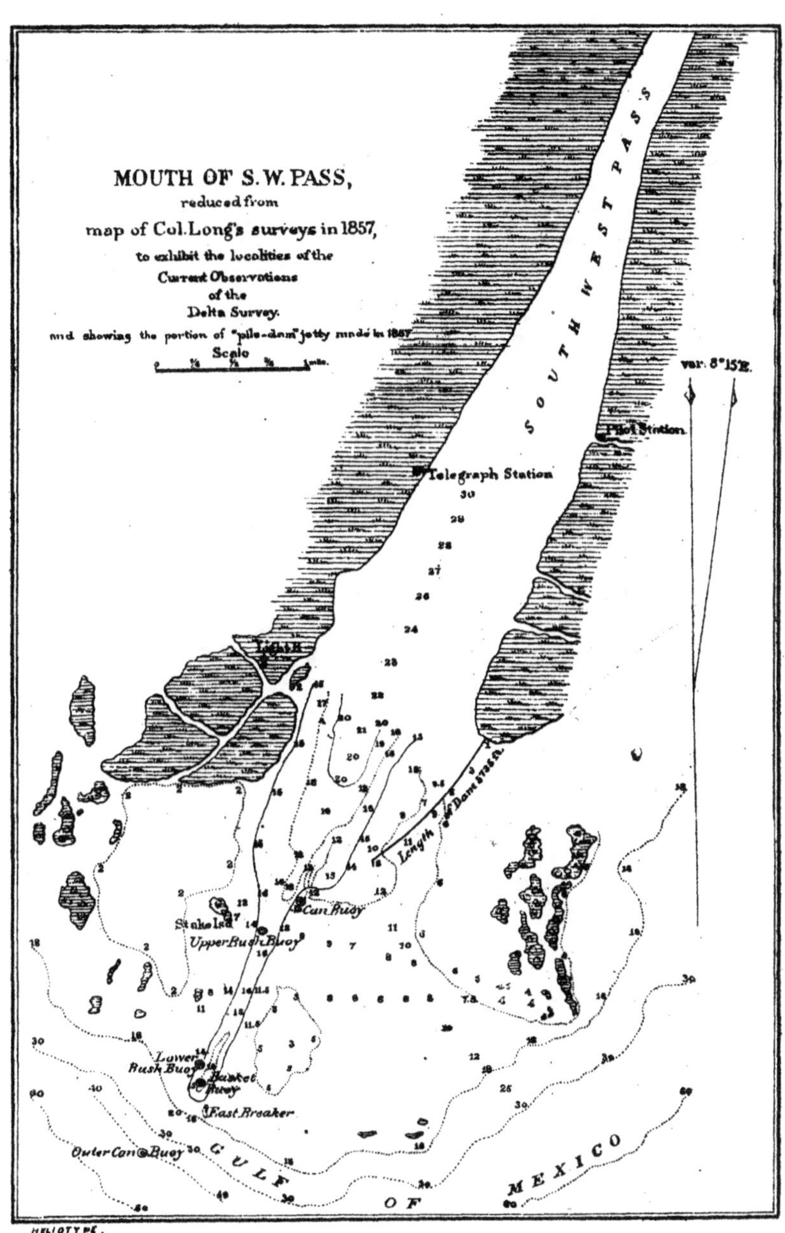

HELIOTYPE.

on its channel side, there being but a few inches of water on its easterly side, the sand being compact and hard against the dam."

It should be remembered that a year previous to this last date, *i. e.*, in December, 1857, when the pile-dam had attained the length of 5 733 feet, the contractors found their resources exhausted (they had made, according to their own statement, an actual expenditure of $66 079.27) and were constrained to apply to the Government for relief. It was finally granted, though not exactly in the form they asked. They obtained an extension of time for completion of their contract to July 1st, 1858, and, what was more important, a relaxation in regard to the *depth* prescribed, by which 18 feet depth was substituted instead of the 20 feet originally contracted for.

The contractors then abandoned their jetty construction and resorted to "harrowing," "scraping" and "blasting with gunpowder;" the latter agent applied principally to the "mud-lumps" at Pass á Loutre.

On May 29th, 1858, Col. Long reported, after personal inspection and soundings, that a channel 300 feet wide with depth from 18 to 22 feet, existed at the South West Pass; and on September 23d he reported, from his own personal examinations, a channel opened at Pass á Loutre with an average depth considerably more than 18 feet, and, at its narrowest part, 325 feet wide;* and hence, in accordance with the stipulations of the modified contract in so far as they relate to the "*opening* of these channels," the compensation to be made for the opening thereof ($125-000 for each) "is now payable to the contractors." It was accordingly paid.

The foregoing particulars† are given in relation to these contracts with Craig and Rightor, because, involving nominally the use of jetties, it has been inferred on the one hand that the jetty system failed; on the other that the attempted jetties were of such frail construction as to be

* The engineer officer now in charge of the dredging of the delta mouths having in his recent annual report (1874) stated (see Ex. Doc. 1, 43d Cong., 2d Session) that he "has satisfied himself that the depths and widths of channels reported in 1853, 1857, 1858, 1859, 1860, have been erroneously reported," it is proper to remark that the only cases in which specific *widths* as well as depths were reported were those of 1853 and 1858, when, under *contracts* for specified *widths* and *depths*, large sums of money were to be paid and, on the certificate of the U. S. engineer officer, *were paid*. These cases were as follows: in 1853, $75 000; in 1858, $125 000 for (severally) the S. W. Pass and Pass á Loutre channels, or $250 000 in all. The official records of Col. Long's inspections and reports have been published in Ex. Doc., H. R. No. 5, 36th Cong., 2d Session. Gen. Beauregard, who was the engineer officer in charge of the execution of the first contract (that of 1853) has seen proper to publish an answer to so much of the so-called "expose" as concerned himself.

† At the Pass á Loutre, about 1 000 feet of "pile-dams" were made by Craig and Rightor, before they resorted to other methods.

quite incapable of endurance. Slight as the construction was, it has been shown by what precedes, that most of it stood firmly during a whole year ; but what is more noteworthy, and what till recently was not generally known is, that though now very much worm-eaten it has endured *to the present time.*

To have carried out the jetty system in its application to this pass (the South West) required at lowest computation that this commenced "pile-dam" should have been extended beyond the bar crest (*i. e.*, about 3 miles further), and that another, starting from the opposite shore, should converge towards this one.

It may very well be doubted whether this "pile-dam" construction would have stood in depth very much greater (12 feet) than that where the incomplete work terminated. It has demonstrated, nevertheless, that the shoals extending from the extreme points of unsubmerged land towards the bar channel have adequate compactness and tenacity to support well adapted engineering works.

A few words must finish this retrospect. If the contractors (Craig and Rightor) abandoned the jetty system, the cause is obvious. Their own funds had given out and the amount of compensation ($125 000) they were ultimately to receive was utterly inadequate for a proper application of that system. But the terms of their contracts required *only* that, at a certain date, they should exhibit *a certain depth* (and width) *of channel.* To exhibit such a result they then resorted to the *temporary* expedients of scraping &c. the bar surface, and by so doing arrived at the result desiderated.

But their contracts *further* provided that they should *maintain the prescribed depths for a period of five years for* $40 000, *i. e.*, $8,000 per annum. Had they effected the increased depth *by jetties*, as they originally intended, they doubtless believed that the maintenance for five years would not be costly. But it was clear enough that a *dredged* channel could only be maintained by incessant dredging, for which the Tow-boat Association, which had already had *experience* in this matter, demanded in their competing bids, $75 000 per annum. Craig and Rightor, after making a futile petition that the compensation be increased to the modest sum of $17 000 per annum, abandoned the work, and the channels which they had made gradually filled up.

There still remained an unexpended balance of the appropriation of 1856, of over $60 000. An abortive contract for reopening the South West Pass channel was, in 1859, entered into and canceled, and then

Col. Long, hiring by contract a suitable steamboat, with scraping apparatus, undertook the operation himself; Mr. C. A. Fuller, (a graduate of the Military Academy, for many years an assistant engineer to Col. Long) being in immediate charge. A channel 18 *feet deep* was, through parts of the years 1859 and 1860, maintained; the width is not stated, but according to Mr. Fuller, it never was so great as 300 feet. The civil war interrupted operations for the time.

Subsequently, the government resumed the work, and a boat (the "Essayons") for dredging, or rather for "stirring up" the bottom, designed by the late Major McAlester, U. S. Engineers, was constructed at Boston under his supervision. The stirring instrument consisted of propeller blades extending below the keel. This machinery, improved by Maj. Howell, by the addition of the "deflector," which more effectually directs the stirred-up material into the upper currents, has since been in operation.

It is stated by Maj. Howell, in an official letter to the President of the first ship-canal Board (of 1873), that with full control over the use of the channel and two dredge-boats, a channel may be made and maintained with 20 feet depth, at a cost of $150 000 per annum running expenses, and $50 000 per annum for wear and tear; and this is reiterated in his annual report for 1873. His report for 1874 does not sustain these assertions.*

A wide "open mouth"—not a mere sub-aqueous "ditch" of uncertain depth and an irremediable narrowness of *less than* "300 feet width"—is evidently the kind of navigable outlet the great river needs.

To furnish an outlet which should evade the bar obstructions of the mouths, a "ship-canal" had long before been proposed; first in 1832, by Mr. Benj. Buisson, State Surveyor; and again, in 1838, by Maj. W. H. Chase, U. S. Engineers; and the project was referred to by the Board of 1852, as one to "fall back on" in case of failure of all efforts to procure an open mouth; thus placing it in its rightful category of a *dernier resort*. This project was revived by the following resolution of Congress, passed March 14th, 1871.

* Maj. Howell, in his last annual report, states that his former reports "do not show the maintenance throughout any one year of a channel 18 feet deep and 300 feet wide." They certainly affirm that "natural causes effecting a blockade of the mouth of the Mississippi have been overcome by the system of dredging adopted, so far as regards obtaining a 20-feet channel across the bar of the South West Pass, is evidenced by my reports." "300 feet width" may be a *desirable* width; but when a "20-feet *channel* across the bar of the South West Pass" is spoken of, a channel of *sufficient width* for the purposes of navigation is necessarily supposed, whether 300 feet wide or not.

"Resolved: that the Secretary of War be, and is hereby requested to cause an examination and survey, with plans and estimates of cost, to be made by an officer of Engineers, for a ship-canal to connect the Mississippi River with the Gulf of Mexico, or the navigable waters thereof, of suitable location and dimensions for military, naval and commercial purposes, and that he report upon the feasibility of the same to the House of Representatives."

In the summer of 1873, a Board of Engineers, of which the writer was President, was convened "to consider and report upon" a plan which had been in the mean time prepared in fulfillment of the above. The question submitted to the board was widened by the request of the Chief of Engineers, at the suggestion of the President, to consider "the expediency of improving the navigable outlet of the Mississippi, by the Fort Saint Philip Canal, as an alternative to, or a simultaneous measure, perhaps, with, the improvement of the passes."

The majority of that Board favored the construction of the canal and embodied their views as to jetties in the following paragraph.

"Upon a review of the practical difficulties which the adoption of the jetty system of improvement at the mouth of the Mississippi would entail, and a due consideration of the original cost of construction and of annual extension, entertaining doubts, moreover, of the succcessful issue of the attempt, the Board do not consider it advisable to recommend it."

The single dissenting member took the ground "that before resorting to an artificial work of the difficult and costly character of a ship-canal, a more attentive consideration of the superior advantages of the natural mouths, and of the fair probabilities of utilizing them, is needed."

And again: "the advantages of an open river mouth are inestimable. The needs of a navigation so great as that which now exists, and which in the future of the great Mississippi valley must be fifty-fold increased, demand it."

"It is said that the 'time has come' when the needs of commerce demand the canal; but I answer that the *time will come* when there will be the same cry for navigation unimpeded by locks—an *open river mouth*—which we now hear for a canal."

The argument, as put in this last quotation, contains the very pith of the question. No seaport in the world would substitute a ship-canal, with locks, for an open sea entrance, if the latter be not *unattainable.*

Would New York, for example, accept as adequate a ship-canal, for her sole channel of access to the sea? And what limit shall be placed upon the magnitude of the freight-commerce which shall pour out of the great Mississippi valley through its only outlet to the sea?

A ship-canal can be but a make-shift, a *pis aller*, only to be accepted on *proof* that there is no *reasonable hope* of an "open mouth." How shall that reasonable hope be established save by reference to what *has been done* elsewhere, and by an appeal, not to theories—for theories simply mock the subject by their impotence to grasp the complicated conditions—but to such simple elementary *facts* as may guide our estimate of probabilities? Here all the burden of proof is thrown on the opposer.

To say, in face of the highest authorities* on this subject, in face of *achieved success* in numerous instances, that there *are no probabilities*, or that there are none which justify an attempt which has for its end a result so indispensable to a great navigation, requires not merely transcendent engineering abilities—it requires something like *prescience.*

The question is *not*, therefore, purely an engineering one. To fail (if the contingency of failure be admitted) is far from being an *engineering* failure; for the undertaking is not merely justified, but *demanded;* unless, indeed, the engineer can deny even the *possibility* of success.

While no engineer, it is presumed, would trust his prescience so far as to deny a *possibility* of obtaining by jetties an "open river mouth," there are a few simple arguments on which to assert—*first*, the strong probability of success; *second*, that the *maintenance* of the accomplished open mouth need not be regarded as involving an unreasonable expenditure or an excessive amount of work.

As to the *first point;* no one, whether "engineer" or otherwise, has yet denied the certainty of *obtaining* by jetties the desired result.

Hence the *second point* only, requires to be dwelt upon. In the draft of a minority report, dated New Orleans, December 6th, 1873, this matter is thus set forth:

"Now as to the application of this work. For reasons which will appear hereafter, I should select Pass á Loutre for experiment. A glance at the chart will show that from the point in the Pass where the depth of 25 feet ceases to obtain, to the *outer crest of the bar*, is about 2½ miles (at the South West Pass over 4 miles). The natural width of the Pass where 25 feet depth obtains is about ½ mile. * * * By stopping the North

* In Europe, *e. g.*, we have Sir Charles Hartley, engineer of the successful jetty construction of the Sulina; Col. James Stokes, Royal Engineers, British Commissioner for same work; and Mr. P. Caland, engineer of the works at the mouth of the Maas; all advocating an "open mouth" for the Mississippi; nor can the opinions of these eminent engineers be impugned by the allegation that, being foreigners, they are unacquainted with the physical peculiarities of the Mississippi. They have all studied it attentively with access to the most authoritative information; including the work, the "Physics and Hydraulics of the Mississippi."

Pass, and extending parallel, or nearly so,* jetties which, starting at the cessation of 25 feet depth (above the North Pass), extend, a half mile apart, 4 miles to points opposite the outer crest of the bar, the bar must be excavated to 25 feet (*i. e.*, the 25 feet channel will be extended at once 2½ miles); the velocity of current maintained unimpaired up to this point will carry its sediment far beyond, into deep water. The present regime of a shoal bar cannot again be restored, until the vast bottom area now covered with deep water beyond, for a distance of 2½ miles, is raised. That there will be a 25-feet, or even a 20-feet available channel *all* this long time I do not contend. But this I do contend, viz.: * * * that once extended out to the crest of the existing bar, jetties do not require the incessant *following up* supposed; that they may *ultimately* require extension I do not dispute."

The recent Board of Engineers (of 1874), to which the whole subject was recommitted, used, in giving its decision in favor of jetties, substantially, but quite independently, the same argument, though more fully and clearly developed.

"At present, the muddy water issuing from the South Pass spreads out in somewhat of a fan-shape, the handle of the fan being at the mouth of the pass and the ribs several miles in length."

"If the proposed jetties were instantly completed, and the new channel scoured out, essentially the same amount of sediment would be spread out in fan-shape, but, from the greater velocity of the issuing water, the ribs of the fan would be longer, while the handle would be narrower. More of the sediment would at first be deposited far out in the Gulf than before.

"But with the present rate of advance, the 25 feet curve 120 years ago was about 12 000 feet above its present position; and if the volume of water carried by the pass is kept the same, neglecting the slight difference in slope of the Gulf bottom outside the present bar, in about 120 years a new end for the pass will probably be formed of the same general shape as the lower 12 000 feet of the present pass. It makes little difference, in the whole time required to accomplish the work, whether the same volume of water flows out at starting over the present shallow bar or from between two dikes which force the water to take a depth of 30 feet. In an average of many years, the rate of progress must be about the same as now, namely 100 feet per annum, the volume of water being kept as at present; and it is on this basis that the average annual cost of extension, namely, $130 000, has been computed."

"It has already been stated that it is proposed to obtain a depth of 30 feet between the jetties, in order that some years may elapse before the shoal which will form beyond the jetties can have on it less than the

* "Perfect parallelism is not necessary; large deviations may be made to select the best location."

required depth of 25 feet in the channel through it. There are no precise data for estimating this period. Going seaward from the upper end of the proposed dikes, the slope of the bottom of the South Pass is about $\frac{1}{440}$. This slope doubtless depends mainly on the velocity of the water flowing through it and on the lifting of the fresh water by the salt. As the causes remain essentially the same, it would seem natural that the new end of the South Pass to be formed by the sediment passing through the jetties should at least have the same bottom slope. If this assumption were true, the bottom would at least shoal from 30 to 25 feet in a distance of $5 \times 440 = 2\,200$ feet, and the time required would be about twenty-two years."

Mr. Eads in his pamphlet entitled "The Jetty System Explained" (printed in 1874), pages 6–7, dwells on and develops the same principle, justly reasoning from the facts of nature, that between the lowest point at which there is 60 feet depth in the South West Pass (whether that *final* 60 feet be in the unmodified pass, or suddenly realized, by means of jetties, on the site of the *present* bar) and a bar having only 15 feet, there must be a distance of 7⅓ miles—and the *time* for the creation of a new bar (if by jetties the present bar be deepened to 60 feet) must be equal to the number of feet in 7⅓ miles divided by the amount in feet of the *present annual* advance; a quotient which he assumes to be 178 years.

The arguments are *essentially* identical in all the three independently exhibited forms. These reasons are in themselves the broad and indisputable *facts* of observed configuration. All that has, in a different and conflicting sense, been arrayed is—where not pure assumption—based on theories* which have themselves, no sufficient inductive basis.

But the matter may be somewhat otherwise stated, thus—the passes can prolong themselves no faster than they can build up their base of formation; the broad *bank* on which their bed is laid and that serves as the solid *trough* (as it may be called) which conveys them to the sea. The *front* on which the fan-like expansion over which the great delta arms are laid, has an extent measured on the 100 feet (depth) curve of about 40 miles. The material if all laid *within* (and we know it is transported far beyond) the 100 feet line, cannot advance this front much more than 300

* The two most prominent and sharply defined "theories" of bar formation are those of Mr. Ellett, (the vertical *eddy* theory,) and of the "Physics and Hydraulics of the Mississippi," pages 445–6, 7, 8, refuting the former and attributing the bar formation to the heavier sediments "pushed along the bottom," but which also calls for "vertical eddies" and a "dead angle, where the river-water meets and rises upon the salt-water." Were this latter theory *proven*, it would be far from sustaining the inverse rule-of-three computations of enormous bar *advance*, under influence of contraction by jetties, based on it in Ex. Doc. 220, page 31.

feet per annum. Or if we take the South West Pass by itself (forming a kind of salient on the western extreme of the general configuration) its base measured at the same depth is 10 miles, (even on the 18 feet curve the base is 5 miles,) and this same configuration obtains whether we refer to Talcott's chart of 1838 or the Coast Survey chart of 1867, during which interval there has been a *general* progression of 1½ miles. The side banks, from the pass to lateral deep water, are quite pertinently compared by Mr. Eads to completed natural jetties; and as such, they must complete themselves as they advance. There is every reason to affirm that the advance, whether the material be projected with high velocity over a bar crest 2 000 feet long, or with low velocity over one 11 500 feet long, cannot be made on a base of *less width than we observe to be essential to the natural advance.**

Stress is laid on this exhibition of the case because it discards all theorization, and all subsidiary and disputable questions of "littoral currents," "tide," "winds" or "waves." If in the final minority report of the writer stress is mainly laid upon *precedent,* it is because successful precedent *is enough* to prove the claim that the "open mouth" should be striven for at the Mississippi; and because the greatest possible brevity was aimed at.

It will be noticed doubtless, that in the passage quoted from the minority report as first drafted, preference is given to Pass á Loutre, not because the analogy between the South Pass of the Mississippi and the "Sulina" (both bearing about 8 per cent. only, of the total discharge) had not already attracted the attention of the writer; but because in sketching out, under great pressure as to time, some outline of an application of the jetty system to the Mississippi delta, it was deemed inexpedient to select an obscure pass—one which has never been known to navigation—for the purpose. Pass á Loutre is, on the other hand, in some degree a rival of the South West Pass, while the application there would involve very much less expense than to the latter. Preference was subsequently given to the South Pass for reasons fully set forth in the minority report.†

In the foregoing, I have endeavored to give a concise history not only

* The following from the "Physics and Hydraulics of the Mississippi," page 449, is but another *form* of the above affirmation: "The oscillating motion of waves, when meeting bottom, is changed into a motion of translation, and this tends to arrange the deposit made by the river *into the same gentle slope at which it disposes similar material at corresponding depths along the shores.*"

† Ex. Doc. 220, page 124.

of actual operations at the delta mouths, but of the various projects for providing an adequate outlet, whether by operating on the mouths themselves, or by canalization. I have, at the same time, endeavored to make plain the grounds on which an "open river mouth" may be confidently hoped for.

In this matter the recent Board (of 1874), in all essential matters, is in unison with me. Its plans or its estimates are doubtless able and thorough, and, in absence of any precedent for the kind of work it proposes, are naturally founded on the best foreign precedents, which are those furnished by the practice of Holland, and more especially by recent works at the mouth of the Maas.* These works were visited by me in 1871, and fully described with full details of the fascine and ballast construction ("zink stukken," &c.) in Professional Papers, Corps of Engineers, No. 22, and the methods indicated as likely to "prove especially available in Louisiana." But at the same time they can but serve as *models*. In practice and adaptation to the peculiar locality, I believe they may be much simplified and the desired results of the jetty application be arrived at more speedily and economically than by following rigidly the board's model.

In all that relates to the rival project of a canal, the recent Board has given incomparably the best solution of that problem yet offered. Nevertheless, while always admitting the *practicability* so far as the mere question of construction (a difficult one though it be), I am far from believing it to offer a reasonable assurance of success, if by *success* is meant the furnishing of an outlet at all adequate; I doubt much whether in its *working*, it will fulfill even that degree of success which would be justified for similar canals in other localities, and I feel sure it could not be maintained for the small annual sum estimated.

Before closing this paper I would advert to the case of the Rhone mouth, upon which much stress has been laid as an unsuccessful attempt to apply jetties. I have before me a copy of the "Rapport sur les Projets presentés par les Ingénieurs chargés de la Navigation du Rhone," † made by a "Commission" of the "Ponts et Chaussées."

---

* These, even in Holland, were the *first* applications of this kind of work to an *open sea exposure*. So successful has it proved that the lower legislative body of Holland reports that "*the complete success of the works at the Hook of Holland has removed all doubts as to the possibility* "*of making piers at sea*" (*i. e.*, jetties) "*on our coast.*"

The construction, wholly of beton blocks at the sea entrance of the new North Sea Canal, has not proved so complete a success.

† Furnished to Gen. Wright, President of the Board of 1874, by M. Malezieux.

Stating that the General Council (*Conseil General*) of the Ponts et Chaussées had already been engaged with this subject in connection with two projects presented by Mr. Surrell, it mentions the *first* as that for a "canal maritime," &c., &c., and the *second*, as one for *concentrating the waters of the Rhone in one single arm*, that of the "Grau de l'Est;" the Council referred to, stating the principle upon which rested this project to be, "that the depth over the bar of a river mouth emptying into the sea is the greater, the greater the quantity of water which is discharged through it."

Thus we find laid down authoritatively, at the very outset of this matter, not the *jetty* method but (see enumeration, page 107, made by the Board of 1852) a distinct and very different one, *i.e.*, that, specified in the words of the board just cited, as "closing the useless passes." And, indeed, through the forty closely written manuscript pages of the report before me, this, and this only, is dwelt upon and discussed in all its bearing, without even an allusion to the very distinct notion of jetties or, as more generally known in Europe, that of "parallel piers."

That the actual construction assumed somewhat the semblance (as far as they went) of "parallel piers," is due simply to the fact that it was deemed indispensable to connect the *dams*, which stopped the "useless passes," by dikes running over the low, intervening islands (*theys*) —that, on the east side it was found easier and more economical to make a *continuous* dike, riverwards of the islands, than isolated dams.

Finally, this Commission, concludes as follows: "Whereas," * * *

"3d. The delta arms (*graus*) of Piémanson and Rouston, which are the first derivations, up stream, from the main river, receive more than half of the total discharge.

"4th. That the closing of these arms will constitute a valuable experience from which may be derived useful information.

"Therefore, the works to be executed for the improvement of the Rhone mouth should be confined to the closing of the Píemanson and Rouston arms."

The government, however, decided to carry out the plan of Mr. Surrell in full; and now let us hear in the language of M. Malézieux (September 10th, 1874) *what* was done.

The works constructed constitute a continuous dike ("*endiguement*") upon the two banks of the Rhone, from the Tower of St. Louis to the bar; that on the left has a total length ("*developpement*") of 7 kilometres (4½ miles), and *stops at* 1 531 *metres* (a mile less 80 yards), *inside the* *crest of the bar;* that on the right has a length of 6 500 metres (4 miles), and stops at 1 460 metres ($\frac{9}{10}$ mile) *inside the crest.* * * * "The result of these works was to *concentrate the waters of the Rhone in one arm,*" &c., &c.

And again, the official journal, "Annales des Ponts et Chaussées" (1863, 2d semestre), refers to this matter in these words (translated) : "After having attempted to improve the mouth by concentrating all the water *in a single channel,* the administration" (*i. e.*, of the Ponts et Chaussées) "renounced their fruitless efforts and had recourse to the construction of a maritime canal," &c., &c.

It seems scarcely necessary to remark that the jetty system has never been applied to the Rhone mouths. The method of closing useless passes having resulted in failure, the work was abandoned without even an attempt to apply the true jetty system, and the alternative project of Mr. Surrell—a "canal maritime" (ship-canal)—made. This, in the words of the report of the recent board, "is more than adequate to the wants of commerce." Inasmuch as at that locality there are comparatively trifling wants to be supplied, in *our* sense of such needs, one might suspect a vein of irony in these words, when we consider what a "*canal-maritime*" would be to the wants of commerce of the port of New York. Even *those* wants should not rival the exigencies of the now enormous, but yet undeveloped, freight-commerce of the Great West through its only outlet where the Father of Waters bears to sea the spoils of half a continent !

CIX.

ON THE MEANS OF AVERTING BRIDGE ACCIDENTS.

Reports by James B. Eads, C. Shaler Smith, Thomas C. Clarke, Julius W. Adams, Alfred P. Boller, Charles Macdonald and Theodore G. Ellis, Members of the Society.

Presented March 3d, 1875.*

REPORT I.

To the American Society of Civil Engineers:

The Committee appointed, under the resolution of May 21st, 1873,† to enquire into the "most practicable means of averting bridge accidents," begs leave to report as follows:

After a careful examination into the causes of the more disastrous accidents which have occurred during the past few years, it finds that they can readily be divided into three different classes. First, where bridges are erected by incompetent or corrupt builders, and accepted by incompetent or corrupt railway or municipal officials. Second, where bridges of good design and sufficient material fail from absolute neglect on the part of their owners, or from injury to the material during transportion or erection. Third, where bridges, good or bad, are knocked down or destroyed by derailed trains moving at a high rate of speed, or where the growth of a neighborhood has brought a class of traffic on a bridge, which it was not originally designed to bear, either by the builders

* At the regular meeting of the Society, March 3d, 1875, ordered printed and set-down for discussion at the Seventh Annual Convention to be held at Pittsburg, Pa., June 8th, 9th and 10th, 1875.

† At the Fifth Annual Convention, held at Louisville, Ky., May 21st and 22d, 1873, it was:—

"Resolved: in view of the late calamitous disaster of the falling of the bridge at Dixon, Ill., and other casualties of a similar character that have occurred and are constantly occurring, that a committee * * * be appointed to report at the next Annual Convention the most practicable means of averting such accidents."

The committee appointed consists of Messrs. James B. Eads and C. Shaler Smith of St. Louis, Mo., I. M. St. John of Quinnimont, Va., Thomas C. Clarke of Philadelphia, Pa., James Owen of Newark, N. J., Alfred P. Boller, Octave Chanute and Charles Macdonald of New York, Julius W. Adams of Brooklyn, N. Y., and Theodore G. Ellis of Hartford, Conn. Mr. Alfred L. Rives of Mobile, Ala., was appointed on the committee but resigned or the owners. How to treat each of these classes of causes will now be considered in the order above stated.

Accidents occurring from the first class would certainly not have taken place had the wrecked structures been correctly designed and had they possessed the proper sectional areas in their different parts—but failure from faulty design, is not nearly so frequent as failure from insufficient material. One great difficulty in the way of protecting the public from the results of imperfect design or scanty material lies in the absence of a fixed legal standard of loads and stresses for all classes of these structures, and another is the negligence of those controlling public works or those engaging in their construction, in securing skillful professional aid.

It would seem, therefore, to be our duty as a Society to establish in a few general terms—such as can be readily embodied in a law—a standard of maximum stresses and a table of least loads for which bridges should be designed, and to add thereto a practicable suggestion as to the necessary legislation required to give the public that protection which an adherence to this standard would afford. First, as to the standards for the least live loads to be used in proportioning bridges; a law which would provide that all railroad bridges should be built to carry not less than the following loads, would be well within the mark of safety.

For highway and street bridges the standard loads should not be less than as in first table on next page; for city and suburban bridges and those over large rivers where great concentration of weight is possible, as in column *A*; for highway bridges in manufacturing districts, or on level, well ballasted roads, as in column *B*, and for country road bridges, where the roads are unballasted and the loads hauled are consequently light, as in column *C*.

Spans.	Pounds per Square Foot.		
	A.	B.	C.
60 feet and under.	100	100	70
60 to 100 feet.	90	75	60
100 " 200 "	75	60	50
200 " 400 "	60	50	40

With the highway bridge the floor-beam strength is especially important, because of the great concentration of weight which may be carried on a single pair of wheels, therefore the floor system of each class of bridge should be—per floor-beam for each wagon-way—for city bridges, 6 tons; turnpike bridges, 5 tons, and county bridges, 4 tons.

SPAN OR PANEL.	POUNDS PER LINEAL FOOT OF TRACK.	SPAN OR PANEL.	POUNDS PER LINEAL FOOT OF TRACK.
Under 12 feet	6 000	Under 75 feet.	3 000
" 15 "	5 500	" 100 "	2 750
" 20 "	5 000	" 150 "	2 500
" 25 "	4 500	150 to 175 "	2 500
" 30 "	4 000	175 to 200 "	2 400
" 50 "	3 250	200 " 300 "	2 250

The panel weights for railroad bridges are obtained by using the standard weight per foot for short spans. In computing all web members, one panel of panel weight is to be considered as preceding the standard span load. The proposed law should also provide that with the foregoing loads, the stresses on materials shall not exceed the following :

For wrought-iron in tension, long bars or rods, 10 000 pounds per sq. in.
" " " " short links, (for floor beams)............... 8 000 " " "
" " " against shearing force..... 7 500 " " "

and for wrought-iron in compression, as in this table:

DIAMETERS.	POUNDS PER SQUARE INCH.		DIAMETERS.	POUNDS PER SQUARE INCH.	
	SQUARE ENDS.	ROUND ENDS.		SQUARE ENDS.	ROUND ENDS.
10	10 000	7 000	30 to 35	6 000	4 000
10 to 15	9 000	6 500	35 " 40	5 000	3 500
15 " 20	8 000	6 000	40 " 50	3 800	2 500
20 " 25	7 500	5 500	50 " 60	3 000	2 000
25 " 30	6 800	5 000	....	....	....

Where one end is square and the other end is rounded, a mean is to taken between the two.

Cast-iron to be used in compression only, in lengths not exceeding 22 diameters, and at the same stresses as those prescribed for wrought-iron.

The shapes under compression in the above are assumed to be hollow struts either square or cylindrical in section; other shapes than these to have the stresses varied as actual experiment may dictate.*

For wood, the greatest allowable strains shall be as follows:

For oak in flexure.............1 200 pounds per square inch.
" pine " " ....1 000 " " " "

and in compression as in this table:

Diameters.	Pounds per Square Inch.	
	Oak.	Pine.
10	1 000	900
10 to 20	800	700
20 " 30	600	500
30 " 40	400	300

The above standard should be changed or elaborated more fully, from time to time, as future experience and experiments on material suggest.

In order to secure to the public the full measure of benefit from the adoption of this standard, the law in question should provide for the appointment by the governor in each state, of an expert whose duties would consist in having cognizance of the construction and maintenance of every bridge intended for public travel in the state or states for which he was appointed. The law should also make it imperative that the expert so appointed shall pass an examination as to his mathematical and mechanical competency, which, it is suggested, should be by a standing committee of this Society, regularly constituted for the purpose, and that the appointment of any such expert who fails to receive the endorsement of this committee shall be null and void. Under the proposed law it should be the duty of all railroad, city, county or state officials having charge of the letting or construction of bridges to call upon this expert—first, to examine the strain-sheet of the proposed structure before work has been commenced, to certify to its correctness if correct, or to make such alterations as may be necessary if it is faulty in design or scant in material according to the legal standard ; next, to be present on the completion of the bridge, and then and there to make

* Further experiments can alone determine the values to be used for other than square or cylindrical cross sections.—A. P. B.

a critical examination of the work in all its details, comparing and verifying the sections on the strain-sheet with those of the actual structure, and if these last are insufficient, to forbid the use of the work until the law is fully complied with ; and, lastly, if the bridge is up to the standard in all its parts, to obtain from him a certificate to that effect, copies of which certificate shall also be given to the builder, and filed on record in the proper department of the state government. This officer shall also see that a tablet or plate is placed on a conspicuous part of the bridge, bearing the names of the builders, his own name, and that of the officer of the railway or corporation who accepts the work, together with the strength of the bridge as designed, and the year of its erection.

Accidents arising from the first class of causes would be nearly, if not quite prevented by the general enforcement of the foregoing provisions. Against accidents occurring from causes of the second class, the law should further provide that all railway or other corporate bodies, when having a bridge built, to be used for public travel, shall be compelled during the erection of the work, to keep on the spot a competent inspector, who shall have power to reject any piece of material which may have been injured in transportation or while being placed in position. Also that all railroad and city bridges shall be inspected once every month by a competent person in the employ of the corporation owning the bridge, for the purpose of seeing that all iron parts are in order, all nuts screwed home, that there are no loose rivets, that the iron rails are in line and without wide joints, and that all wooden parts of the structure are sound and in proper condition.

It should also be the duty of the state officer before mentioned, upon any bridge being reported as in a neglected condition—whether the report be an official one or made by one not connected with the corporation—to proceed to the spot and examine for himself, and if he finds the bridge in a neglected or dangerous condition, he should cause the owners to put it in safe order without delay.

In relation to the third class of causes—destruction by derailed trains, high winds, or by concentration of living weight owing to the growth of cities or neighborhoods—prevention is less easy, but much can be done by carefully designing the structure. In most of our railroad bridges the floor system is the weak point. The cross-ties are short, the stringers are proportioned for a train *on*, not *off* the rails ; and the guard-timbers are too low, and are insufficiently bolted. A derailed engine on such a floor as this, plunges off the end of the cross-ties into the open space between the stringers and the chords, and generally wrecks the bridge. To obviate this, the law should provide that, first, —all cross-ties shall extend from truss to truss, they shall be placed so close to each other that if supported at the proper intervals it will be impossible for a derailed engine to cut through them, and the stringers shall be so spaced as to give them this support. Next, the guard-timbers shall be scantlins not less than 9 × 10 inches, and they shall be strongly bolted or spiked to at least each alternate cross-tie. And lastly, the clear width between the trusses on through bridges shall be so great that the wheels of a derailed train will be arrested by the guard-rail before the side of the widest car can strike the truss. Where switches are placed at the end of a bridge, the Wharton or some other form of safety switch should be used.

Against the majority of accidents from high winds, a provision in the law requiring that all lateral bracing shall be sufficient to resist a pressure of 30 pounds per square foot of truss and train, will be sufficient. Lateral bracing can be proportioned at 15 000 pounds per square inch against this particular strain, as it is of very rare occurrence.

The last case in the third class of causes of accidents is where a bridge built originally for a neighborhood or country road becomes too weak for the requirements of a growing community or possibly of a newly established manufactory; also where a railroad bridge, intended only for that class of traffic, has a highway floor subsequently added to it. Against the first contingency, the vigilance of the state official and the chance that some one of the users of the bridge may occasionally notice the tablet setting forth its strength, would seem to be about the only safeguard; but in the second case, the law should provide that—except by permission of the state officer in charge of bridges—no corporation or other bridge owner shall add to the dead weight on a bridge without at the same time making the proper addition to its strength.

The foregoing provisions, if embodied in a law, will afford the public about all the protection which is readily obtainable in the case.

No mention is here made of the quality of the material, as the proposed officials engaged in carrying out the law will be men who have been passed on by the Society, and the very fact of their surveillance will be apt to produce care in this regard. In addition to this, the standard stresses have been placed so low that the use, whether accidental or fraudulent, of low grades of iron will hardly endanger the work. A provision in the law that all bridge details shall possess the proper proportional strength to that of the main members of the bridge, and a series of instructions from the examining committee of the Society to those who pass their examinations for appointments under this law, in reference to these proper proportions, will protect the purchasers of bridges from insecure details of construction.

In addition to his duties, as above defined, the state officer in charge of bridges should also visit the scene of any accident in his district as soon as possible after the occurrence, and remain during the removal of the wreck, or until he is able to ascertain the true cause of the failure. The facts in the case should then be reported by him to the examining committee of the Society.

In conclusion, it is here advised that a committee be appointed to draft such a law as is outlined in this report; that a resolution be passed by the Society recommending the adoption of this law by the different state legislatures, and that printed copies of this report, the proposed laws and the accompanying resolution, be sent to the members of the Society with a request that they move actively, each in his own state, towards procuring the passage of the specified law by the various state legislatures during the coming winter.

JAS. B. EADS, Chairman.

October 30th, 1874. C. SHALER SMITH. *

---

* In advocating the views presented in the foregoing report, the undersigned is actuated by the following reasons:

First—the resolution under which the Committee is acting requires from it "the most practicable means of averting—*i. e.*, preventing—bridge accidents"—rather than the mode of sitting in judgment on them after they occur.

Second—as the national legislature has for some time been passing laws for the protection of life on the navigable waters of the United States, prescribing qualifications and standards for engineers and pilots, the proportions of safety valves, &c., for boilers, and appointing examiners and inspectors under these laws—so, sooner or later will the question of the proper construction of railways be taken up and legislated upon.

Third—many mistakes have been made in these laws, owing to ignorance on the part of those passing them, and the undue influence of interested inventors and manufacturers, and each succeeding Congress has had amendments to make in order to repair some injustice or supply some omission.

Lastly—as laws regulating the construction of railroads and bridges will certainly be enacted, and official positions will assuredly be created by them—it is far better that this Society should take time by the forelock, dictate a law which will be just and equitable, and hold control of the appointments under it, than that it should stand in the background, until an aroused public opinion compels legislation which may be injurious to the profession, especially if enforced by political appointees who may be utterly unfit to fill such positions. All laws are written by some one, and the greater the knowledge of the subject matter on the part of that person is, the more probable is the production of a good and wise statute.

Hence the undersigned believes that the fixing of the standards as proposed, the preparation of such a law as suggested, and the professional surveillance of the appointees under it, are eminently the province of this association, and that all legislation on the subject should be both inspired and dictated by the most competent authority in the premises—the American Society of Civil Engineers.

April 18, 1875. C. SHALER SMITH.

REPORT II.

The undersigned differ from the views expressed in the foregoing report, and present the following as an expression of their own :

I.—They agree with the report, that it is desirable the American Society of Civil Engineers should publicly declare what it considers to be a standard bridge, anything below which is not to be deemed as a safe or durable construction. But they do not think it is desirable to go much into detail, as they believe it to be impossible to construct a specification that will meet all cases. Incompetent engineers cannot be prevented from building bad bridges by any specifications however elaborate ; they therefore are content with laying down general principles, leaving the application to others, and offer the following standard specification for bridges of iron and wood :

1. Every highway bridge shall be capable of carrying, in addition to its weight, a moving load per square foot of roadway and sidewalks as follows :

SPANS—FEET.	POUNDS.	SPANS—FEET.	POUNDS.
100 and under.	100	300 to 400	60
100 to 200	80	Over 400	50
200 " 300	70	....	......

2. Every railway bridge shall be capable of carrying on each track, in addition to its own weight, 2 locomotives coupled, weighing 30 tons on drivers in space of 12 feet, and whose total weight, including loaded tenders, is 65 tons each ; said locomotives to be followed by so many loaded coal cars weighing one ton per lineal foot, as will cover the remainder of the span.

3. Bridges shall be so proportioned that the above loads shall not strain any part of the material over one-fifth of its ultimate strength.

II.—The signers of the foregoing report, propose to cause future bridges to come up to the standard by a system of inspection, the inspectors to be passed by the Society before being appointed. The undersigned believe that in the present state of public opinion this is impracticable. If any inspectors are appointed, it will be by political influence, and the results will be worse than at present, as the inspection will be inefficient, and yet, to a great extent, relieve the owners of bad bridges from legal responsibility.

The undersigned consider that the most the Society can hope to do, is to provide means in case of the fall of a bridge, by which the responsibility of imperfect construction (if this was the cause of the accident) may be fixed on the designers and builders, and iron manufacturers.

It is therefore recommended that the Society prepare and present to the state legislatures, a petition embodying the following data :

1. That the standard of the American Society of Civil Engineers shall be the legal standard, and in case it shall be found that any bridge is of less strength than this, it shall be taken as *prima facie* evidence of neglect on the part of its owners.

2. That no bridge shall be opened for public traffic until a plan, giving the maximum loads it was designed to carry, the resulting strains, and the dimensions of all the parts, sworn to by the designers and makers, and attested by the signature of the proper officer representing the municipality or corporation by whom it is owned, be deposited in the archives of the Society, and that the principal pieces of iron in the bridge be stamped with name of maker, place of manufacture and date.

The result of this will be, that in case of the fall of a bridge, the responsibility can be directly and easily traced to the right party, which at present cannot be done, and the Society should willingly aid to such a purpose. This, it is recommended, should thus be done ; the Society to appoint a committee—with compensation to be fixed by law—which, upon the call of the executive of any state, should visit and report upon any fallen bridge, care being taken that no parties interested in the construction of the bridge be upon the committee.

It is believed by the undersigned, that the knowledge all bridge builders would have that their misdeeds, if any, could, by this process, be traced home to themselves, would make them very careful in the future, and eliminate all failures from imperfect design or material.

As to the inspection of existing structures ; if the Society assumed the first duty, this would soon fall under its jurisdiction, and if it would volunteer the duty—in case any plan was deposited obviously unsafe—to protest against it, that also would be well ; such would have prevented the fall of the Dixon bridge, and the lamentable loss of life and limbs there occurring.

THOMAS C. CLARKE.
JULIUS W. ADAMS.

February 1st, 1875.

REPORT III.

The undersigned differ from the views expressed in the foregoing reports, and respectfully present the following :

1. The members of the committee agree that it is meet and proper the American Society of Civil Engineers should determine the standard of strength for all bridges to be built in this country, and they further agree in the main, what this standard should be. The differences in opinions grow out of the methods for incorporating this standard in the every-day practice of the country. Two general modes present themselves for so doing ; the one legislative and compulsory, and the other looking forward to directing public sentiment to right conclusions by a thorough dissemination of the adopted standard.

2. The undersigned advocate the latter method as the true policy of the Society, believing that any attempt to influence the enactment of laws that would be so far-reaching as the ones proposed, is impracticable, if not contrary to the genius of the Society itself. They further believe that when once public sentiment is aroused by the publicity which should be given to the adopted standard, it will compel the passage of laws covering the question.

3. The undersigned therefore suggest that the report to be accepted be simply one covering a standard strength for all bridges, in as general terms as possible, with a recommendation that such standard be widely disseminated by circular and the public prints, and that copies be distributed among the legislative bodies of the several states.

The following standard, culled from the forcgoing reports, is proposed for adoption :

4. For highway bridges, as submitted in Report I, page 123.

5. For railroad bridges :*—the structure shall be at least capable of carrying on each track, in addition to its own weight, 2 locomotives coupled, weighing 30 tons on drivers in space of 12 feet, and whose total load, including tender, is 65 tons each. Said locomotives to be followed by as many loaded coal cars, weighing one ton per lineal foot, as will cover the remainder of the span.

Bridges to be so proportioned that the above described loads shall not strain the several parts in excess of one-fifth or one-sixth of the ultimate strength. In determining the strains produced by the above stand-

* Being the same as submitted in Report II, page 129.

ard, it is to be understood that the chord system is to be computed for a uniform loading, while the web strains must be based upon the irregularly distributed or concentrated loads produced by the above described train, in its passage from one end to the other.

The following table represents the uniform distributed moving load for different spans :

Span or Panel.	Pounds per Lineal Foot of Track.	Span or Panel.	Pounds per Lineal Foot of Track.
12 feet.	5 250	75 feet.	3 000
15 "	5 250	100 "	2 750
20 "	5 000	150 "	2 500
25 "	4 500	175 "	2 400
30 "	4 200	200 "	2 300
50 "	3 250	200 to 300 "	2 250

The extreme panel weight for all spans is obtained by using the standard weight per foot for short spans.

6. Under the standard loading, as expressed in above table, materials should not be strained in excess of what is submitted in Report I, page 124.

All of which is respectfully submitted.

Alfred P. Boller.
Charles Macdonald.

March 1st, 1875.

REPORT IV.

While agreeing in many important particulars with the report of the Chairman of this Committee, the undersigned holds the views expressed by some of the other members regarding the expediency of compulsory legislation on the subject. It is believed that the opinions of this Society as a body, advanced for its interest and benefit and that of those who should choose to be governed by them, would have more weight and influence than though the Society should assert itself as the only competent authority upon bridge construction. If this Society adopts a well defined standard of strength for bridges, it is believed that the public generally will wish to conform to it, and engineers even who are not members will be glad to avail themselves of the united opinion of so many of the profession.

There seems to be a unanimity of opinion among the members of the Committee as to what constitutes the ordinary load upon a railway bridge, and but a slight difference of opinion as to its amount.

From an examination of the weights carried upon many of the principal railways in the United States, it is found that the heaviest engines weigh about 2 830 pounds per foot; and that three, and sometimes four, are coupled. The heaviest weight on one pair of drivers is from 21 000 to 24 000 pounds, and the weight on all the drivers, generally not exceeding 12 feet wheel-base, is from 72 000 to 84 000 pounds. The heaviest trains may be assumed to weigh 2 250 pounds to the running foot, exclusive of the engines. As the coupling of more than two engines is mainly upon snow roads, it is not believed they should be included in a general rule for proportioning bridges, but should be classed among those exceptional cases for which a general provision cannot be made.

In view of the above, it is believed that all railway bridges should be proportioned for a rolling load of 3 000 pounds to the foot for the total engine length, and for 2 250 pounds to the foot for the remainder of the bridge; that the bracing on each system should be proportioned to sustain 84 000 pounds on any 12 feet of track, and that any point on the track should sustain 24 000 pounds.

It is not believed that the system of expressing the loads that a bridge should carry, by so much per foot with a varying amount for each length of span, is the best; but if such a standard is to be adopted, the table* in the report of the Chairman is believed to be the best of those given, although it is somewhat below the loads actually carried by many roads in this country.

The floor-beams of railway bridges should be proportioned for not less than the following loads:

Spaces.	Pounds.	Spaces.	Pounds.
4 feet apart, or less.	28 000	12 feet apart, or less.	42 000
6 " "	31 500	15 " "	45 000
8 " "	35 000	More than 15 feet apart	3 000 to the foot.
10 " "	38 500		

* Page 124.

The following table is offered as embracing the foregoing loads when reduced to so much per lineal foot :

Span or Panel.	Pounds per Lineal Foot of track.	Span or Panel.	Pounds per Lineal Foot of track.
12 feet or under.	7 000	50 feet.	3 000
15 feet.	6 000	100 "	2 800
20 "	4 800	200 "	2 600
25 "	4 000	300 "	2 500
30 "	3 600	400 "	2 450
40 "	3 200	500 or over.	2 400

For intermediate lengths of span the proportional number of pounds per foot should be taken.

These loads do not include the extraordinary weights that are sometimes drawn over railways in this country ; such as heavy pieces of machinery, blocks of stone, or a locomotive of different gauge on a truck car, nor more than two engines coupled. These are exceptional cases which can be provided for when they may be expected to occur, and the weight can ordinarily be distributed so to cover a sufficient length of track as not to exceed the loads above given.

For the effect of wind, the maximum strain is believed to be about 40 pounds per square foot horizontal, and about 20 pounds per square foot vertical.

For highway bridges, the following table is offered as a substitute for that given in the report of the Chairman* for the three classes of bridges named.

Spans. (Intermediate lengths in proportion.)	Pounds per Square Foot.		
	A.	B.	C.
100 feet and under.	100	75	60
200 "	80	60	50
300 "	70	50	50
400 "	60	50	50
500 " and over.	50	50	50

* Page 123.

The floor-beams and flooring should be of sufficient strength to sustain the following loads on four wheels :—Class A, 24—B, 16—and C, 8 tons respectively. These do not include the extraordinary loads sometimes taken over highways. They are exceptional cases and the weight can generally be divided.

With regard to the factors of safety to be used, it is believed that a less factor is required for the permanent and unchanging dead load, than for the vibrating and uncertain live load, which may, by accident, be increased beyond the limit for which it was computed. This, together with the fact that a larger factor for the dead load gives no additional strength to the bracing near the middle of the span, but only at the ends, leads to the following substitution for the factor offered in the report of the Chairman.

For wrought-iron and steel in both compression and extension—for the dead load including snow, $\frac{1}{3}$—for the live load including wind, $\frac{1}{5}$ the ultimate strength.

For cast-iron in compression only, and for lengths of not more than 20 diameters—for the dead load $\frac{1}{5}$, and for the live load, $\frac{1}{10}$ the ultimate strength. For large masses, as in arches, a factor of $\frac{1}{4}$ the ultimate strength may be adopted.

Bridges should be tested with the maximum loads which they are intended to sustain. A less load would seem to be of but little use, and a much greater one might unnecessarily strain the structure. The load should be applied gradually, and the moment any undue deflection or crippling is observed, or the slightest diminution in the transverse section of any bar is occasioned, the load should be immediately removed and never repeated. If no actual rupture occurs, the bridge will probably be safe with 0.4 of the test applied. The acceptance of all bridges, after being constructed with proper proportions for the material used, should be subject to such a practical test.

THEODORE G. ELLIS.

April 20th, 1875.

CX.

ON THE FORM, WEIGHT, MANUFACTURE AND LIFE OF RAILS.

A second Report, by Ashbel Welch, C. E. (Chairman), Member of the Society.

Presented May 5th, 1875.*

The members of the Committee† on Rails desire, when they make their final report, to present some definite results, which a wide experience alone can establish. They therefore earnestly beg their professional brethren to state their experience on the subject, in response to the interrogatories issued by the Committee last year,‡ or in any other way they may think best.§ In the meantime, a few points now settled will be presented, and a few questions raised for the consideration of the Society.

Forms of rails on the same principles as those recommended by the Committee have been adopted on three of the great railroad systems of the country—the Erie, Lehigh Valley and Pennsylvania. The Pennsylvania has also adopted the plan of a deeper head for main lines, on nearly the same base as a shallower head for branches ; the base for main lines is 4½ inches.

The Committee considers it settled, that with the present weights on a wheel, a thickness of the middle of the stem of seven-sixteenths inch

* At the adjourned regular meeting of the Society, May 12th, 1875, presented, ordered printed, and set down for discussion at the Seventh Annual Convention at Pittsburg, Pa., June 8th, 9th and 10th, 1875.

† Appointed January 8th, 1873, to determine the "the best form of standard rail sections of this country; the proportion which the weight of rails should bear to the maximum loads carried on a single pair of wheels of locomotives or cars ; the best methods of manufacturing and testing rails ; the endurance, or, as it is called, the 'life' of rails; the causes of the breaking of rails and the most effective way of preventing it, and the experience of railways in this country in the use of steel rails."

The committee consists of Messrs. Ashbel Welch, of Lambertville, N. J., M. A. Forney and Octave Chanute, of New York, and I. M. St. John, of White Sulphur Springs, W. Va.

‡ Referred to in Proceedings, Vol. I., page 76.

§ The Chairman of the Committee is instructed by his colleagues to give "particular Jesse" to the members of the Society who have furnished no answers or information ; being utterly unskilled in handling that terrific weapon (if it is a weapon), he asks each recusant to consider himself the recipient of a tremendous poke, and keep the fear of a similar punishment before his eyes hereafter—if he continues in default.

AMERICAN SOCIETY OF CIVIL ENGINEERS.

INCORPORATED 1852.

TRANSACTIONS.

NOTE.—This Society is not responsible, as a body, for the facts and opinions advanced in any of its publications.

XCVIII.

UPRIGHT ARCHED BRIDGES.

A Paper by JAMES B. EADS, C. E., Member of the Society.

READ JUNE 10, 1874.

In a report on the Illinois and St. Louis Bridge, in 1868, I advanced the proposition that, for railroad purposes, an upright arched bridge could be more cheaply constructed than was possible by the suspension system. This postulate called forth soon after, some dissenting views from engineering journals to which I had not, at the time, the leisure to reply.

In this paper I will endeavor to show that upright arched bridges can be more economically constructed than is possible by any other method whatever, no matter what length of span may be required. As the cost of the span (excepting the cost of roadway) will, by any system, increase at least as rapidly as the square of the distance spanned, the length of span will be limited in all cases, by financial difficulties, before grave engineering ones are encountered.

I will first point out some of the disadvantages of the system adopted for the superstructure of the St. Louis Bridge, which was the best method of arch construction then known to me, and will respectfully venture to indicate such improvements as have suggested themselves, in consequence of these difficulties being so forcibly thrust upon my attention in the progress of that work. An earnest wish to make these and their remedies thoroughly understood, will I trust, excuse in me much that may seem commonplace or didactic.

In the St. Louis Bridge the upper and lower members, which constitute a single rib of the span, are tubular in form, the tubes being each 18 inches outside diameter. The rib thus formed is 12 feet deep from centre to centre of the tubes, and the two lines of tubing are braced together by a single triangular system of vertical bracing, formed of flat bars secured to the tubes at points about 12 feet distant from each other throughout the length of the rib, the bars being placed in pairs, one on each side of the tubes, and secured to them by pins passing through the ends of the bars and the couplings of the tubes. An upper and lower line of tubes thus braced constitutes one rib of an arch or span. The curve selected for the ribs was, for greater convenience of manufacture, the segment of a circle. Each individual tube is straight, the curvature of the rib being accomplished at the junction of these individual members, each of which is about 12 feet long. The curve of the rib differs from a parabola but a few inches.

If the effects of temperature could be avoided, and the curve were a parabola, an equally distributed load on a rib would, of course, be borne by the upper and lower tubes equally, that is, half on each ; and the only strain on the bracing would be in transferring half of the imposed load to the lower tube. In this case the tubes could be together and the bracing dispensed with. We should then have, in the two lines of tubes, the least possible section requisite to sustain this equally distributed load. To brace the arch against unequal loading, the tubes were placed 12 feet asunder.

The medium temperature was assumed at 60° Fah. The effect of temperature (ranging from — 20° to + 140° Fah.) increases the length of the rib about 6 inches. This extension causes the crown to rise, which relieves the lower tube of compression at the abutments, and hence that tube does not then support any portion of the weight of the rib or the load. These are borne wholly by the upper tube at the abutments, and hence its section there must be increased accordingly. At the crown, the strains are likewise changed. There, however, the *lower* tube does all the duty, as the upward bending of the rib, relaxes the compression in the upper tube at this point, hence the lower one must be increased at the centre of the rib to enable it to do this double service. It is thus seen that the upper tube at the abutments, and the lower one at the crown, must, when the temperature is at its maximum, perform the whole duty of sustaining the rib and its load. The strains in the respective tubes decrease from these points toward the haunches of the arch, where the centre of pressure passes through the middle of the rib. At the haunches the compression is borne in nearly equal portions by the upper and lower tubes. The extra section required by temperature, therefore, becomes smaller in the tubes as we leave the crown and abutments.

These are the effects of expansion. As the ribs are formed for a medium temperature, contraction by cold reverses these strains. The crown of the arch falls, and the *upper* tube at that point must be reinforced, because it must then sustain the entire compressive strain, which, at medium temperature, is equally borne by both; while, at the abutments, the *lower* tubes have now to carry all the load. Thus it is seen that, both at the abutments and the crown, the upper and lower tubes must be each of greatly increased section on account of the changes of temperature.

These changes, in very extreme cases, will probably tend to withdraw the one tube or the other from the abutments, as extreme heat or cold affects the rib. At the suggestion of my chief assistant, Col. Flad, to give greater resistance to a change of form of the rib under unequal loading, the skewbacks in which the tubes are fastened are rigidly held to the abutments by anchor bolts. Thus, at times, a tube at the abutments may not only be relieved of all compression, but may bear tension and pull upon its skewbacks, by which an additional compressive strain may be transferred through the braces to the other tube. For this contingency additional section had to be provided at the abutments in the first two or three tubes.

Greater depth of the rib would have increased all these strains of temperature, and would thus have involved larger sections at the crown and abutments. By lessening the depth, the strains would have been diminished, but a more flexible rib, under unequal loading, would have resulted. Between these evils on either hand, after various calculations, the most economic and satisfactory results were obtained with 12 feet depth of rib.

A diagram of the strains of the central arch, on which my remarks are based, is appended, (Fig. 25). From these it will be seen that effects of temperature have compelled the use of a much larger quantity of metal in the ribs, than would have been necessary if these effects could have been avoided.

No one will, I think, deny that the cheapest possible form in which steel or iron can be used to span an opening and support an *equally* distributed load, is the catenary or suspended arch. It is equally evident that if an upright arch has the same span, weight and curve of any given catenary, the strains in the one form would be no more intense than in the other. In the upright arch they would be compressive strains, and in the suspended arch they would be tensile ones. In the suspended form, the section of metal may be solid; in the upright, it must be hollow, tubular, or of some construction that will resist buckling; but to be of equal strength it must not necessarily be more weighty. If either form have an equally distributed load placed on it, no bracing will be requisite to preserve its normal curvature. The same load, if within the elastic limit of the metal, can be borne by either with the same amount of material. Hence, the only difference in material required for the two systems for any given span and load, must lie in the difference of bracing them to resist distortion when *unequally* loaded. I refer here simply to the span between the supporting towers in the one case and the abutments in the other. Between these points, with the same curvature, the sectional areas of each may be the same, under equal loads. In this I, of course, assume that the iron or steel can be trusted with equal strains in tension or compression. In compression, tubular or other sections are quite capable of sustaining, in wrought-iron or steel, all that it is safe to apply in tension if the lengths of the compressive members do not exceed 8 or 10 diameters. In the St. Louis Bridge however, they are but 8 diameters.

The section of arch is doubled by doubling the span, and in the suspension cable it is evident that a long span involves equal sectional areas also in the shore spans, or portions between the towers and anchorages. Whereas, when the stream is spanned by a long arch, the need of such extra section in the shore spans does not exist, because they can almost always be short spans. Mr. Peter W. Barlow, C. E., in 1860, published a pamphlet on the Niagara Railway Suspension Bridge, from which I quote the following remarkably clear explanation of the fact that in all known systems of girders, with any given depth, *four times* as much metal is required to obtain the same rigidity as is needed with the arch or the cable.

"Let *A C B*, Fig. 1, represent an arch supported on abutments *A* and *B*, and let the deflection produced by a given weight, loaded equally, be represented by unity. Now, let us consider the effect of making this arch into a self-supporting structure, or bowstring girder, by removing the abutments and substituting a tie, *A B*, Fig. 2.

" Assuming the same weight, w, to be placed equally all over, the deflection will be 2, the points A and B being no longer rigid, because the tie $A\ B$ will extend as much as the arch $A\ C\ B$ will compress. Therefore, to produce the same rigidity in a bow string girder four times the metal is required as compared with the arch. The same result arises in a cable $A\ C\ B$, suspended from the two fixed points $A\ B$, Fig. 3.

" If the back chains are removed, and a compression tube $A\ B$ substituted, the metal is doubled and you have a structure with only half the rigidity. The Chepstow Bridge on the South Wales Railway is an example of this arrangement.

" The mechanical combination in the Saltash Bridge is represented by substituting the arch $A\ D\ B$ for the tie $A\ B$, Fig. 4, forming a combination of a suspension chain and an arch. The arch $A\ D\ C$ will not perform the duty of compression unless it is connected with the chains by the ties $a\ a$, $a\ a$. When thus connected both the cables and the arch assist in supporting the weight of the load. The points $A\ B$ now become fixed points, and as both the arch and the chains assist in supporting the weight, the deflection will only be half that of the simple suspension cable with double the weight of metal. It therefore appears :

"1. To convert an arch supported on two fixed abutments into a bowstring girder, four times the metal is also required to support the same weight with the same deflection.

"2. To convert a cable suspended from two fixed points into a Chepstow girder four times the metal is required to support the same weight with the same deflection.

"3. To convert the same cable into a Saltash combination (which consists of a bowstring and Chepstow girder combined, so that the horizontal tie in one case neutralizes the compression tube in the other, by which they are both avoided), the deflection is reduced one-half, with double the weight of material, or the same weight of material will produce the same deflection with the same load, as in the case of the simple arch or cable. But this is obtained at the expense of double the depth ; and if the arch or suspension cable was of the same depth as the Saltash, only one quarter of the metal would produce the same stiffness.

" In the preceding illustration, the bowstring and Saltash girders are referred to—parallel girders are more commonly used—but they present no economy over the simple bowstring, and however perfect their arrangement and proportions, they will still require not less than four times the metal of a simple cable of the same depth and span to produce the same deflection."

Enough is shown by Mr. Barlow in these extracts to prove a far greater economy in the metallic arch or catenary than is possible with any truss system known. In practice, however, the chief causes which have conspired to lessen this evident economy are : 1st, the bracing requisite to preserve the form of the arch when unequally loaded ; 2d, the effects of temperature, and 3d, the necessity of heavier masonry to resist the pull of the cables or the thrust of the arch.

I cannot better illustrate the notably small amount of bracing or "girder-power" required to resist the effects of unequal loading in the suspended arch or cable than by again quoting from the same distinguished author. Mr. Barlow says :

"If the beam *A B*, Fig. 5, be divided into two beams by being supported at *C*, the two half beams, *A C* and *B C*, will deflect one-eighth of the amount of the entire beam *A B* with the same weight. Let us assume this to be a girder attached to a chain, and a load placed at *D*, the effect will be to distort it into the shape shown in Fig. 6. The deflection by the weight at *D* will cause a corresponding elevation at the point *E*, and the girder will assume the shape represented by dotted lines in the figure, to produce which a force equal to double that for a given deflection on half the beam is required, from which it is evident that the wave produced by a given weight at *D* will only amount to one-sixteenth of the deflection the same weight will produce on the entire beam resting on its two ends.

"In the above proposition it is assumed that the beam is supported at its centre point only; in practice, when attached to a suspension cable, it is supported at various points of its length, the difference between the wave of a supported girder and the deflection of an unsupported girder will therefore be greater than one-sixteenth."

"In order to arrive at the result by experiment, I had a model of the proposed Londonderry bridge on a scale $\frac{1}{33}$ of the actual span, the length being 13 feet 6 inches between the bearings, a length exceeding that of the average of the models used by the Iron Commissioners in their experiments, and is amply sufficient—due allowance being made for the scale—to determine the accuracy of the deflections on the actual girder. The principal object of these experiments was to ascertain the deflection of the wave of a girder attached to a chain, as compared with the deflection of the same girder detached, which being obtained, it is perfectly easy to arrive at the deflection of the wave of any required suspension girder, because we have sufficient experiments on actual girders of various dimensions to obtain the deflection from a given load on the same girder not attached to a chain. These experiments gave a mean result of $\frac{1}{25}$, so that, it being first determined what amount of deflection is to be the limit with a given load in a given bridge, you have only to arrive by calculation at the sections of metal of a girder of the same depth which would deflect 25 times that amount."

The economy of a continuous girder, resting on a central support, depends upon the several supporting points remaining absolutely stable, or in line. The sinking of one or the elevation of another, creates extra strains in the girder which may destroy all the advantages of continuity. The great economy of girder power theoretically shown by Mr. Barlow is not attained in any suspension bridge of which I have knowledge, because the effects of temperature have not been avoided in their construction. The extension and contraction of the cables cause the central part of the girder to fall and rise, whilst the ends of the girder remain at a constant level. This is not avoided even where the towers are of iron also. Additional strains are thus created in the girder, for which increased sections are required. These strains can be avoided however, by jointing the cables at the centre of the span, and cutting the girder in two at the same point. By this means each half length of girder trusses the half length of cable to which it is attached. If the end of each half girder be securely fastened to the central joint, the economy of a continuous girder may be attained, because the effect of the load in bending the one half girder down is resisted by the other, just as it would be if the two were continuous. The loaded one cannot deflect without distorting the cable above it, and the cable cannot deflect, without rising where it is unloaded, which movement could only occur by bending up the unloaded half girder beneath it. In this case the cable must be likewise jointed at the towers, as each half of its length is rendered rigid by its connection with the half girder, and the half girders must also be allowed to expand and contract at the towers.

Fig. 7 illustrates this method of eliminating the strains of temperature from the suspension bridge, and securing the fullest benefit of "girder power" with the greatest economy attainable by this system of bracing. If Fig. 7 be reversed, as in Fig. 8, the dotted lines will show that exactly the same economy of bracing or "girder power" is attainable in the upright arch by this method, except that in one case the vertical connections act as *ties*, and in the other as *struts*, and inasmuch as the compressive strains on the long struts will necessitate greater sections than the tension strains require in the ties, a slight advantage is found in the suspended arch. Owing to the weight of the cables, this advantage will be increased by a difference in the expense of wind bracing. In this last item, the difference will be found to be less, however, than is generally supposed.

This fact may be thus illustrated; if a column of metal be suspended by its upper end, its weight will resist the deflection caused by a current of wind that would blow it over, if standing on its base. It must be remembered, however, that if suspended, the resistance of the weight is only effective *after* the centre of gravity of the column has been moved. When vertical, its resistance is *nil;* the maximum effect being exerted when the horizontal position is reached by the column. Therefore to preserve the lower end absolutely from movement by the wind, would require as strong a brace or guy as would be needed to preserve the same stability at the upper end if the column were standing. The case is identically the same in the suspended and upright arches. The bridge should be braced against all movement by wind as far as possible, and hence the stability of the cables due to their weight, will not, on investigation, be found to possess as much importance as has been claimed for it. The plan of spreading the arch at its bases, as proposed by Telford in his 600 feet span for the Thames, has been applied in its reverse form to the suspension bridge, as a means of securing greater stability against wind pressure. Either application of this feature, suspended or upright, involves the necessity of increased section in the cable or arch, the supporting power of either being lessened as the plane of the curve inclines from the vertical. The increased section therefore involved in this means of securing stability should be charged in the estimate of wind bracing.

The illustration I have given of the suspended and standing column, may likewise be referred to here, to show that for rigid structures, the weight of the cables in preserving the suspension bridge from a change of form under unequal loading is not an element of so much importance as advocates of that system claim. Let *A B*, Fig. 9, be a suspended arch loaded at *D*, and *C* be the point to which the greatest curvature has been removed by the load from the centre *E*, of the span where it was when the cable was in equilibrium. By reversing the figure, we see at once that in the upright arch, the flattening from *A* to *C*, increases the thrust of that portion against the remainder of the arch, which being without load, and of inferior weight, can only be sustained by the strength of its bracing or girder power. This change of form in the arch lessens its ability to resist the effect of the load, and even increases the power of the weight, to further distort it by the additional horizontal pressure against the portion *C B*, due to the flattening of *A C*, whilst the curvature of *C B* becomes less favorable for resisting this horizontal pressure. In the cable, these conditions are exactly reversed. The effect of gravity upon the flattened portion tends to resist a further distortion of the catenary. The tensile strains in this portion increase with the straightening between *A* and *C*, and thus equilibrate the effects of the load at *D*.

If we apply the illustration of the column in explaining these phenomena, we see that if a force shall have *already* deflected the suspended column, the application of a load to its lower end will tend to restore its vertical position, and will lessen the strain on any horizontal brace or guy employed to resist the deflecting force ; but if the column be placed on end and deflected, the imposition of an additional load upon its upper end will tend to overthrow it, and will increase the strain on the brace or guy, resisting the deflection. These effects are precisely the same with the arch, when suspended and upright.

If we desire to prevent any appreciable deflection of the suspended column from its normal or vertical position, it is evident that we must apply the same amount of horizontal bracing to resist the deflecting force that would be required to preserve the column vertically against the same force if the column were standing on its end, for so long as the suspended column remains vertical, the resistance due to its weight or that of the load is *nil,* as before stated, and so long as its vertical position is maintained when standing on end, its own weight cannot be added to the deflecting force, and hence it will need no more bracing than if suspended. It is *after* distortion has occurred that the effect of the weight of the cable or the arch is felt ; in one case to restore equilibrium, and in the other to increase its disturbance.

For railroad purposes, as well as to insure durability in the structure, this distortion, should be prevented as far as possible, and I have no doubt with a proper degree of stiffness in the roadway of both systems, the bracing of the upright arch can be quite as economically accomplished as that of the suspension cable. Just in proportion, however, as we permit greater undulations in the roadway of the bridge, the economy of bracing will incline in favor of the suspension system.

Recurring to Fig. 8: if half the span of the upright arch be loaded, a horizontal impulse is given to the arch at the crown, tending to move its central point towards the unloaded half. To prevent this horizontal movement of the centre of the arch, is one of the most important problems with which we are dealing. If the unloaded half be kept from curving upward, the movement of the center horizontally cannot occur, and then the undulation of the roadway will be reduced to the minimum. Evidently the slightest bending of the girder will result in a horizontal movement of the centre of the arch and cause a wave in the roadway, hence depth of girder is an important element in stiffening the arch. This movement naturally suggests as an expedient that the ends of the lower chord of the girder be firmly fixed to the masonry, by which means one-half of the girder would resist this movement by tension, and the other half by compression, which would certainly reduce the wave. But owing to the effects of temperature, the ends of the girder, at the abutments, must be left free to move horizontally, or they will push or pull the masonry to its injury or destruction.

Another effect will be noticed as a result of the load being on half of the span ; see Fig. 8. The top chord of the loaded girder, as well as the arch itself, is in compression whilst the lower chord acts in tension to resist the thrust from the upper chord ; therefore, on this side we have two longitudinal compressive members, and as these strains are reversed in the unloaded half, we find two similar tension members there. It is evident that if the struts were run up to the upper chord and tension diagonals were introduced from the top of the first strut at the chord, to the bottom of the second one at the arch, and so on to the centre, the arch would supply the tensional resistance for the upper chord, and the lower one could be dispensed with in the loaded side and the tension chord in the other half. This modification simply substitutes spandrel bracing for the girder, and when jointed at the crown, forms the system used in the jointed arch bridge at Szegedin. From an examination of Fig. 10, which is a skeleton drawing of that bridge, the strains of the various members of one of its ribs will be seen, as given by M. Ritter, from whose work the drawing is copied.

The resistance to deflection by this and the preceding form of bracing would evidently be increased by greater depth of girder. In the Szegedin bridge the large sections of the braces and chords near the centre of the structure are due mainly to the shallow depth of the rib, while this depth has evidently been kept shallow, because of the increased length required for the struts and braces. These being alternately in compression as well as tension, are by economy limited in length. The span of the bridge is but 135 feet. In a structure of 400 or 500 feet length of span these members would be of great length, and hence the advantage of depth would be lost by its greater proportionate cost.

The half girder system of stiffening the arch will be found more economic than any method of spandrel bracing, because vertical members only are required between the arch and half girder, whilst greater proportionate depth is practicable without involving such long compression members. But for another important reason, greater economy and greater rigidity can be attained by it than by spandrel bracing. In resisting the horizontal movement at the central joint by spandrel bracing, the diagram of the Szegedin bridge shows that the chord over the unloaded half arch acts wholly in tension. Its large sections in the central panels of the half rib, being about one-third of those of the arch, indicate the great pull brought by it upon the unloaded half arch, while stiffening it to resist the buckling impulse from the loaded one. This pull increases the compression in the unloaded arch, and thus increases the tendency in the central joint to move towards the unloaded side of the structure. When it is remembered that the deflection of the loaded half depends almost wholly on the horizontal movement of the central joint, it will be evident that any system of bracing which, while tending to stiffen the arch increases the impulse to move its centre in the direction of the unloaded half span, must be in conflict with economy, at least in theory, if not in practice. As the loaded half produces compressive strains at the same time in the chord over it, and these by the braces at the central joint also tend to increase its horizontal movement in the same direction, resistance to these strains can only be had by increased material. These objections do not exist in the girder system, whilst all spandrel braced arches are open to them, whether jointed or not. Therefore spandrel bracing will invariably prove more expensive, theoretically, than girder bracing, for the arch.

If the chords in the spandrel bracing referred to, be placed *beneath* instead of *over* the arch, as in Fig. 11, these objections vanish, because the strains are reversed. Under the loaded half they become tensile strains and resist the horizontal movement at the central joint by pulling directly against it, and this serves to prevent the spread or flattening of that half. By a system of struts, between this member and the arch above it, the chord becomes virtually a suspension cable and acts in unison with the arch to sustain the load, in the manner of the Saltash girder.

This brings us at once to the most economic solution of the problem, of preventing the horizontal movement of the centre of the arch, and as a sequence, to the most economic system of superstructure that is possible.

If we examine the effect of this arrangement on the unloaded side of the span, we find the chord here has become a compressive member and also resists the horizontal force at the crown. The intermediate strut work acts in tension and prevents the rising of the unloaded arch, as well as the fall of the chord. Exactly such strains in tension as are borne by the loaded chord will be the sum of those borne by the unloaded one in compression. On the unloaded side, the arch and its chord or counter-arch act simply as a strut to transmit the horizontal and vertical forces at the central joint directly to the abutment at the unloaded side. The necessity of preventing, as far as possible by any method of bracing the arch, any horizontal movement at the crown, should not be lost sight of, as it is of the first importance in insuring rigidity. By no method can this be so economically accomplished, as by the counter or inverted arches shown in Figs. 14 and 15, which give also diagrams of strains of a 500 foot span on this plan.

By reference to these diagrams it will be seen that a notable uniformity of section is obtained in all of the members of the structure, a circumstance very favorable in construction. Perhaps the most remarkable result, however, that is developed by the diagrams will be the fact that with a steel arch, with maximum compressive strains of 20,000 pounds per square inch and all the other members of wrought iron, with 10,000 pounds maximum strains per square inch, and with 10 per cent. added for joints, it is practicable to sustain on a 500 feet span, a moving load of 2,500 pounds per linear foot by a superstructure weighing (including rails, floor bed and everything) only 1,500 pounds per foot.*

This remarkable result is due—

1. To the fact that every strain from temperature is completely eliminated.

2. By combining the arch and cable, great depth of girder or bracing is obtained.

3. No struts longer than one-half the versed sine of the arch are requred and but few that long.

4. No great strains, such as are incident in almost every other system, are thrown on the struts. When the roadway is suspended beneath the arch as in the case of the diagrams of strains (Figs. 14 and 15), the compression on the struts is much reduced.

5. Long struts being unnecessary, a greater versed sine or more economic depth of arch is practicable.

6. The least disturbance of equilibrium brings every member of the structure into play to resist it.

* The correctness of this statement has been ascertained by carefully estimating the weights of the span from detail designs, and calculating the strains induced by the weight of the structure and its variously proportioned loads. The result given in Figs. 14 and 15, as well as the requisite sizes and weights of road-bed, rails, &c., have been all carefully verified by my friend Col. Henry Flad, and may be accepted with confidence.

I will not stop to compare the relative economy of this method of stiffening an arch, with that of any girder system as at present applied to suspension bridges, but will call attention to some of the facts disclosed by the diagram.

To span an opening 500 feet long with a bowstring girder, and attain equal stiffness would involve, as is shown by Mr. Barlow, the use of four times as much metal as the arch would require. The average strains in the arch in the diagram equal 1060.6 tons of 2,000 pounds, hence a bowstring girder would involve four times as much, and would require an average sectional area in its two members, equal to the resistance of 4,242.4 tons. To stiffen the arch in the diagram, an average section in the counter-arch is required equal to the resistance of 184.8 tons, or about $\frac{1}{23}$ part of the weight of the bowstring girder. Mr. Barlow obtained by his experiments with models a result of $\frac{1}{25}$ as the weight of his stiffening girder. The similarity of his experimental results, with those of the careful scientific deductions shown in the diagram, seem to me quite remarkable. It will be observed that his proposition as to the necessity of quadruplicating the weight of the girder to get the stiffness of the arch relates to the sustaining members only, and omits the bracing or web needed in all girders between the upper and lower chords. In his experiments this was of course included.

Respecting the relative strength required in a stiffening girder for a suspension bridge, as compared with the strength of a girder for the same span suited to bear an uniform load of the same intensity, Rankin says (in a note, page 375, "Applied Mechanics," 5th edition): "Hence, it appears that if the chain be supposed inextensible, the proportion borne by the strength of the stiffening girder to that of a simple girder of the same span, suited to bear an uniform load of the same intensity with the traveling load, ought to be as 0.138 to 1; while if the chain is supposed very extensible, as in the approximate solution, that it is found to be $\frac{4}{27}$ or 0.148 to 1; so that in the intermediate cases that occur in practice, no material error will be committed if that proportion be made as 1 to 7 or as 0.143 to 1."

The wide difference between the proportion of $\frac{1}{25}$ obtained experimentally by Mr. Barlow, and the $\frac{1}{7}$ mathematically deduced by Prof. Rankin, arises chiefly from the fact that the one relates to *stiffness*, while the other refers to *strength*. Mr. Barlow's illustration, shows that with double the metal and the same load, the deflection of the bowstring will be twice as great as that of the arch, but as the strains would not be increased thereby, it follows that double the metal in the girder should (theoretically) give the same strength of the arch, whilst four times the metal is required to give the same stiffness. After making this allowance, however, the proportions of Prof. Rankin are nearly twice as great as those of Mr. Barlow. This may arise from difference in the assumed proportions of depth and length of girder and chain on which the Professor's calculations were based, and those of Mr. Barlow's models.

Leaving this discrepancy to be explained by others, I will point to the fact that by the diagram the average strains in the counter arches are only 184.8 tons of 2,000 pounds, while those in the arch are 1060.6, or 5¾ times as great. Hence, as it requires at least twice the metal of the arch to convert it into a bowstring girder of equal strength, it will be seen that the girder would weigh eleven and a half times as much as the counter arches by which the proposed arch is stiffened, or 65 per cent. less than the weight of stiffening girder required for the suspension bridge according to Rankin. While the stiffness of the arch over that of the bowstring girder is maintained under the whole load, the form and depth of the counter arches give far greater resistance to undulation under the movement of partial loads, than is possible by any practicable depth of stiffening girder yet proposed for a suspension bridge.

I am confident that a careful investigation of the system suggested and the facts stated, will convince those interested, that it is entirely practicable to brace the upright arch more effectually and with equal, if not greater economy, than is possible by any known method of stiffening suspension bridges; and that the proposed system avoids all the disadvantages resulting from temperature. These two difficulties have hitherto prevented the most perfect economy of superstructure from being attained. By overcoming them, the cost for long spans is wonderfully reduced, compared with the most economic truss systems yet devised. By any method of girder construction hitherto known, it is impossible to span a clear opening of 500 feet, with less than three times the dead weight of the arch on the proposed system, with equal strength of girder and with the same material and allowable strain. More than twice the quantity would be requisite in any case, but when the span becomes so great, a less economic depth of truss must be taken, and the length of truss must considerably exceed that of the arch, because the girder must rest upon the masonry, whilst the arch rests against it. In addition to this great excess in its cost, the girder will have twice the deflection of the arch under equal loads.

The arch, as hitherto constructed, being still much cheaper for the superstructure, it is evident that a great saving in the substructure must have existed in the girder systems, to enable them to be introduced during the last thirty years in all parts of the world, almost to the exclusion of the arch. The difficulty of stiffening the arch, and the inconvenient effects of temperature, together with the greater cost of masonry, have given the different girder systems a degree of public favor which must disappear when these objections to the arch are removed.

Having shown how the cost of the arch in superstructure may be brought to the lowest possible point, by economic and effective bracing and by the avoidance of the effects of temperature, I will proceed to suggest such methods as will in almost every case, render in combination with the arch the economy of the girder *substructure* available. Evidently if the cheapest possible form of superstructure can be combined with the cheapest methods of substructure, we shall have attained the most economic system of construction that is possible.

The greater masonry required for the arch arises solely from the horizontal forces resulting from the weight of the arched span and its load, and from those which are induced by temperature. By reducing the weight of bracing to a minimum, and by eliminating the strains of temperature, we not only arrive at the greatest possible economy of superstructure, but by thus lessening the horizontal pressure upon the masonry to the lowest possible point, we also reduce the cost of the substructure to a minimum, so far as the arch *per se* is concerned. Therefore, to reduce still more the cost of masonry and approximate, if not equal, the economy of girder bridges in this item, we start from an already advanced point in our problem.

Where timber is abundant, an economic method of saving masonry in the piers of arched bridges may be employed where the bridge consists of two or more arches, by introducing wooden chords in them against the skewbacks or piers and abutments. These wooden chords would act in compression only and form a series of *compression* members instead of a line of *tension* members or chords from abutment to abutment, as in the case of bowstring girders. They need not, however, be in compression unless the bridge is loaded. If there be a series of long spans together, however, the loading of an arch at one end of the series would produce compression throughout the entire line of chords in the other arches, and this might shorten those chords so much in the aggregate as possibly to allow the loaded arch to spread too much, and thus produce objectionable deflection in the roadway of that arch. In this case it would be desirable to make the abutments stronger and put an initial compressive strain in all of the chords of the system by means of screws or wedges against one end of each line of chord timbers.

In a series, for instance, of five arches of 500 feet span each, where the maximum horizontal force of the load is 500 tons on the chords, if an initial compressive strain of 400 tons be produced in the entire system, from abutment to abutment, when the bridge is unloaded, then this initial strain will be taken out of the chords of the first arch so soon as it has its maximum load on it, while the compression in those of the unloaded ones will be only increased 100 tons, and therefore the shortening of those chords would only be one-fifth part as great as if they had no initial compression ; hence the deflection by load on any one arch in the system would be reduced accordingly, and would be really less than what it would be in an ordinary bowstring girder. In this case, the maximum stress on the abutments, when all the arches are loaded, would be 500 tons load + 400 tons initial compression + (the force from unloaded arches say) 300 tons, making a total of 1,200 tons ; while the piers would be subjected to vertical pressure only, and hence they could be as cheap as if for ordinary girders.

If the timbers were secured together to resist tension, of course the compressive strains would be so much lessened, and the abutments proportionately reduced in cost. With such a system of wooden chords used only in compression, the repairs of the timber would be very simple and easy. The sticks should be squared at each end and butted against each other throughout the span, vertical movement being prevented by the connections of the floor beams with the arch, and lateral movement, by the wind bracing of the floor. To remove any defective stick it would only be necessary to withdraw the wedge, or slack the screw at the end of the line in which it was located, and by which the initial compression was created, and every piece in that line would then be released and any one easily removed.

The initial compression could be so great that no tension could be produced in either chord by wind pressure, and hence no jointing of the sticks together would be necessary to resist wind.

The track stringers and every longitudinal timber in the floor-way could be thus utilized to resist the thrust of the arches, and in this way, where timber is cheap, a very durable and economic structure can be erected. As no thrust in such a bridge can come on anything but the abutments, and as these can generally be located on the high banks of the stream, the cost of the entire substructure would exceed very slightly that which would be required in a truss bridge with spans of equal length. It would probably be best to make the arches of such a series, uniform. The thrust at the abutments will be the same whether there be but one or many arches in the system. The stress on the chords (except initial) would be due entirely to the unequal loading of the various arches.

This method is applicable to parallel truss bridges, and by it the iron lower chord or tension member may be omitted and wooden compression members substituted therefor. The objection to the combination of wood and iron in bridge construction, owing to the difficulty of repairing the bridge, does not exist in this method. In all others, the wood is either under tension or compression and therefore difficult to be removed. In this, the entire chords of any one arch could be removed without endangering the stability of that arch or of any other one of the series; for it is plain, that if any temporary weight were placed on the floor beams, which would equal the weight of the chords to be removed, the equilibrium of the whole series would be undisturbed by their removal, so long as the whole bridge remained unloaded. In repairing it would never be necessary, however, to remove any one chord entire at once, but only to replace such pieces as were found defective.

Where the use of timber is found objectionable the cost of masonry in arched bridges may be greatly reduced by the following method also. Suppose *A B*, Fig. 2, be a bowstring girder, whose arch produces a horizontal force of 500 tons; and that the load increases this force to 1,000 tons. The iron chords of such a girder will require a sectional area of 200 inches if we allow a strain of 5 tons per square inch. Suppose two such girders, Fig. 11, constitute a bridge with abutments capable of resisting a horizontal force of 1,000 tons, and that each arch abuts against the other at the central pier, then it is evident that the section of the chords may be at once reduced one-half or to 100 square inches; for the thrust of one arch will balance that of the other, and the only strain which can come on the chords of either will be from the effect of the load, and this cannot exceed 500 tons. No horizontal strain can come on the central pier, for any unbalanced thrust will be borne by the chords. If both arches be equally loaded, or both be unloaded, no strain whatever will be on the chords of either.

If the arch *A* has its maximum load imposed, its chords will be strained in tension to 500 tons, but if the chords of both arches be formed to resist compression as well as tension, 250 tons of this strain will be transferred in compression to the chords of *B*, and by it to the abutment of *B*, while the tension in the chord of the loaded arch will be reduced to 250 tons. Instead of a central pier which would have to sustain a horizontal force of 500 tons if no chords were used, we now have a pier subjected to vertical pressure only; and instead of bowstring girders, with chords of 200 square inch section, we need only one-fourth of that. As the chords of a bowstring girder are in great part supported by the arches, if we can reduce the chords 75 per cent., we at the same time lessen the requisite section of the arch itself, by relieving it of this much dead weight.

The only difficulty in carrying out this suggestion is the expansion and contraction of the chords by heat and cold. Suppose that to the end *A* of the lever *A B*, Fig. 12, we attach one end of the chord *C* of one arch, and to the end *B* we attach one end of the chord *D* of the other arch, and that the fulcrum *E* be secured to the central pier, whilst the other ends of the chords are attached to the abutment ends of the two arches. Now, if the inner ends of the arches be made to abut against the fulcrum of the lever, it is evident that the two chords may expand or contract without moving the central pier, or in any manner disturbing the arches. Such expansion or contraction of the chords will simply cause the lever to turn upon its fulcrum. A force against the fulcrum from either side of it will not, however, tend to turn the lever at all. Such force would be resisted equally by both chords, one in tension and the other in compression. One half of the force—500 tons due to the load on one arch—acting in the direction of the arrow, would be received on *C* in compression, and one-half on *D* in tension, whilst the only movement of the lever or fulcrum would be that due to the stress on *C* and the tension on *D*. The lever could be made in the form of two circular disks fitted in circular rests in the skew-backs, the axes of the disks being coincident. The end of the chord from one arch would be fastened between these disks by a suitable pin passed through that chord and the upper part of the disks, and the other chord would be fastened by a similar pin through it and the lower part of the disks. The effect of heat or cold on the chords would simply cause a rotation of the disks in their rests without strain and with no horizontal movement of them or the skew-backs. This lever arrangement is illustrated by Fig. 13, which shows a skew-back in perspective, seated on a series of rollers resting on the cap-plates of the pier. The object of the rollers is to avoid any possibility of horizontal strain on the pier, arising from the extension of one set of chords and the compression of the others in two adjacent spans, when the load on one span is greater than that on the other. This movement will be so slight, however, in spans of ordinary length, that if the central pier were proportionately high, the rollers would be unnecessary.

The chords of the arches are, in Fig. 13, attached to the disks by links pivoted to them. One end of a link is inserted between the two disks, and a pin is passed through its end and through the two disks *above* the centre of the disks, while the link from the other chord is similarly secured by a pin passed through the disks and link *below* the centre of the disks. The other ends of the links are pivoted to the adjacent chords of the two arches. This, in effect, constitutes a vertical lever attachment for the ends of the chords, of greatly stronger design and more compact than would be possible with a vertical lever having a central fulcrum pin through it. The links must, of course, bear compression as well as tension.

This plan of disks is best used in two-span designs, but can be used with great economy in those of but one, or of more than two spans.

When both arches of a two-span bridge are loaded, the abutments will of course receive as much thrust as with an ordinary arch, for the chords are only strained when a greater load is on one arch than the other. But the central pier has nothing but vertical pressure on it, and may be greatly reduced in cost, while the chords are only one-quarter the weight that would be needed in ordinary bowstring girders. If four spans be desired, the central pier need then only be strong enough to resist the thrust due to unequal loads on the arches, as the thrust from the dead weight of the arch on one side of it will be balanced by that of the one on the other side of it.

In the case of a single arch, let us suppose that one end rests upon one abutment capable of holding but half the thrust of the arch, and at the other abutment we locate a skew-back, designed substantially as in Fig. 13. Let a chord be secured to the end of the arch, at the first abutment, and to the inner link at the other abutment. Now, if the end of the second link be secured in this abutment so as to resist compression, it will throw against this abutment one-half of the thrust of the arch, while the chord will receive the other half in tension. By such a modification one-half the weight of the chord of an ordinary bowstring girder and one-half of the masonry that an ordinary arch would require will suffice. The skew-back with the disks in it would have to move on rollers in this case, and would make one-half of such movement as would be due to the elongation of the chord from temperature and from the load also. By very simple modifications of the system this movement could be divided so as to occur equally at both abutments. This movement would, however, be no more objectionable than that of the ordinary iron girders on their piers, while the deflection, by preventing the arch from spreading, would be 25 per cent. less with a single arch, and 50 per cent. less if two arches are used, than with any girder bridge of equal depth and strength now known.

By combining with this modification of the bowstring girder, the counter-arch method of bracing the arch, before suggested, and with central and abutment joints in the arch, we have a system of bridge construction from which the effects of temperature are absolutely eliminated, and which will be found to greatly surpass in economy of superstructure anything yet devised, and which admits of such reduced cost of substructure as to almost, if not quite, equal that applied to the various kinds of girder bridges.

The construction of the arches in half-length ribs, with the counter-arch bracing, enables the ribs to be easily erected, even if the spans be enormous in length. Each segment or half of a rib could be easily erected by a temporary tower placed in the stream, midway in the span, either on floats or piles, to support the inner ends of the segments, and on this, and on the abutments, should be placed machinery sufficient to lift a segment. When it is understood that such a segment, with its counter-arch and bracing for a span of 500 feet to carry 2,500 pounds per linear foot, weighs less than 50 tons, if the arch be of steel, and that the hoisting machinery needs only to lift each end of such a segment, or 25 tons, the ease with which such arches can be put together will be at once manifest.

No suspension bridge system, yet devised, possesses anything like the resistance to change of form which this does, owing to its great depth of bracing ; while for equal length of span it possesses greater economy. The catenary to span the same opening, must be longer than the arch, by the diameter of one tower, as it extends from centre to centre of towers, while the arch will spring from the faces of the masonry. This advantage possessed by the arch, will quite compensate for the joints required in its construction, and which are not needed in wire cables.

Where great height of span is desirable, the cost of masonry to hold an ordinary arch may become so great as to forbid availing of its unquestioned economy. In such cases the chord with its compensating lever or disk attachment, at one or both ends of the arch, will relieve the piers of any desired amount of the thrust, just in proportion to the relative lengths of the lever arms, or relative distances from the centre of the disks, at which the pins are located.

It is, however, when we compare this system with other parts of the suspension system, that its great economy over that system is seen. When we leave the great central span, the chief feature of nearly all suspension bridges, and examine the large sections that must be maintained in its cables over the reduced spans between the towers and anchorages, and compute the necessary weight and great cost of the masonry required to resist the tension of the cables, and compare these features with the shorter and more economic spans and light piers which this system admits of in the approaches, we perceive its remarkable economy over the best suspension system yet devised. To the economy and rigidity secured by the system proposed, we must add in its favor also the important elements of safety and durability, which are secured in a higher degree by using the material of the chief sustaining member of the structure in compression, instead of tension.

There is no limit except a financial one, to the length of span which may be safely constructed by this system, and spans of 1,500 or 2,000 feet will be found to be entirely within a practical or profitable limit of expenditure.

Figs. 16, 17, 18, 19 and 20 represent a bridge with two spans of 400 feet each, on the proposed system, for a double-track railroad. Table I contains a summary of quantities and weights of materials for its construction. Table II contains the quantities and weights of a bridge with five spans of 250 feet each, all the piers being of masonry. Figs. 21, 22, 23 and 24 illustrate the five-span bridge. Both tables have been carefully prepared from complete designs for both bridges. (See pages 235, 236.)

Mr. Charles Macdonald—I would not presume to discuss the paper just read without opportunity for full consideration, nor will I at this time attempt an examination of the argument presented in favor of the economy of the arch over the suspension system.

We, as engineers simply, too often loose sight in bridge construction of a very important element, the cost per pound of the material and the facility for erection, while instead we are considering—also an important element—the reduction of weight. Those who examine the St. Louis Bridge, must be impressed with the great accuracy in workmanship required to fully carry out the theory of the design. The most expensive material was used, to withstand the strains which was said in Capt. Eads' first report to exist in the members. All this increased the cost per pound of the structure, and I doubt whether in the construction of another bridge, he will again adopt this design for the purpose of saving a few pounds of metal.

In my judgment, and from a practical point of view, great increase in lengths of spans generally seems unnecessary. In most cases the problem of covering a given space is best solved, and with greatest economy, when the cost of superstructure about equals that of its supports. I will refer to a recent instance; bids were asked for a bridge on the Cincinnati Southern Railway, over the Kentucky River, where the depth from the rails to the water was 275 feet, and the opening was 1,225 feet. Ten or twelve proposals were received, only one of which was for a suspension bridge, and that was the most expensive offered; the others were for spans varying in length up to 270 feet only. In this case the engineers who bid, did so with reference to cost, and without regard to "glory"; each in designing his structure endeavored to get the most economical arrangement of parts and length of span.

More attention should be given to the cost per pound, and a preference to shapes of iron most easily and cheaply made, and which are most economical in the end. There may be a little more or less difference in weight in consequence, but where the cost of the whole bridge is taken into account, it is hardly necessary to make so nice calculations as have been just read.

Mr. Ashbel Welch—I wish to endorse as strongly as possible what Mr. Macdonald has said about cost of structures, and to remind this body of Civil Engineers of a cardinal principle to be regarded always in practice—that engineering is best which most fully answers its purpose at the least cost.

Mr. J. Dutton Steele—I will mention a historical anecdote relative to the Suspension Bridge built by Telford over the Straits of Menai, which will be found recorded in the history of that structure. It was his intention to construct a cast-iron arch, such as he had put up in many places in Great Britain; to support the *voussiors* during erection, he designed a suspension system, similar to that employed at St. Louis but more elaborate, which when complete, was found sufficient in itself without the arch, hence he abandoned his first design and put up a suspension bridge.

Mr. Willard S. Pope.*—In this paper is stated the broad and sweeping proposition, that "Upright arched bridges can be more economically constructed than is possible by any other method whatever, no matter

* This and the following discussions were presented at the meeting of the Society, held September 16th, 1874.

what length of span may be required;" the general reasons are given on which this opinion is based, and in explanation and corroboration thereof are appended diagrams and estimates of materials in upright arched bridges of various spans, in accordance with the designs.

This proposition is a startling one. During the past quarter of a century the necessities of commerce have stimulated bridge construction utterly beyond precedent, and consequently great and earnest attention has been paid to this specialty of engineering. All over the civilized world engineers have devoted their best capacities to the study of this subject, and the concurrent action of almost all has been in one direction. Without consultation with each other, and certainly without undue bias, reasoning out their conclusions from different data and by different processes, they have, with surprising unanimity, departed from the simple arch and gravitated toward other forms of structure. Of the multitudinous bridges for railroad purposes that have been constructed in metal during the past twenty years, those that are of the pure arch form are insignificant in number. The bridge at St. Louis is almost the sole modern example.

If the proposition so boldly affirmed is correct, it shows that the general tendency of modern bridge engineers is in the wrong direction; that they have been misled and are all astray. It is surely proper, therefore, to examine with care the reasons on which this revolutionizing statement is based.

Action and reaction are equal. In a structure of the kind known distinctively as the truss, the compressive action of one member is met by the tensile reaction of its corresponding mate, and so the superstructure is of itself in equilibrium. In the suspended or the upright arch, the direct reaction is taken by the substructure, which must be enlarged accordingly. Therefore, both substructure and superstructure must be considered together in making any comparison between the economic merits of different forms of construction.

Here let me commend the characteristic fairness with which the writer has met the case. He recognizes the fact just stated, and very properly considers the entire bridge as a unit. Whatever may thought of his conclusions and the reasoning on which they are based, he certainly confronts the problem boldly and squarely.

First, as to the difference between a suspended and an upright arch. Here, as the reaction in both cases is borne by the substructure, that element of cost may, for the purposes of the comparison, be disregarded.

In the suspended arch, the cables which carry the structure must be extended full size over and beyond the supporting towers to the anchorage behind them. Thus the actual length of the bridge is considerably greater than the effective length. This item of cost is saved in the upright arch, and so far, therefore, the comparison is in its favor. In many cases, however, short spans are required at each end of the main span, in which case the extended cables answer for such support, so that such extension is not necessarily a total loss.

But the cables or chains of the catenary are in tension, while the ribs of the upright arch are in compression. It is doubtless the fact, as stated in this paper, that iron or steel can be trusted with equal strains for equal sectional areas, whether in compression or tension, although the almost universal practice is to tax the metal less with the former than with the latter duty. But in compression the ratio between length and diameter is an essential element, while in tension this is not considered. To get the full value of the compressive capacity of the materials named, the length of the member must not exceed ten or twelve times its diameter. This at once introduces the necessity of bracing the upright arch to secure its permanence, a necessity which does not at all apply to the suspended arch.

That we may get a clear insight into this matter, let us leave entirely out of view for the present the lateral strains induced by wind or by moving loads, inasmuch as these are common to both forms of structure, and material must be provided to resist them alike in each. Let us also disregard for the present the necessity (also common to each) of providing for a variable load, and assume that the weight to be carried is definite and uniformly distributed. The data being the same, the strains are alike in each, only of an opposite character; and it may be granted for the sake of the argument that the net sectional area of metal and consequently the net weights are also alike.

What, then, are the conditions respectively? Each single cable of the catenary is complete in itself. To perform its functions it needs no other or auxiliary connections. It is entirely independent, self-supporting, and carries its load without outside help. It is of simple construction, compact, solid, without objectionable joints, and contains within itself no element of destruction. It is easily and safely erected in place. Application of reasonable load, and indeed its own weight, serves only to increase its stability. All the forces of nature act with it, and it is in entire harmony with the immutable laws that govern all matter.

In the upright arch, most of these conditions are reversed. Each rib is by itself utterly helpless, even to carry its own weight, and must, therefore, be connected with other ribs by an elaborate and expensive system of lateral bracing. Its construction must be tubular, or rectangular, or of some similar form suitable to resist flexure, and all such forms are expensive. It abounds in joints, each one of which must be carefully and perfectly fitted. The lateral bracing must be so complete as to thoroughly secure the various ribs at intervals of not greater than ten or twelve diameters. To erect it in place is a difficult and dangerous task. The centre of gravity is high relatively to its base, and, consequently, the forces of nature act against rather than with it. No human work can be perfect, and defects of workmanship, that would be almost immaterial in the catenary, become serious when in the upright arch. It is impossible, even if it were desirable, to make a structure which will be absolutely rigid; oscillations and undulations that would be harmless in the catenary might prove ultimately fatal to its rival.

These are some of the inherent and broad differences between the two forms of construction. Other matters, such as provision for variable load, for side strains from wind, &c., &c., are common to both, and so need not enter into the present computation. And, in the opinion of modern engineers, it is these differences that have so generally influenced the substitution of other forms in place of the arch.

Indeed, the fact is not to be disguised that, on general principles, most engineers prefer to avoid compressive strains in metals as much as possible. It is easy to know perfectly our material and all its capacities in tension; but, in the present state of our knowledge so many elements of uncertainty enter into the use of iron in compression, that such use must be attended with much risk. It is one of those subjects concerning which we feel that a little knowledge is a dangerous thing, and prudent engineers are careful to err designedly on the side of safety.*

If an upright arch is to be used at all, the suggestion of a counter-arch for variable loads has much merit. The difficulties that were encountered in the designs of the St. Louis arch-bridge, from the effects of changes of temperature, are fully and forcibly detailed. In this

* The great desirability of more information in regard to the practical compressive capacity of metals is illustrated by the action of the Society in appointing a committee (of which Capt. Eads himself is a member) to procure the assistance and co-operation of the Government in making a thorough and elaborate series of tests and experiments on the capacities of metals. No more important subject than this can engage the attention of the Society and its members.

structure, the two members composing one rib are intended to act together, each bearing its proportion of compression, and at medium temperatures they do so act, but in extreme cold weather the rib deflects, changing of course its curvature, and then at the crown the upper member and at the springing the lower member, does all the duty, which duty is still further increased by an actual tensile strain brought upon the opposite member at those points. In extreme hot weather this action is reversed. Thus the novel experience is had, of certain portions of an arch subjected to tensile duty. This tension was found so considerable as to render it necessary to firmly bolt the skew-backs to the masonry. Doubtless the counter-arch jointed at the crown and at the skew-back would have obviated the difficulty, and indeed, it would seem that, even with the present construction, if the two members composing the rib had been brought together at the springing and at the crown, the trouble would not have occurred. As the bridge is designed, it appears impossible to tell how much duty each skew-back is at any time actually performing; just as it is impossible to tell precisely how much weight comes upon each leg of a four-legged table.

Accompanying Capt. Eads' paper are plans and estimates for a bridge on his design, with a span of 400 feet, and a rise of 50 feet, the floor being suspended below the arches flush with the springing. A thorough system of lateral and diagonal bracing between the respective arches and counter-arches is shown, so thorough indeed, as to quite block up the roadway, the lateral strut between the counter-arches nearest the springing being only about 6 feet above the floor, while the lateral ties seem to extend quite down to the floor.*

But assuming that a clear headway of 20 feet above the floor is needed for the passage of trains, no lateral strut or tie could be placed between the main arches for a distance of 40 feet from the springing, or between the counter-arches for a distance of 120 feet from the springing. For these distances therefore, the arch and counter-arch could only be stiffened laterally by knee braces from the floor; inasmuch as the entire floor is simply suspended from the arches this would not prove a very reliable security, and for just this locality where the lateral bracing is the weakest, the need of it is the greatest, as it is exactly here that the strains are the heaviest.

Indeed, the demands of an upright arch for continuous and effective lateral bracing between the ribs are so imperative and absolute that it

* This, however, is evidently an oversight of the draftsman.

is almost a necessity that the flooring and passage way should be placed either entirely below the springing or above the crown. The vertical space between the springing and crown is fairly interdicted for such service, and any intrusion therein is at the expense of the stability or economy of the structure. The grade line of the floor being generally the governing consideration, if the arches are placed above it sufficiently for the necessary head-room, they are raised very high, which of course adds to masonry, and so to cost. If the arches are placed below the grade line, they not only take up what may be valuable headway for navigation but also necessitate a heavy and costly system of struts for the support of the roadway on top of the haunches.

It is furthermore pertinent to consider that so far as bridges are or may be built over navigable streams, an arch placed below grade usurps more of the head-room for vessels than does any other form of structure. A law decreeing a certain specified clear space between high water and the crown of the arch may prove very deceptive as a protection to the interests of navigation.

Leaving, now, the comparison between the upright and the suspended arch, we come to a consideration of the devices suggested to secure economy in masonry. These are ingenious, and so far as I know, novel; they can be best understood by a reference to the paper. That the line of timber chords suggested for a series of arches would answer the purpose I have no doubt; to secure them firmly however, would require a large amount of bracing, both vertical and lateral. They would not be especially ornamental, and would be liable to decay and to fire. To decide as to their ultimate economy would require a calculation for each particular case. I imagine that engineers generally will hardly urge their adoption.

The other and more elaborate plan provides for dividing the thrust into parcels, and apportioning a certain definite part to the abutments and a certain other part to a system of longitudinal tie-rods or lower chords; in other words, the arch now becomes partly an arch, and partly a bowstring girder. In the case of two adjoining spans, if they are both empty or both uniformly loaded, the abutments receive the entire thrust and the chords carry nothing. But if one arch is loaded and the other empty, then the chords are strained to the extent of one-half of the thrust from the live load, and the arrangement is such that of this thrust one half is borne in tension by the chords of the loaded arch and the other half in compression by the chords of the unloaded arch; the chords being so constructed as to resist both tension and compression. In any case the pier sustains nothing but vertical load. The device is ingenious in the extreme and well worth careful study.

The reflection presents itself however, that possibly there may be some practical difficulty in harmonizing three distinct agents, viz., the abutments in gravity, the lower chords of one arch in compression and of the other in tension, so that each will always do exactly its allotted duty, for if one does less, the other must do more, and thus be overburdened. It is somewhat similar in effect to a continuous bridge resting upon several supports, so long as each does its work fully and fairly, so long is the structure effective; but if one settles or in any way shirks its duty, new, unexpected and dangerous strains are at once developed in the girder. Another pertinent illustration of the difficulties attending a divided duty, is found in the practice formerly so common of uniting an arch and a truss in the same bridge. Experience showed that it was impossible to harmonize them—one did all the work, and the other, instead of being a help, was really an incubus and a nuisance; the better modern practice has, I believe, entirely abandoned the plan.

Even assuming that it is entirely practicable to parcel out the thrust of the arch, as it is proposed to do, yet the plan will not be without cost; inasmuch as a lower chord 400 feet long, to resist even limited compression, must be well and thoroughly braced both vertically and laterally. If it were simply suspended from the arch as shown in the drawing, it would be as limber as a whip-lash.

After all, it is largely true that in such matters each particular locality forms a law unto itself. A structure that is admirably adapted for one place may be utterly unsuitable for another, and he is the best engineer who best fits his plans and designs to the peculiar demands which they are to serve, and who thoroughly accomplishes the desired purposes with the least expenditure of money.

The entire paper is exceedingly interesting and suggestive. It is a bold and vigorous attack upon the labors and opinions of the great majority of modern bridge engineers, and both for the brilliant professional repute of its author, and for its own merits, it will command and receive earnest attention.

Mr. Thomas C. Clarke—It must be a source of gratification to the Society that a member, so much occupied with public business as Capt. Eads, should find time to present such an elaborate paper as this.

During the last seven or eight years the proper construction of iron bridges has been investigated with great ability. It will be observed, however, that almost the whole of this effort has been directed towards one point—elucidating the action of the strains caused by a load upon the main trusses or girders. Very little attention has been given to the bridge as a whole—that is regarding it as a complex piece of framing, subject to impact, vibration and the swaying from side to side, caused by a rapidly moving train ; unless all these points are carefully attended to, the bridge cannot be considered a perfect structure—time will develop its defects.

It is with some hesitation that a criticism of the plan here presented is ventured upon, from this point of view. Assuming for the present, that the main arches do what is here claimed for them—require less material than any other system—yet it will be seen that a platform merely suspended from them will not possess much lateral stability, and must sway from side to side under a rapidly passing load. In what is termed a "through" bridge, the floor is held in place not only by its iron system of horizontal bracing, but also by the posts and knee or angle braces which connect it with the upper chord. Horizontal bracing alone will not prevent lateral motion, for the lower chord being in tension will vibrate like a stretched string. It is necessary to connect the floor by rigid angle bracing with the upper chord, which being in compression, never leaves a straight line. If this were done in the bridge proposed by the writer, some of the economy of material claimed for it would disappear.

Moreover, practice has shown that a bowstring girder is the worst possible form to brace against horizontal motion, on account of the very acute angle at which the ends of the arches meet the chords. Practice has also shown that the deflections on a bowstring girder are very great at each end, owing to the want of height of the truss at these points. The locomotive seems to fall upon it with a blow or shock on leaving the pier, instead of gliding on over a curve gradually increasing toward the centre, as in a parallel girder.

In its present shape, the bridge proposed is not well suited for a rapidly moving load ; it may possibly be modified, but this will add material again.

In the next place, the economic merit of this system does not appear to be borne out by the figures presented. The weight of five double track spans of 250 feet each, in iron, is estimated at 3,010,300 pounds. The weight of five equally strong parallel girder spans would not exceed

3,300,000 pounds, and on account of their greater simplicity of construction, would cost enough less per ton to more than compensate for the difference in weight. If we add to the plan as it now is, enough iron to make it laterally stiff, the cost would somewhat exceed that of the parallel girder.

But when we come to consider the quantity of masonry required by the two systems, we see the great economy of the parallel girder. The masonry in these two piers (which, like those under a parallel girder, receive no pressure except a vertical one) is estimated at 1,410 cubic yards, while those two which receive the semi-thrust of the arches require 3,630 cubic yards, or more than double as much. It is difficult to see wherein this lever-disk arrangement, which by the paper under consideration seems to save half the iron in the chords and double the amount of masonry, is so economical.

Finally, the conclusion to which we arrive is this—economy in bridge construction is to be attained by saving in the cost of piers and abutments so as to allow of shorter spans, rather than in the cost of iron in order to build very long spans. There are of course, other questions than those of economy which come into consideration, such as exceptionally long spans required in navigation, or because good pier foundations cannot be obtained, but this is foreign to the subject of the paper, which challenges the parallel girder system on the ground of *economy alone.* We say that the case has not been proven ; because the cost of the piers and abutments which should make up at least one-half of the cost of the whole—but which in the case of this system, would absorb considerably more than one-half—has been omitted.

Mr. Louis Nickerson—In discussing the bridge before us, it would be well to examine somewhat the short review of arch bridges by Mr. Barlow, which has been used as a postulate. He therein claims, that for certain reasons, an arch bridge is more economical than a truss of triangular or trapezoidal elements. I think that this is an error. For even as a theory, it is founded on the assumption that the deflection of a truss of any kind is the manifest point, from which the investigation should be made. Now the Fink bridge, though rather more costly in original construction, than some other well-known forms, is one of the cheapest as regards maintenance, and one of the safest as regards stability, that is used. Yet the Fink bridge deflects more than any other known bridge ; I think twice as much as the Warren girder improved by Fink. But the same cause which makes its entire deflection great—the advance of the stress towards the center, and the uniform flexure of the chord from compression—entirely eliminates the reverse curve common to other bridges, which it is most our duty as engineers to get rid of, and which, so far as my knowledge extends, is much worse upon arch bridges, metal for metal, than upon any other. It is this partial and wave-like deflection preceding and following the engine in its course, which breaks the back of the bridge, destroys its fastenings and abutting surfaces, and which engineers have attacked since the substitution of more elastic material for stone. The design before us really strives against this, with an effect which we will attempt to measure hereafter.

As regards practical economy, the case seems to be as follows: place a bowstring bridge on piers and a similar simple arch between abutments (their stiffening webs may be supposed equal), then if the chord of the bowstring costs more than the extra abutting masonry, the open arch is the cheapest; if the chord cost less, then the open arch is the dearest. This refers to the amount of materials alone.

In constructing an ordinary triangular or trapezoidal truss bridge, it is not necessary that the handicraft be very perfect. An error of $\frac{1}{64}$-inch in length is not perceptible in practice, and as regards safety more may be allowed with impunity. By bringing to bearing little imperfections it will rather improve than otherwise during a year's service, after which they seem not to exist. Now, to arrive at this $\frac{1}{64}$-inch costs but little per pound of material, because it is easily approximated by ordinary machine tools, but to finish with the same perfectness the abutting surfaces in the long and by itself flexible curved member and also the bracing members of an arch bridge, requires much more care, and even when not carried to scrupulous excess, involves a much greater working cost per pound; whence a rectangular bridge can be built at less first cost, and all things considered, with a really more economical result than can an arch bridge.

If you were asked "what is the lowest priced bridge, so far as amount of material is concerned, that can be built?" I think the unanimous answer would be "that rectangular bridge which, with the greatest height of truss is least liable to 'buckle' the same area of web"—the Whipple bridge, and we know (whatever faults it may have) the Whipple bridge is not only cheaper in cost, but, metal for metal, has much less haunch deflection than an arch bridge. Arch bridges, as hitherto constructed, can neither be considered economical nor very rigid.

Notwithstanding his use of Mr. Barlow's text, the author of the bridge before us realizes the difficulty of the reversed curve in the chord; this is shown by the fact that he has made no special attempt against the bridge deflection, but has struck strongly and well against the haunch deflection, and whether successful or not, he deserves our praise for the essay. Fortunately for your patience, the best way to arrive at the measure of this is the most simple and expeditious one.

First, in regard to stiffness, let us remember a fact too often forgotten—that no system of bracing, however complicated, can have any other influence upon the effects and directions of the forces in a girder, than the most simple plan that an engineer could imagine. If the braces be removed from the "loup" girders of this bridge and replaced with plain plates of the same resistance, the status of the girders or the bridge has not been in the least altered. Take an ordinary bowstring bridge of the same span and height—a similar bridge—and replace the web of that with a corresponding plate; we could mark upon it with chalk the exact saving of metal with but little computation,—and from this deduce the form of the two "haunch" girders.

Remember, that the rigidity or flexibility of a bridge does not at all depend upon its height of truss, *but on the depth of web within the truss*, and as no form of bracing within the limits of a truss, however ingeniously conceived, can vie in depth with the web that fills the truss, therefore none can be so stiff. With arch and bow-string girders then—which are already in fault with respect to flexibility—the change is not an improvement.

Second, in regard to strength;—this quality and that of stiffness are fully separated in the design. As we have only been called on to treat of one in discussing the arch arrangement, so we are almost exclusively confined to the other when we come to examine the lower chords and lever attachment. That the arrangement is highly ingenious all must at once see, yet it seems to me it must fail from the same cause that several attempts of the same kind have failed—notably, the construction of a trussed girder of which the beam should bear one-half the load and the rods the other portion, or with the same idea the attempted combination of arch and truss.

For, supposing first only tensional chords, and that the loaded span would elongate and its arch move outwards against the heel of the other, as described in the paper, the unloaded arch would then move slightly inwards, thereby being relatively weaker to resist thrust than before, and an additional strain would thus be thrown upon the chord of the loaded truss. Then this must further elongate, the loaded arch spread, and the unloaded arch be again forced inwards, becoming still less capable to resist thrust; so repeating until *the security being sufficient*, the engine would cross the first arch, strike the second and cause it to recoil with a jerk; the same action to be partially reversed upon the other when the load had entirely passed onwards. Safety then would probably depend upon there being sufficient *security* to allow the chords to resist the *full* horizontal strain.

But supposing the chords capable for compression (and they would then probably cost as much as full-sized tensional chords), we must remember the inequality between the elongation and depression of material within elastic limits, and even at low strains, so that to shorten one chord a certain distance, and to lengthen the other the same distance (a *sine qua non* to the attempt), would require very different amounts of force (per square inch), a fact at once seen to be inadmissible with equal chords. Hence, at no moment could there be a mutual assistance.

In the two cases mentioned, the trussed girder and the arch and truss, the first was too obviously in error to hold a place in mechanics long, and in regard to the second, it has been found necessary and more economical, to make one or the other member sustain the load, because by no combination would the materials act together in such unison as was required. It seems to me, with all diffidence, that in the case before us, either a sufficient chord or a sufficient abutment is necessary for safety and economy.

MR. SAMUEL H. SHREVE—The paper before the Society appears to be an acknowledgment of "the disadvantages of the system adopted for the superstructure of the St. Louis Bridge," which the writer says were forcibly thrust upon his attention in the progress of that work.

He says of the bridge: "If the effects of temperature could be avoided, and the curve were a parabola, an equally distributed load on a rib would, of course, be borne by the upper and lower tubes equally, that is half on each"—but the effects of the temperature are inevitable, and consequently the above supposition, if correct (which it is not), is without value. He further says: "This extension (from the temperature) causes the crown to rise, which relieves the lower tube of compression at the abutments, and hence that tube does not then support any portion of the weight of the rib or the load. * * At the crown, the strains are likewise changed. There, however, the *lower* tube does all the duty, as the upward bending of the rib relaxes the compression in the upper tube at this point."

Suppose the crown to rise, the lower tube if relieved of compression at the abutments, would not be strained at any point. Bracing beneath a parabolic arch unformly loaded can receive no strain and is useless, and if the curve of the tube considered is not a parabola, it is so near it, that the strains which are transferred by the braces to the lower tube are too small to be noticed. The conclusion is unavoidable, that the upper tube at times must bear the whole load, and even more, for the tubes "are rigidly held to the abutments by anchor bolts," and a large extra amount of strain is in this manner brought upon the loaded tube. Now consider the opposite condition: "As the ribs are formed for a medium temperature, contraction by cold reverses these strains—the crown of the arch falls," and the lower tube must just as surely take the whole load and the upper one be useless. Suppose a still different case; when the tubes are affected by the temperature, one may, and probably does, expand or contract more than the other, and the condition is still worse.

The result is simply this: each tube must contain a quantity of material sufficient to resist the strains caused by a full load, and more (on account of the bolting down of the abutments) or be injuriously strained.

This doubt as to which members the strains will affect should not exist in regard to any truss, and the axiom may be laid down, that a plan in which such ambiguity of strains obtains is sufficiently defective to be rejected without further examination.* This complication may be prevented in a simple manner, and the strains confined to their respective members which then need not be proportioned to bear all that can possibly come upon any part of the truss.

Suppose that of a framed arch the lower arc member at each abutment, and the one of the centre are removed, the structure will then be of the form shown in the figure (next page), divided into two parts, jointed together at the centre and similarly joined by the same tube or arc to the abutments. Expansion and contraction will not affect this truss, and the upper arc has its work well defined, which work cannot be added to by any action on the part of the lower arc.

The horizontal component of the strain in the upper arc is

$$H = \frac{w\,s}{8\,h}, \qquad (1)$$

where w is the maximum load uniformly distributed, s the length of the

* There is no difficulty in calculating the strains in a correctly planned arch truss; they are readily determined by simple mathematical reasoning as in any horizontal truss. The labored and uncertain theory of arches as applied to masonry, has no more bearing upon arched trusses than it has upon a Howe truss or a king-post bridge.

span and h the height of the centre of the arch above the points where it is joined to the abutments.

The segments of the lower arc are sometimes subject to compression and sometimes to tension, according to the position of the load. The braces are needed only under partial loads. That the greatest tension in the lower arc of either segment is when that segment alone is fully loaded, is self-evident; to determine the amount of strain and the requisite quantity of material, some calculation is necessary.

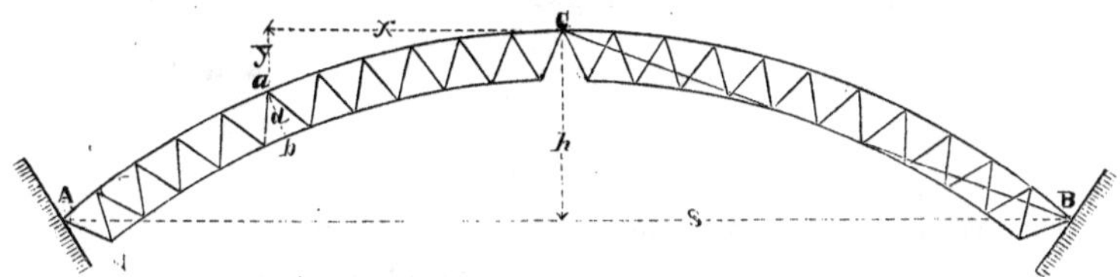

Let the arch be loaded uniformly (horizontally) from A to C, then since w represents the full load of equal density, the weight borne by the abutment B, or its vertical reaction, is $\frac{w}{8}$. The load upon $A\,C$ produces a strain which must pass through C and B, and which may consequently be represented by the strain line $B\,C$, of which force h will represent the vertical, and $\frac{s}{2}$ the horizontal component. This vertical component is $\frac{w}{8}$ $\therefore\ h : \frac{s}{2} :: \frac{w}{8} : \frac{w\,s}{16\,h}$, hence $\frac{w\,s}{16\,h}$ is the horizontal component of the force through $C\,B$, or the horizontal reaction of the abutment B: it also is evident that there are the same forces acting at C as at B.

Take moments at any point a, where the braces meet in the upper arc in the loaded part, distant x from the centre C, and we obtain for the longitudinal strain in the opposite member of the lower arc, $L \times d$, (d being the depth of the arc) $=$ the vertical reaction at $C \times x$. which $= \frac{w\,x}{8} + \frac{w\,s}{16\,h} \times y$ (the term being the horizontal reaction at the same place, $\times\ y$ the vertical distance of C above the point a) $- \frac{w\,x^2}{2\,s}$ (the load on x); collecting these we have

$$L\,d = \frac{w\,x}{8} + \frac{w\,s\,y}{16\,h} - \frac{w\,x^2}{2\,s}. \tag{2}$$

Since the curve is a parabola, y may be expressed in terms of x, thus: from the properties of the parabola, $x^2 = 2\,p\,y$, and $\frac{s^2}{4} = 2\,p\,h$

$\therefore 2p = \frac{s^2}{4h} \therefore y = \frac{4hx^2}{s^2}$, hence

$$Ld = \frac{wx}{8} + \frac{wx^2}{4s} - \frac{wx^2}{2s}, \therefore L = \frac{wx}{8d} - \frac{wx^2}{4ds}. \qquad (3)$$

From this equation we can find the strain in each member of the lower arc of one segment when that alone is loaded. It is seen that when $x = \frac{s}{4}$, L reaches its maximum value and becomes $= \frac{ws}{64d}$.

For convenience in calculating, let d bear a certain proportion to h, say $d = \frac{h}{4}$, as this is somewhat near the facts in the St. Louis Bridge, and then

$$L = \frac{ws}{16h}. \qquad (4)$$

As the load passes on and gradually covers the whole arch, this tension diminishes until when the arch is fully loaded, it entirely disappears. When the arch is half loaded, as in the case supposed, the upper arc in the loaded part is subject to much less compression than when it is fully loaded. When one segment is loaded, the upper arc of the other is subject to tension and the lower to compression; a glance at the figure will show that the pressure from C in the direction of B will tend to cause a bending upward of the segment CB. Here again we can easily find the strain; take the moments around a point distant x to the right of C, the left segment being loaded, and we have the same equation as before,

$$Ld = \frac{wx}{8} - \frac{wsy}{16h},$$

the forces at C acting in opposite directions.

As the load comes upon this segment, these strains gradually disappear, and unlike the previous case, are diminished by the weight of the arch. The tension in the upper arc can be entirely prevented by giving sufficient depth to the arch. To do this in the St. Louis Bridge, 12 feet will be found to be ample; that is, a depth of 12 feet in this arch will prevent any tendency in the unloaded segment to rise when the other segment is loaded.

These investigations have been made to obtain formulæ whereby the quantities of material may be compared. The cubical quantity of material in any member of a truss is the area of its cross section multiplied by its length, and the area of the cross section varies directly as the strain upon it, so that if the strain is multiplied by the length of the member supporting it, the product will be all that is needed for the purposes of comparison, and a quantity from which the weight may be directly calculated. For compression members a certain percentage to prevent buckling or bending must be added, which generally may be put at, say 25 per cent.; in tension members this addition is unnecessary, and in comparison no extra material need be allowed for joints, as this may be assumed to be the same in the different cases.

In the centre arch of the St. Louis Bridge, the span is 515 feet, the rise at the centre 51.5 feet, and the length of the arch in even numbers is 529 feet, or about 2½ per cent. longer than the span. The horizontal component of the strain throughout one arc or tube when fully loaded is $\frac{w\,s}{8\,h}$, and bears about the same proportion to the longitudinal strain that the span does to the length of the tube, or the longitudinal strain,

$$L = \frac{1.025\ w\,s}{8\,h}, \tag{5}$$

multiply by the length of the tube, 1.025 s, and we have the quantity,

$$Q = \frac{1.0625\ w\,s^2}{8\,h}; \tag{6}$$

next add 25 per cent. for stiffening, and

$$Q = \frac{1.0625\ w\,s^2}{8\,h} + \frac{1.0625\ w\,s^2}{32\,h} = \frac{5.3125\ w\,s^2}{32\,h}. \tag{7}$$

Now, as each tube of the St. Louis Bridge is liable to be subjected to the whole load, the quantity of material required for the two tubes in one rib, is

$$Q = \frac{5.3125\ w\,s^2}{16\,h}, \tag{8}$$

Compare this with the quantity of material in an ordinary horizontal truss of equal length and depth. The quantity in either chord is represented by the contents of a parabola, whose base equals the length of the truss, and whose height is equal to the strain at the centre of the truss, or,

$$Q = \frac{w\,s}{8\,h} \times \frac{2\,s}{3} = \frac{w\,s^2}{12\,h};$$

add the 25 per cent. for the upper chord, and

$$Q = \frac{5\,w\,s^2}{48\,h}; \tag{9}$$

for the lower chord,

$$Q = \frac{w\,s^2}{12\,h}. \tag{10}$$

Adding (9) and (10), and

$$Q = \frac{9\,w\,s^2}{48\,h}. \tag{11}$$

Comparing these quantities we find that the chords of the horizontal truss require less than 57 per cent. of the material needed in the ribs of the arch. I do not know how much material the tubes contain, but if they are properly proportioned to bear the loads, there must be that difference, which will hold good if the arch and truss are subject to the same strain per square inch. This enormous difference being considered, it is hardly worth while to discuss the comparison of the quantities in the braces. No argument further is needed as to the merits of these two systems.

To compare the arch of the St. Louis Bridge with that of the figure, we have, in the upper arc of the latter, the same quantity as in one of the tubes of the former, or

$$Q = \frac{5.3125\, w\, s^2}{32\, h}.$$

In each segment of the lower arc the strains vary as in a horizontal truss, and are equal to the contents of a parabola whose base $= \frac{s}{2}$ and whose height $= \frac{w\, s}{16\, h}$, hence $Q = \frac{w\, s}{16\, h} \times \frac{2}{3}$ of $\frac{s}{2} = \frac{w\, s^2}{48\, h}$,

and for two segments, $$Q = \frac{w\, s^2}{24\, h}; \qquad (12)$$

add this to the quantity for the upper arc, and

$$Q = \frac{19.9375\, w\, s^2}{96\, h}, \qquad (13)$$

which is 62 per cent. of the material in the St. Louis arch. The horizontal truss has still the advantage even of the arch properly constructed; the latter does not need so much material in the braces, but the roadway is to be supported, and other expensive items added that will probably more than compensate for the difference.

The form of arch which the writer now recommends is certainly a great advance upon his previous one, but it is doubtful if it possesses great advantages over an ordinary bowstring. His views in this particular seem rather extreme, and will hardly be accepted by engineers, who are likely to be satisfied, for the present generation at least, with what has already been done in the construction of steel arches.

TABLE I.

Estimate of Weights and Quantities of Double Track Railroad Bridge of Two Spans, each 400 feet between Skew-back Pins; with Lever Arrangement.

Weight of structure for a main arch of steel—1.28 tons per foot, and of wrought-iron—1.93 tons per foot. Live load—2.5 tons per foot. Versed sine—$\frac{1}{8}$.

1st. Main arch of steel. (Ten per cent. having been included for weight of joints.)

DESCRIPTION.	Steel.	Wrought iron.	Cast iron.	Timber.
	Pounds.	Pounds.	Pounds.	Pounds.
Weights in one span—Main arch	253,630			
Counter arch		110,880		
Main bracing		147,550		
Lower chord and track stringers—				
Chord in centre		48,720		
2 outside chords		84,800		
4 track stringers		137,600		
Cross beams		60,523		
Wind bracing of main arch—				
Struts		20,000		
Rods		46,466		
Diagonals		10,000		
Wind bracing of tracks		27,048		
Suspension rods		21,000		
Cross-ties and planks				25,440
Rails		32,000		
Joint in centre			7,000	
Total	253,630	746,587	7,000	25,440
Total weight of span 1,032,657 lbs.=1.29 tons per lin. foot.				
Weights of both spans	507,260	1,493,174	14,000	50,880
Castings above piers			63,000	
" " abutments			36,000	
Ends of main arches			20,400	
Levers and pins	4,620			
3 columns of centre pier			141,000	
Wind bracing		20,000		
Lanterns			4,500	
Total	511,880	1,513,174	278,900	50,880
Masonry (estimated from 50 feet below superstructure)—2 abutments, 6,506 cubic yards.				
2d Main arch of wrought iron:				
Weights in one span		1,520,587	7,000	25,440
Total weight of one span 1,553,027 lbs. = 1.94 tons per foot.				
Weights of both spans		3,041,174	14,000	50,880
Castings on pins and abutments			99,000	
Ends of main arches			20,400	
Levers and pins	4,620			
3 columns of centre pier			141,000	
Wind bracing		20,000		
Lanterns			4,500	
Total	4,620	3,061,174	278,900	50,880
Masonry (estimated from 50 feet below superstructure), 2 abutments, 7,386 cubic yards.				

TABLE II.

ESTIMATE OF WEIGHTS AND QUANTITIES OF DOUBLE TRACK RAILROAD BRIDGE OF FIVE SPANS, EACH 250 FEET, BETWEEN SKEW-BACK PINS; WITH LEVER ARRANGEMENT.

Weight of structure of main arch of steel—1 ton per foot: and of wrought iron—1.2 tons per foot. Live load—2.5 tons per foot. Versed sine—$\frac{1}{8}$.

1st. ONE SIDE SPAN. (Ten per cent. being allowed for joints.)

DESCRIPTION.	MAIN ARCH OF WROUGHT IRON.			MAIN ARCH OF STEEL.			
	Wrought iron.	Cast iron.	Timber.	Steel.	Wrought iron.	Cast iron.	Timber.
	Pounds.	P'nds.	P'nds.	P'nds.	Pounds.	P'nds.	P'nds.
Main arch	183,000	......	......	86,000	....		
Counter arch	44,500	......	......	......	44,540		
Main braces. Struts	24,000	......	......	......	24.000		
Rods	29,880	......	......	......	29.880		
Joints	5.000	......	......	......	5,000		
Lower chords and stringers	169,250	......	......	......	169.250		
Cross beams	41.700	......	......	......	41.700		
Wind bracing	18,644	......	28,380	......	18 644	......	28,380
Diagonals and wind bracing of counter arch	4.000	......	......	......	4,000		
Wind bracing of arch. Stays	6,076	......	......	......	6.076		
Rods	6,992	......	......	......	6,992		
Couplings and eyeplates for rods	2,000	......	......	......	2,000		
Suspension rods	6,154	......	......	......	6,154		
Bolts and nails	688	......	......	......	688		
Rails (60 pounds per yard)	21,000	......	......	......	21,000		
Joints in centre	....	6,000	......	......	....	6,000	
Total	562,924	6.000	28,380	86,000	379,924	6,000	28,380
Total weight of ones ide span	597,304 pounds. = 2,400 pounds per lineal foot.			500,300 pounds. = 2,000 pounds per lineal foot.			
2d. CENTRE SPAN : *							
Total weights	533,600	6,000	28.380	86,000	350,600	6,000	28,380
Total weight of centre span	568,000 pounds. = 2,272 pounds per lineal foot.			471,000 pounds, = 1,884 pounds per lineal foot.			
3d. FIVE SPANS:							
Centre span	533,600	6,000	28 380	86,000	350,600	6,000	28.380
4 side spans	2,251,700	24,000	113,520	344,000	1,402,400	24,000	113,520
Castings on top of piers and abutments	....	150,000	......	......	....	150,000	
Ends of main arches	....	30,000	......	......	....	30,000	
Levers, pins and connecting rods	12,000	......	......	6,000	....	......	
Lanterns	....	3,000	......	......	....	3,000	
Total	2,797,300	213,000	141,900 ft.B.M =37,300	436,000	1,753,000	213,000	141.900 ft.B.M. =37,300
Masonry (estimated from 50 feet below superstructure.)							
2 Abutments	4,910 cubic yards.			4,636 cubic yards.			
2 Piers	3,630 " "			3,630 " "			
2 Piers	1,410 " "			1.460 " "			
Total	9.950 cubic yards.			9.726 cubic yards.			

* The centre span is not a bowstring girder with chord, but purely an arch ; the thrust of which is received by the piers between which it is placed. Hence it is lighter than the other spans.

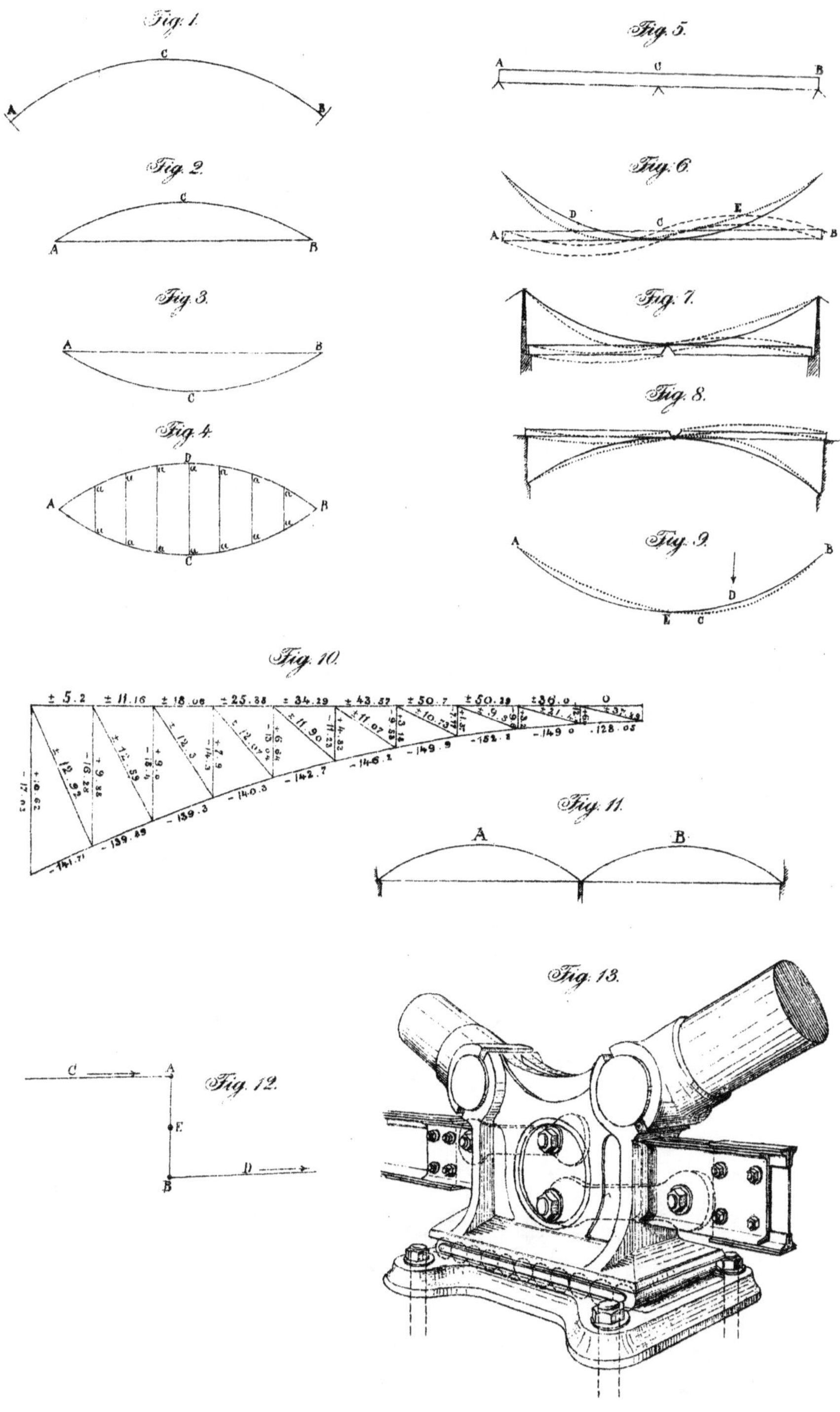
Fig. 1.
Fig. 2.
Fig. 3.
Fig. 4.
Fig. 5.
Fig. 6.
Fig. 7.
Fig. 8.
Fig. 9.
Fig. 10.
Fig. 11.
Fig. 12.
Fig. 13.

Fig. 14.

Diagram showing Strains in Braces, lower and upper Member of 500 feet Archbridge

Permanent Load 0.7 tons per lineal foot, Movable Load 1.25 tons per lineal foot going from the Left to the Right, supported by the lower Joints.

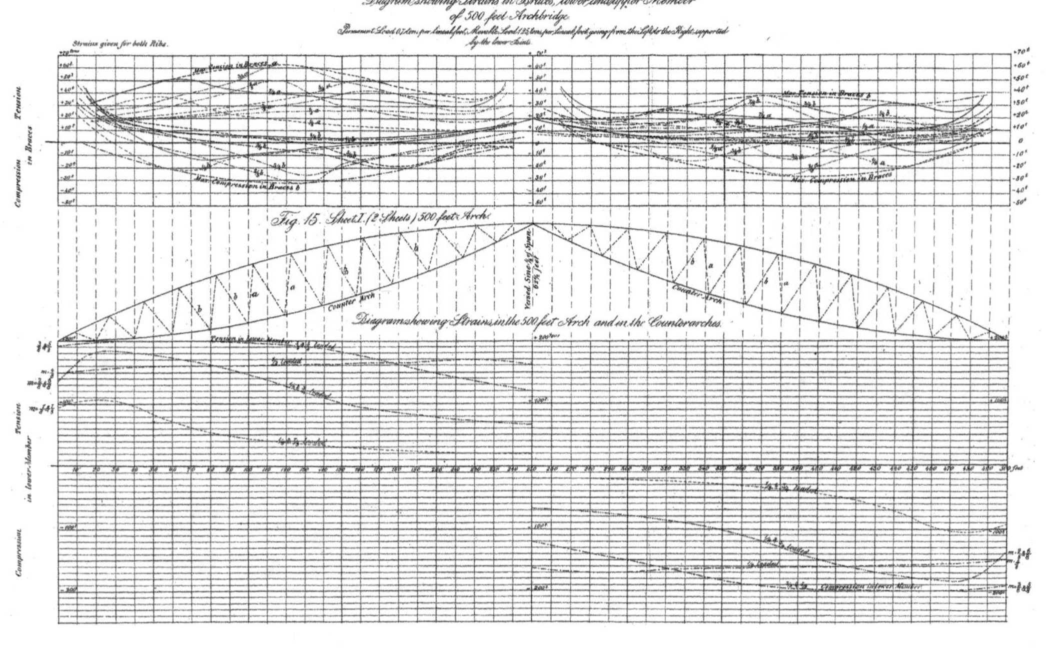

Fig. 15. Sheet II.

Diagram showing Strains in the 500 feet Arch and in the Counterarches.

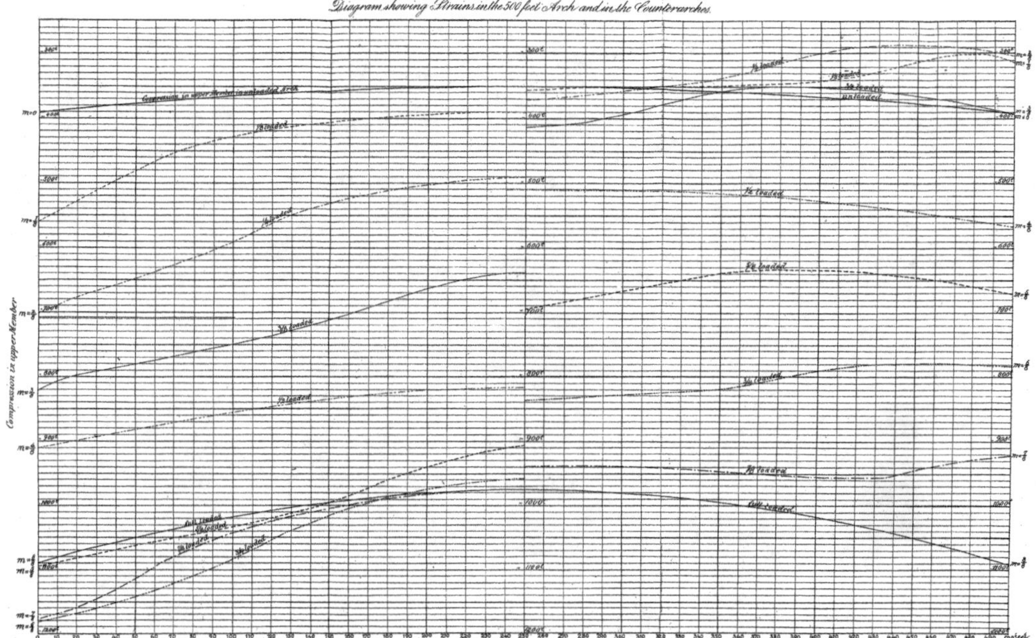

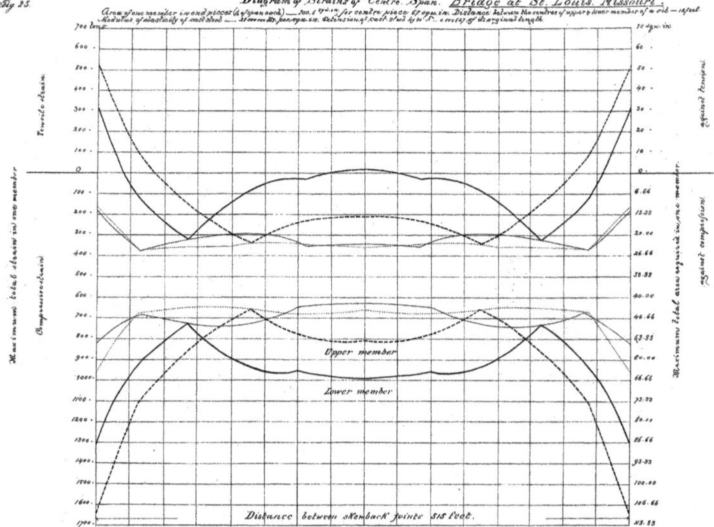

The light lines show the maximum strain curves without regarding the influence of temperature.

Railway grade crossings will be free from accidents if guarded at the intersection by signals which block one road when they open the other, and which are repeated when necessary at suitable distances on either side. No sane engineer will run past a red light in full view, into an obstructed crossing.

We have laws requiring trains to come to a full stop before passing such points, which is well, but well devised signals are better, on the principle that an engineer in a hurry will be more likely to take risks by breaking the laws of the land than by breaking his own neck; we hear much of the carelessness of engineers as the cause of accidents, but as a class they have so high an appreciation of their lives and of the risks of their calling as other men and will not be found running into known danger. In a majority of cases the want of care will be found more with those who have charge of the roads and running arrangements, and they should take full share of the responsibility.

Tunnels cannot be safely worked except by the full block system. Hoosac, with her five miles of length, cannot be safely worked on any other principle, although such an amount of business may be conceived, as would make a block station desirable inside of tunnels so long as this.

The Committee is without necessary information to treat intelligently what may be termed the railway vocabulary of the semaphore, but American ingenuity will find no difficulty in supplying the deficiency. This report is closed by repeating the recommendations of the Institution of Civil Engineers, that uniformity should be obtained:

First.—In signals of danger, caution, stop, go ahead, and go back,

Second.—In the character of the fixed signals used upon our several roads, for distinct purposes, such as switch, block and station, and

Third.—That the signals should be as few and simple as possible.

For the Committee,

April 24th, 1875. J. DUTTON STEELE,

Chairman.

DISCUSSIONS.

ON UPRIGHT ARCHED BRIDGES.*

MR. SAMUEL H. SHREVE.—In replying† to the criticisms on his paper on "Upright Arched Bridges," Capt. Eads enumerates so many errors in my remarks upon the St. Louis bridge, that I seem liable to a charge of inaccuracy. It is true his assertions are unaccompanied by proof, yet the time and thought he has devoted to this subject give his positive declarations more weight than they would otherwise be entitled to. At the time of making my previous remarks, I had not sufficient data for numerical calculations of the strains affecting the arches of the St. Louis bridge, and was, therefore, obliged to give only general formulæ. I have now the information I then needed, and while briefly noticing some of the points of difference between us, I propose to devote this paper chiefly to a careful analysis of the strains affecting the ribs of the centre span of this bridge, basing it solely and entirely upon Capt. Eads' statements of the condition of the arch at different times, the weights given by him and the actual dimensions of the members of the tubes, as the upper and lower chords of the ribs composing the arch are termed. If these are found not to possess sufficient strength, it is unnecessary to examine the braces, joints and other parts of the structure. and if it were necessary, I should be compelled to limit myself, for want of space, to the matter I have chosen.

The St. Louis bridge is a fair subject for criticism. It differs from any other metallic bridge in this country, it has cost a vast amount of thought, labor and capital, and if it possesses one-half the merits Capt. Eads claims for it, it is time that bridge engineers should examine it more closely than they have yet done, and compare its strength and economy with the other styles that are now so much more popular throughout the world. Engineers are by no means a bigoted or prejudiced class, and if it can be shown that the St. Louis bridge has any great advantages over the more common types, they will not be slow to follow the example it presents them. It is purely a question of form and not one of material.

---

* Continued from page 85.

† Vol. III, page 319.

But first they require a clear and complete analysis of its strains and the proportions of its different members ; these have not yet been given. The pamphlet of investigation published some years ago undoubtedly does credit to Capt. Eads' ability as a mathematician and shows him expert in the use of the integral calculus ; but it is incomprehensible, I am inclined to think, to the majority of engineers, and is, consequently, unsatisfactory. This investigation gives no rules or formulæ for determining strains in an arched truss, and is only an illustration of the fact, which must be remembered, that the calculus will not determine strains affecting a truss, whether arched or horizontal.

Before proceeding with the analysis, I wish to allude, in as few words as possible, to some of the points in my former paper* which Capt. Eads has termed mistakes, and has numbered so that there may be no difficulty in referring to them.

The reply of Capt. Eads has these words : "Mr. Shreve says, 'the paper before the Society appears to be an acknowledgment of the disadvantages of the system adopted for (the superstructure of) the St. Louis bridge.' "† In his paper under discussion on "Upright Arched Bridges," Capt. Eads' language is, "I will first point out some of the disadvantages of the system adopted for the superstructure of the St. Louis bridge."‡ My first error seems to be in assuming that Capt. Eads acknowledges the disadvantages which he himself "points out." If he will not go this far, we can hardly expect him to acknowledge the "disadvantages" others may "point out." The next three errors may be summed up in the fourth, which is, that I declare "that each tube must contain a quantity of material sufficient to resist the strains caused by a full load."§ These errors may be better judged of when we come to the analysis.

Again Capt. Eads writes: "Hence Mr. Shreve makes a fifth mistake when he asserts that 'bracing beneath a parabolic arch uniformly loaded, can receive no strain and is useless.' " ‖ For this error, I think I am pardonable when I offer as an excuse, that Rankine, Stoney, Weisbach and every other author I have read, who treats the subject, has made the same mistake. It is, too, an error one is likely to commit, since the most simple methods of determining strains, the method of sections and the graphic method, lead one so easily into it. Capt. Eads himself has not escaped it ; in speaking of the upright and the inverted arch, his words are : "If either form have an equally distributed load placed on it, no bracing will be requisite to preserve its normal curvature."¶ In other

* Vol. III, page 227. † Do. page 323. ‡ Do. page 195. § Do. page 228. ‖ Do. page 324. ¶ Do, page 198.

places in the same paper he gives evidence of his falling into the same mistake which he attributes to me.

The eighth mistake is in making the assertion "that the greatest tension in the lower arc of either segment is when that segment alone is fully loaded." * Capt. Eads then declares that "greater tension will occur in the lower members when the maximum load per foot has advanced so as to cover either three or five-eighths of the entire span,"† and claims that this is shown graphically in one of the figures accompanying his paper. This assertion has been made, I think, rather hurriedly, as there is nothing shown graphically in any of his papers concerning the bridge. A diagram of strains is not a graphic solution and proves nothing whatever.

The remark just quoted is applied to a jointed arch, such as I have previously suggested, as well as to the St. Louis bridge, and is almost wholly incorrect. There is but one point, in the case alluded to, in the jointed arch where a three-eighths load will produce the greatest strain, and there is most positively, no point in the lower arc of the fully loaded segment where an ounce more on the other segment will produce a greater tension than the half load. When one segment is loaded, any weight whatever, in any position on the other segment, will lessen the tension on the lower arc of the loaded segment. I respectfully invite Capt. Eads to prove, mathematically or graphically, that he is correct on this point. He need not have recourse to the calculus, as there are three points through which all strains must pass.

The greatest tension at any point in the lower arc produced by a uniform load is when its length extends a certain distance from the abutment bearing a fixed proportion to the distance of the point ; a formula for this strain may be very readily determined.

There are other errors of which I am accused, which, however, are not of much consequence in this discussion, and with which I do not think I would have been charged had Capt. Eads read my paper a little more carefully. Two of my errors were in assuming that each tube must at times bear the whole load and must be so proportioned ; upon this assumption I made my calculations and comparisons, showing the economy of the chords of an ordinary horizontal truss over the ribs of the arch.

I propose to admit these errors and to make a new analysis and a numerical calculation of the strains upon the ribs of one of the arches of

---

* Vol. III, page 229. † Do. page 325.

the centre span, assuming nothing, but basing my whole argument upon premises furnished by Capt. Eads' own statements contained in his papers which have appeared before the Society.

Capt. Eads writes as follows : "The medium temperature was assumed at 60° Fah. The effect of temperature (ranging from—20° to + 140° Fah.) increases the length of the rib about 6 inches. This extension causes the crown to rise, which relieves the lower tube of compression at the abutments, and hence that tube does not then support any portion of the weight of the rib or the load. These are borne wholly by the upper tube at the abutments, and hence its section there must be increased accordingly. At the crown, the strains are likewise changed. There, however, the *lower* tube does all the duty, as the upward bending of the rib, relaxes the compression in the upper tube at this point, hence the lower one must be increased at the centre of the rib to enable it to do this double service. It is thus seen that the upper tube at the abutments, and the lower one at the crown, must, when the temperature is at its maximum, perform the whole duty of sustaining the rib and its load." "The extra section required by temperature, therefore, becomes smaller in the tubes as we leave the crown and abutments."

"These are the effects of expansion. As the ribs are formed for a medium temperature, contraction by cold reverses these strains. The crown of the arch falls, and the *upper* tube at that point must be reinforced, because it must then sustain the entire compressive strain, which at medium temperature, is borne equally by both ; while, at the abutments the *lower* tubes have now to carry all the load. Thus it is seen that, both at the abutments and the crown, the upper and lower tubes must be each of greatly increased section on account of the changes of temperature."

Again—"Thus, at times, a tube at the abutments may not only be relieved of all compression, but may bear tension and pull upon its skewbacks, by which an additional compressive strain may be transferred through the braces to the other tube."*

Before proceeding further, attention should be called to the fact, that more than once, as will be seen in the above quotations, Capt. Eads says the crown of the tubes must be of greatly increased section to resist the increased strain at that point, and the impression is certainly intended to be given that the crown contains a greater quantity of material than the haunches. The truth is, the two tubes are of uniform section throughout, with the exception of the five members at each end.

"The total dead load of the (centre) span is 8 000 pounds, and maximum live load, 6 400 pounds, per lineal foot."† I give below, other data

* Vol. III, pages 196, 197.

† Do, page 326.

for the centre arch, which I have obtained from personal investigation : span, 520 feet ; actual rise of the arch, 47.05 feet. Each tube has an envelope of wrought-iron, $\frac{1}{4}$-inch thick. There are six steel staves in each tube ; outside diameter of staves and envelope, 18 inches ; outside diameter of staves, $17\frac{1}{2}$ inches. The dimensions of the tubes are as follows : the numbers begin with the abutment members in each tube.

No. of Member.	Thickness of the Staves in Inches	Area of one Stave in square Inches.	Total Area in square Inches.
1.	$2\frac{1}{8}$.	17.11.	102.66.
2.	$1\frac{7}{8}$.	15.34.	92.04.
3.	$1\frac{5}{8}$.	13.51.	81.06.
4.	$1\frac{7}{16}$.	12.09.	72.54.
5.	$1\frac{7}{16}$.	12.09.	72.54.
Thence to centre.	$1\frac{3}{16}$.	10.14.	60.84.

From this, it will be seen that only the five members in either tube nearest the abutments, are of increased section. The uniform length of the members of the upper tube is 144.965 inches. The length of the skew-back members of the lower tube is 114.983 inches, of all the other members, 142.622 inches ; vertical distance between the tubes at the centre, 12.05 feet. The total weight of the bridge and load is 7 488 000 pounds ; the weight of one rib and its load is, therefore, 1 872 000 pounds.

Let w = the weight of one rib and load, s the span, and h the rise of the arch and d the depth of the rib at the centre ; then, according to the well known formula, the horizontal strain at the centre,

$$H = \frac{ws}{8h};$$ substituting the values given above,

$$H = 2\,586\,184.9 \text{ pounds.}$$

If we consider each tube as taking half this strain, the compression upon each will be 1 293 092.5 pounds ; dividing this by 60.84, the area of the centre member, we have 21 252 pounds as the strain per square inch—less than the limit, 27 500 pounds per square inch, which Capt. Eads assumes as a perfectly safe load for steel in compression.

This, however, is the strain only when both tubes are equally loaded, a condition which by no means always prevails. When the rib is expanded by the temperature, and rises, the whole strain must be taken by the lower tube, for the upper is entirely relieved, and the whole strain is not simply 42 505 pounds per square inch, or the amount that was before upon the two tubes; for this reason, that while the strain comes upon the lower chord at the centre, the abutments react against the ends of the upper. Hence, the actual rise of the arch is no longer h, but $h-d$, or instead of 47.05 feet, we have 35 feet. The equation therefore becomes,

$$H=\frac{ws}{8\,(h-d),}.$$

Supplying the quantities and dividing by the area, we obtain 57 143 pounds per square inch for the strain upon the central member of the lower tube.

The formula given above is as correct as are the principles of the lever, and the result is simply inevitable. The conclusion is apparent from the figure. No matter what the intermediate shape may be, if it be uniformly

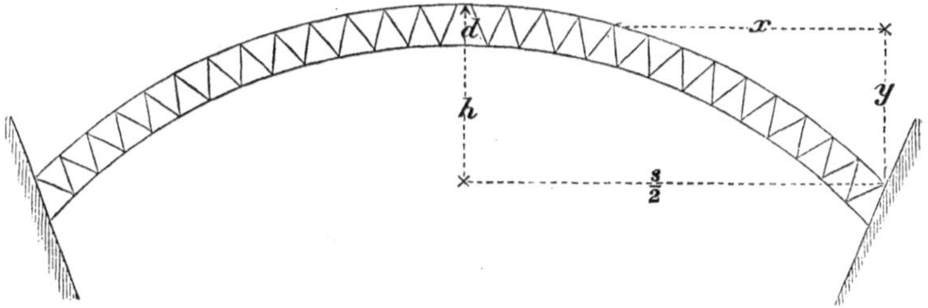

loaded, the weight multiplied by the span and divided by eight times the height of the centre point above the points of contact with the abutments, gives the horizontal thrust at the centre and at the abutments.

This compression of 57 143 pounds to the square inch upon the central member of the lower rib is considerably more than double the allowable strain, and makes an excess of 130 380 pounds over the test to which this member was subjected.* Reasoning upon my erroneous assumption that each tube at times must bear the whole load, the strain in this case would be only 42 505 pounds; an error, as is evident, entirely upon the unsafe side. If the arch be in the same position and unloaded, its dead weight

* (Foot note,) Vol. III, page 326.—"The tubes are all of cast-steel, tested to 55 000 pounds per square inch without permanent set, and the highest maximum strain they must bear will not exceed 27 500 pounds." In the Appendix to Capt. Eads' Report to the Illinois & St. Louis Bridge Company, for 1870, under specifications for cast-steel work, we read, "The staves composing the tubes will be required to stand a compressive strain of 60 000 pounds per square inch of section without permanent set." This latter test seems to have been abandoned as being too severe, though so slightly in excess of the actual strain.

will cause a strain of 31 746 pounds to the square inch, or the compression from the weight of the bridge alone is greater than the maximum strain the member must bear. A strain of 57 143 pounds per square inch is, even for steel, an unusual amount, and it may be questioned whether a structure subject to such compression is safe ; surely an iron bridge, with so low a factor of safety, would be immediately condemned ; but it is probably by such experiments as this that we are to learn the strength and durability of steel.

Formulæ are next needed to determine the strains in the other members of the tubes ; these may be found as follows. Let moments be taken around a point in the middle of the centre member of the lower arc when the arch is extended ; a vertical section at this point will cut no other member subject to a strain, consequently the moment of the vertical reaction of the abutment, $\frac{w}{2} \times \frac{s}{2}$, in one direction must equal the moment of the load on the half span, $\frac{w}{2} \times \frac{s}{4}$, and the moment of the horizontal reaction of the abutment, $H \times (h-d)$, (being at the end of the upper tube,) in the opposite direction, or,

$$\frac{w\,s}{4} = \frac{w\,s}{8} + H\,(h-d),$$

$$\text{whence } H. = \frac{w\,s}{8\,(h-d)}, \qquad (1)$$

Next, from moments around any point in the upper tube where the braces intersect it, distant x horizontally from the abutment, we have, for the moment of the longitudinal strain in the opposite member of the lower tube, the difference of the moments of the load on x and the horizontal reaction of the abutment in one direction and the moment of the vertical reaction of the abutment in the opposite direction, or,

$$L\,d = \frac{w\,x^2}{2\,s} + \frac{w\,s\,y}{8\,(h-d)} - \frac{w\,x}{2}, \qquad (2)$$

y being the vertical distance of the point above the abutment ; it may be expressed in terms of x and thus simplify the equation.

Let the curve of the arch be considered a parabola—from which it differs so slightly as not to affect perceptibly the results of the calculations —and we have from its equation,

$$\frac{s^2}{4} = 2\,p\,h, \therefore\ 2\,p = \frac{s^2}{4\,h};$$

Again, $\left(\frac{s}{2}-x\right)^2=2p(h-y)$, $\therefore \frac{s^2}{4}-sx+x^2=\frac{s^2}{4}-\frac{s^2y}{4h}$;

$$\text{whence, } y=\frac{4h}{s^2}(sx-x^2).$$

Therefore by substituting this value of y in Eq. 2, we obtain,

$$Ld=\frac{wx^2}{2s}+\frac{wh}{2s(h-d)}(sx-x^2)-\frac{wx}{2},$$

which readily is reduced to

$$Ld=-\frac{wdx^2}{2s(h-d)}+\frac{wdx}{2(h-d)},$$

$$\text{therefore, } L=\frac{wx}{2(h-d)}-\frac{wx^2}{2s(h-d)}, \qquad (3)$$

from which the strains may easily be found.

In the same manner, by taking moments around a point in the lower tube where the braces intersect it, we get,

$$Ld=\frac{wx}{2}-\frac{wx^2}{2s}-\frac{ws(y-d)}{8(h-d)} \qquad (4)$$

$$\text{which reduces to, } L=\frac{wx^2}{2s(h-d)}-\frac{wx}{2(h-d)}+\frac{ws}{8(h-d)}, \qquad (5)$$

giving the strains in the upper tube. Moments which tend to produce compression have been given the plus sign and the others the minus sign. It is simpler to measure x from the centre of the arch than from the abutment, and to do this, we have merely to substitute for it, in the above equations, $\frac{s}{2}-x$, when Eq's. 3 and 5 become,

$$L=\frac{ws}{8(h-d)}-\frac{wx^2}{2s(h-d)}, \qquad (6)$$

$$\text{and } L=\frac{wx^2}{2s(h-d)}. \qquad (7)$$

Substituting in these equations the values given above, we have from Eq's 6 and 7

$$L=3\,476\,571.43-51.43\,x^2. \qquad (8)$$

$$\text{and } L=51.43\,x^2. \qquad (9)$$

These apply only when, distended by the temperature, the arch is resting with the upper tube against the abutments; in the lower tube it then decreases, as the ordinates of a parabola, from the centre towards the ends; in the upper chord, from the abutment towards the centre in a similar manner. When the arch is compressed by the cold and sinks, so that the upper tube at the centre and the lower at the abutments take the whole amount of strain at these points, the equations vary somewhat. Owing to the increased height of the arch, the strain is less, but it is again increased by the fact that, while in the extended condition, the weight of the rib as well as the movable load is acting against the effects of the temperature, preventing, as Capt. Eads says, tension in the upper chord; in the depressed arch they both act with the decreased temperature and produce tension in the lower tube at the centre, and thus greatly increase the compression in the upper at the same point and the other at abutments. The equations for this condition, found as before, with the quantities supplied, are for the upper tube

$$L = 2\ 973\ 943.47 - 30.46\ x^2. \qquad (10)$$

and for the lower tube $L = \quad 30.46\ x^2. \qquad (11)$

To apply these, we use Eq. 8, for the upper chord, commencing at the centre, until we reach a point where its value is exceeded by Eq. 10, and then employ the latter to the end of the span; for the lower tube, take similarly, first Eq. 9, and then Eq. 11.

The table on page 173 gives the maximum strains in each member of both tubes: in them x is measured from the centre of the arch horizontally towards the abutments to the point of intersection of the braces with one tube, opposite that member in the other whose strain is sought. The numbers of the members, counting from the centre, the values of x, the amount of strain in pounds, the strain per square inch on the present area, the area of section which must be added to the present area of the different members of the tubes to reduce the strain per square inch to 27 500 pounds, and the total area necessary, are given in the respective columns.

It will be seen from the table that every member of the two tubes is deficient in area; many containing much less than half the material that is necessary.

Since the members in the upper chord are of uniform length (12.08 feet) we may add up the deficiency areas of the fifth column and their sum will equal the area of one member 12.08 feet long. The sum of the areas is 639.56 square inches; multiplying by 12.08, we have the area of a body one foot long = 7 725.88 square inches; next, multiply by 3.4 pounds, the weight of a square inch of cast-steel one foot in length, and the result is 26 267.99 pounds. This is for one-half of the tube; doubling it, we obtain 52 536 pounds, as the extra weight of the steel required in the upper tube to sustain the compression and not allow the maximum strain to exceed 27 500 pounds per square inch.

In the lower tube there are 45 members; the uniform length of all except one at each end, is 11.885 feet; the length of each end member is 9.582 feet. Performing the above operation with the quantities in the tenth column, we shall find the deficiency to be 60 637 pounds for the lower tube, and adding this to the other, we have for one rib a deficiency of 113 173 pounds of cast-steel. To support this additional weight a still further increase must be made in the section of the tubes.

To ascertain the amount of this, an equation may be easily found that will give the weight of an arch which, with a given strain, shall support its own weight and a uniform load.

Let w' = the load and w the weight of the arch, both uniform, l the length, s the span, and h the rise of the arch. Then the strain at the centre of the arch and the horizontal component of the strain at any other point is given by the formula—

$$H = \frac{(w' + w)\, s}{8h}.$$

The longitudinal strain in any member of the tube is to its horizontal component as the length of the member is to its horizontal extent, and it will be sufficiently correct to assume that the horizontal component is to the average longitudinal compression as the span s of the arch is to l, its length, or

$$s : l :: \frac{(w' + w)\, s}{8h} : \frac{(w' + w)\, l}{8h},$$

which may be considered the uniform compression throughout the length of the arch; and if this be divided by 27 500, the number of pounds allowed to the square inch, we have $\frac{(w' + w)\, l}{220\,000\, h}$, for the area in inches. Multiply this by 3.4, the weight of one foot of steel, and by l, the length of the arch, and $\frac{3.4\,(w' + w)\, l^2}{220\,000\, h} = w$, the weight of the arch.

Hence, $\frac{3.4\, w'\, l^2}{220\,000\, h} = w - \frac{3.4\, w\, l^2}{220\,000\, h} \therefore w = \frac{3.4\, w'\, l^2}{220\,000\, h - 3.4\, l^2}$.

Substituting the values—$w' = 113\,173$, $l = 531.5$ and $h = 47.05$—we find, $w = 11\,573$.

Hence, 113 173 + 11 573 = 124 746 pounds, is the additional weight required in one rib, and the four ribs composing the centre span must therefore be reinforced with 498 984 pounds of cast-steel before the compression can be reduced to 27 500 pounds per square inch, or an addition of over 52 per cent. of the present weight of the steel in the tubes.

In comparing the St. Louis bridge with a horizontal truss of the same span and depth, it is only just that the same strain per square inch should be allowed ; since, as has been before remarked, it is a question of form and not of material, nor of the amount of strain per square inch to which that material shall be subject. Capt. Eads cannot, while allowing a strain of over 57 000 pounds per square inch in his structure, insist that other forms shall be confined to 27 500 pounds.

I have made an estimate of the weight of the two chords of a horizontal truss, of 520 feet span and 47.05 feet depth, bearing the same load as one rib of the St. Louis bridge—1 872 000 pounds—and varied the strains so that the members of one chord of one form shall have the same strain per square inch as the corresponding members of the same chord of the other. In the lower chord of the horizontal truss, subject to tension, I have decreased the strains per square inch in the proportion of 27 500 to 20 000, and consequently increased the material, as this is the proportion Capt. Eads gives between compression and tension members.

I have made the panels 13 feet long, and used the formula,

$$H=\frac{w\,l}{8d}-\frac{w\,x^2}{2\,d\,l},$$

—measuring x from the centre—to obtain the strains. In this manner, I find the weight of the chords of one truss to be 145 265 pounds, or 61.48 per cent. of 235 627 pounds, the weight of the tubes of one rib of the centre span of the St. Louis bridge ; which is slightly in excess of the percentage (57) deduced from the formulæ given in my previous remarks on Capt. Eads' paper.

The great importance of immediately strengthening the ribs of the St. Louis bridge can no longer be ignored, and probably the simplest and most speedy method of doing this is to joint the upper tubes at the centre and the abutments and to disconnect the lower ones at the same points. Then the weight of the latter can be allowed to remain as it is, while that of the former will have to be increased only to 173 730 pounds; the present weight being 119 564 pounds, the addition will be 54 166 pounds instead of 124 746 pounds, the weight necessary to be supplied to one rib if the present form be retained.

TABLE OF STRAINS FOR ONE OF THE RIBS OF THE CENTRE SPAN OF THE ST. LOUIS BRIDGE.

	In the Upper Tube.					In the Lower Tube.				
Number of Member.	Value of x.	Total Strain.	Strain per Square Inch.	Deficiency of Area.	Total Area necessary.	Values of x.	Total Strain.	Strain per Square Inch.	Deficiency of Area.	Total Area necessary.
1	2	3	4	5	6	7	8	9	10	11
0	......	....	....	....	....	0	3 476 571	57 143	65.58	126.42
1	5.9	2 972 868	48 863	47.28	108.12	12.1	3 469 042	57 019	65.31	126.15
2	17.8	2 964 270	48 722	46.96	107.8	24.2	3 446 452	56 646	64.49	125.33
3	29.7	2 947 092	48 440	46.33	107.17	36.3	3 408 803	56 029	63.12	123.96
4	41.6	2 921 356	48 017	45.76	106.4	48.4	3 356 093	55 162	61.2	122.04
5	53.4	2 887 083	47 453	44.15	104.99	60.4	3 288 947	54 059	58.76	119.6
6	65.2	2 884 337	46 751	42.49	103.43	72.5	3 206 243	52 700	55.76	116.6
7	77.	2 793 157	45 909	40.73	101.57	84.5	3 109 348	51 107	52.23	113.7
8	88.8	2 733 590	44 930	38.56	99.4	96.4	2 998 635	49 288	48.21	109.05
9	100.6	2 665 676	43 813	36.09	96.93	108.4	2 872 240	47 209	43.61	104.45
10	112.3	2 585 392	42 495	33.18	94.02	120.3	2 732 272	44 909	38.51	99.35
11	124.1	2 504 985	41 173	30.25	91.09	132.2	2 577 738	42 369	32.89	93.73
12	135.8	2 412 540	39 654	26.89	87.73	144.	2 410 119	39 614	26.83	87.67
13	147.4	2 311 871	38 000	23.23	84.07	155.8	2 228 178	36 623	20.19	81.03
14	159.	2 203 883	36 224	19.3	80.14	167.5	2 033 639	33 426	13.12	73.96
15	170.6	2 087 839	34 317	15.09	75.93	179.2	1 825 018	29 997	5.5	66.34
16	182.1	1,964 209	32 285	10.59	71.43	190.8	1 706 285	28 044	1.24	62.05
17	193.4	1 998 912	32 858	11.85	72.69	202.4	1 920 065	31 559	8.98	69.82
18	204.9	2 141 780	29 524	5.36	77.9	214.	2 146 559	29 591	5.52	78.06
19	216.3	2 497 173	34 425	18.27	90.81	225.5	2 383 351	32 718	14.13	86.67
20	227.6	2 764 903	34 109	19.85	100.91	237.	2 622 741	32 356	14.31	95.37
21	238.9	3 044 722	33 080	18.68	110.72	248.5	2 894 328	31 446	13.21	105.25
22	250.3	3 336 426	32 500	18.67	121.33	260.	3 168 412	30 863	12.56	115.22

Mr. James B. Eads. My review* of the comments upon my paper on "Upright Arched Bridges" was written under the pressure of important engagements, and I find that in my haste I expressed myself so carelessly as to be misunderstood in reference to the bow-string girder bridge to which I referred. It is so common to call an entire bridge span, a *truss* or a *girder*, that I have unfortunately misled Mr. Whipple in reference to the bridge design in question, by speaking of it as a "bow-string girder" when suggesting that those who deny the "economy of my proposed system of bracing the arch under unequal loads," should "submit to the Society the details and weights of a *horizontal truss* of 517 feet span on the data given, to show how nearly it approximates to 3 100 pounds per lineal foot in weight."† In a preceding paragraph I stated the moving weight to be 2 500 pounds per foot, "including everything." I intended to say that 3 100 pounds per lineal foot is the weight of this single track bow-string girder bridge, including road-bed, wind bracing and everything ready for the rails.

Mr. Whipple has submitted to the Society,‡ without details, a theoretical calculation showing that a single trapezoidal truss of 517 feet span, "capable (when secured transversely by connection or bracing with one or more similar trusses) of withstanding the vertical action of 2 500 pounds of movable load to the lineal foot upon the whole or any part of its length, with a stress of 10 000 pounds upon iron and 20 000 pounds upon steel," per square inch will weigh, but 2 000 pounds per lineal foot.

His comparison is not complete, and hence gives no approximation to the result of an investigation of the relative economy of the two systems, inasmuch as floor beams, road-bed, wind bracing, &c., are omitted by him. He has given the estimated weight of a single truss, or one side of a bridge, instead of a complete bridge. Of course any comparative design should have regard to equal safety, so that if unusual lengths are required in compression members, the proportion of diameter to length should be regarded. The horizontal steel members of Mr. Whipple's upper chord, being 64⅝ feet long, should be nearly 5½ feet in diameter, if subjected to 20 000 pounds compression per square inch; as the bow-string design, limits the length of compression members to 12 diameters. As the end braces of his truss would be each over 90 feet long, they must be about 7½ feet in diameter, or they would require additional sectional area or additional bracing.

---

* Vol. III, page 319. † Do., page 333. ‡ Page 81 preceding.

DIAGRAM showing Moments resulting from live Load (1.25 tons p.l.ft.)
Span 517'
Dead Load 1.35 tons
Live Load 1.25 tons
M. Part of the arch loaded.
+5000
+4000
+3000
+2000
+1000
0
-1000
-2000
-3000
-4000
-5000
-6000

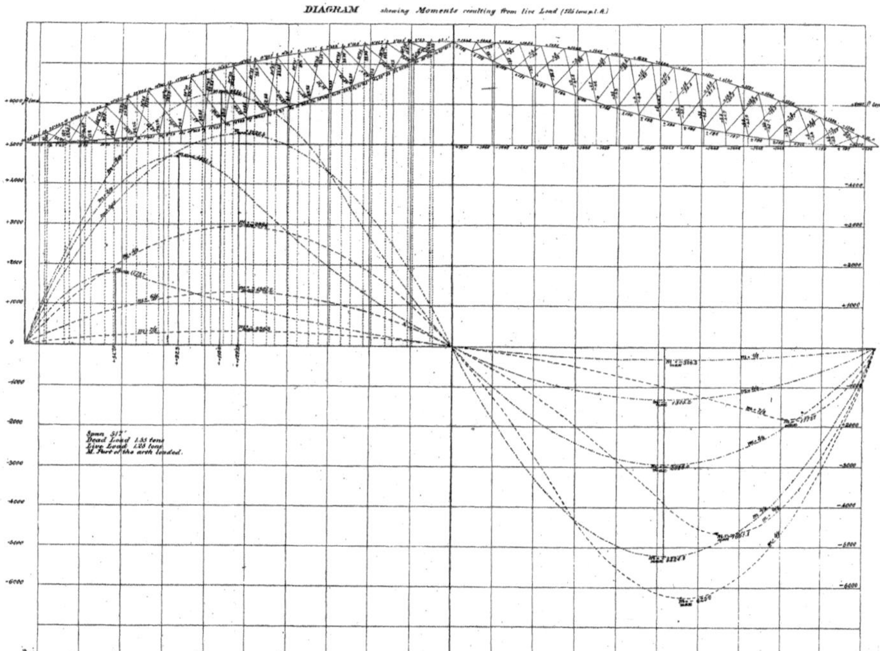

HELIOTYPE

The longest of the braces in the bow-string girder are scarcely half so long as Mr. Whipple's compression verticals; they resist only one-third so much compression as tension, and hence, owing to the weight of the roadway and moving load being suspended from their lower ends, bear but 3 333 pounds per square inch of compression.

The desire to understand every argument advanced by an engineer so deservedly eminent an authority on bridge construction, impels me to ask Mr. Whipple's explanation of his phrase (page 84) "*amount of action* the simple arch and chord alone of the bow-string truss under consideration undergo," and of the deductions following.

Herewith is presented the strain sheet of the design of the 517 feet bow-string girder bridge referred to and estimates of weights and materials; from which it appears that the structure would weigh as follows:

Cast iron..........................	6 600	pounds.
Wrought iron	1 099 499	"
Steel..............................	310 650	"
Weight of metal....................	1 416 749	"
Add weight of timber...............	186 637	"
Total weight of structure.......	1 603 386	"

Equal to 3 100 pounds or 1.55 tons per lineal foot.

Weights and Materials required in a Bow-String Girder Bridge of 517 Feet Span, on the System Proposed.

Description.	Pounds.		
	Cast Iron.	Wro't Iron.	Steel.
Upper Member.			
Tubes	....	....	250 176
Rings of T iron	....	17 504	....
Couplings	....	....	18 240
Centre joint	....	19 760	....
Centre pins	....	....	2 076
Pins	....	....	4 408
Nuts	....	528	....
Counter Arch.			
Links	....	108 648	....
Pins	....	....	12 464
Main braces	....	127 000	....
Nuts	....	684	....
Stays (gas pipe)	....	2 812	....
Bolts in Centre.			
Upper wind bracing	....	936	....
Couplings	3 320	....	....
Stays (gas pipe)	....	11 620	....
Eye-plates	....	3 140	....
Rods	....	11 565	....
Pins	....	926	....
Diagonal rods	....	4 264	....
Pins	....	208	....
Suspension rods	....	37 352	....
Lower Chord.			
Links	....	626 872	....
Pins	....	....	20 202
Cross-beams	....	84 240	....
Castings for cross-beams	3 280	....	....
Bolts	....	377	....
Rods for lower windtruss	....	36 063	....
Pins	....	....	3 084
Eye-plates	....	5 000	....
Total	6 600	1 099 499	310 650

www.ingramcontent.com/pod-product-compliance
Lightning Source LLC
LaVergne TN
LVHW011208110826
845150LV00006B/1356

9781425518998